Maryland State Board of Health

Fifth Biennial Report of the State Board of Health of Maryland

January 1884

Maryland State Board of Health

Fifth Biennial Report of the State Board of Health of Maryland
January 1884

ISBN/EAN: 9783337269203

Printed in Europe, USA, Canada, Australia, Japan

Cover: Foto ©ninafisch / pixelio.de

More available books at **www.hansebooks.com**

[Document Q.]

BY THE SENATE,

January 15, 1884.

Read and one thousand copies ordered to be printed.

By order,

J. M. MILLER,

Secretary.

FIFTH

BIENNIAL REPORT

OF THE

STATE BOARD OF HEALTH

OF MARYLAND.

JANUARY, 1884.

"People who are living in the midst of general unsanitary conditions are in a worse plight than people living in the crater of an extinct volcano; for not only may any one of the severest epidemic diseases break out among them at any time, but they are continually sacrificing unnecessary victims to the demon filth."—PROF. CORFIELD.

ANNAPOLIS:
JAMES YOUNG, STATE PRINTER.
1884.

MEMBERS

OF

THE STATE BOARD OF HEALTH

OF MARYLAND.

J. ROBERT WARD, M. D. - - - - - -	GOVANSTOWN.
C. W. CHANCELLOR, M. D. - - - - -	BALTIMORE.
JAMES A. STEUART, M. D. - - - - -	BALTIMORE.
HON. CHARLES B. ROBERTS, *ex officio*. - -	WESTMINSTER.
J. CRAWFORD NEILSON, C. E. - - - - -	BALTIMORE.
ST. GEORGE W. TEACKLE, M. D. - - -	BALTIMORE.
GEORGE W. BENSON, M. D., *ex officio*. - -	BALTIMORE.

OFFICERS OF THE BOARD.

J. ROBERT WARD, M. D. - - - - - - -	PRESIDENT.
C. W. CHANCELLOR, M. D. -	PERMANENT SECRETARY AND REG. OF VITAL STATISTICS.

PRESIDENT'S REPORT.

Office State Board of Health.

Baltimore, July, 1883.

To His Excellency, the Governor, and the
Honorable, the General Assembly of Maryland:

I have the honor to transmit herewith the fifth biennial report of the secretary of the State Board of Health, in accordance with the provisions of the act of assembly of 1880, which requires that the said secretary "shall at each regular session of the legislature, submit, through the board, a full report, with such suggestions and recommendations as he may deem proper." The present report will be found of special interest, as it contains much desirable information relative to the general hygiene of the state, with suggestions and recommendations, which the board strongly approve and recommend. The report also sets forth in detail the operations of the State Board since its organization, from which it will be seen that a large amount of valuable work, within the peculiar sphere of the board, has been accomplished. The results of such labors cannot be specified or realized, except with the lapse of time.

It is but due to Dr. Chancellor, secretary of the board, to say, that he has assiduously devoted his time to the work of the board. In pursuance of the duties devolving upon him, he has visited every locality in the state, wherever any epidemic or unusual sickness has prevailed, and, aided by his advice and personal labors, the authorities have, in several instances, succeeded in arresting or averting disease. He has, by the direction of the governor, made special inspections of most of the charitable and correctional institutions of the state; also the alms-houses and jails of the counties, of which a detailed account will be found in his report.

By permission of the board, Dr. Chancellor, at his own expense, visited Europe, and whilst there devoted much time to obtaining information in regard to the systems of household and land drainage, city sewerage and school hygiene, as approved and applied in that country. The valuable information obtained by Dr. Chancellor without cost, except to himself, will more thoroughly qualify him for the responsible relation which he holds to this board and the sanitary interests of the state.

The drafts of several proposed laws touching the better sanitation of the state, and the more effective working of this board, such as the registration of vital statistics; the regulation of the practice of medicine in the state; the establishing of local boards of health, to co-operate with the State Board of Health in preserving and improving the health of their respective localities; the local boards having sanitary supervision over the public institutions in their several localities, will be brought to the attention of the legislature, and, as they have received the sanction and approval of a State Sanitary Convention, the board hope they will meet with due consideration at the hands of your honorable body.

Especial attention is asked to the suggestions of the secretary, in reference to the prevention of the ravages of malaria, which, he shows, costs the state annually, in addition to the physical suffering involved, a pecuniary loss of nearly $1,000,000. His recommendations in regard to the acclimatization and cultivation of the eucalyptus tree, and the drainage and utilization of the marsh lands of the Eastern Shore and Southern Maryland, as a measure of health and agricultural prosperity, are worthy the consideration of the statesman and the philanthropist.

Lord Beaconsfield has said, that "the health of the people is the foundation upon which all their happiness and their power as a state, depends, and is, therefore, the first duty of the statesman." Certainly there can be no object of higher importance to the interests of society than its health.

The hygienic education of the young would be an invaluable means of preserving and maintaining public health; by this means, valuable sanitary information would reach the family circle, and in time, by education, the laws of health would be generally known and observed. By act of the legislature of Michigan, hygiene must be taught in all the public schools, the health of the state being regarded as greatly conducive to its permanent prosperity.

We believe that we can point to the past record of the State Board of Health with confidence, that its efforts have met the approval of the people, and if supported by a wise and liberal policy, we shall be enabled to render more efficient and valuable services in the future.

I have the honor to be, very respectfully,

Your obedient servant,

J. ROBERT WARD, M. D.,

President of the State Board of Health.

CONTENTS.

Report of C. W. Chancellor, M. D., Secretary.

Proceedings of the Convention.

Appendix.

FIFTH

Biennial Report

OF

C. W. CHANCELLOR, M. D.,

Secretary of the State Board of Health of Maryland.

JANUARY, 1884.

ERRATA.

Page 12, in line 12, for "in" read *into*.

" 31, " 19, after "have" omit *as*.

" 82, " 6, for "fourteenth" read *seventeenth*

" 173, " 3, for "found" read *founded*.

" 173, " 25, for "statement" read *statements*.

" 182, " 1, for "conclusion" read *conclusive*.

BIENNIAL REPORT

OF THE

Secretary of the State Board of Health

OF MARYLAND,

JANUARY, 1884.

Sufficient time has now elapsed since the organization of the State Board of Health of Maryland to indicate what are or should be its peculiar functions, relations and utility as an integral part of the government of a great state.

Objects of the Board.

The objects of the board, as defined in the act creating it, may be stated under five heads, namely:

1. The supervision of the interests of the health and life of citizens of the state.
2. To make such sanitary investigations and inquiries respecting the causes of disease as may, from time to time, be deemed necessary for the preservation or improvement of the public health.
3. To make special inspections of public hospitals, prisons, asylums and other institutions when directed by the governor or the legislature.
4. To communicate the information obtained and the conclusions arrived at to the governor, the assembly and the public at large.
5. The collection, classification and publication of vital statistics.

Reports of the Board.

The information obtained and the conclusions reached, by patient investigation and study, are communicated to the governor and general assembly, and then, as far as may be, pass into the hands of the people, very many of whom are interested in examining them, as well as the suggestions made for the preservation of health and life. This is evinced by the fact that more than a thousand applications have been made by citizens of the state for the reports of the board, which, it is a matter of regret, could not be furnished for the reason that only one thousand copies are printed by the state for the use of the members of the legislature, and, consequently, comparatively few copies are placed in the hands of the board for distribution. In addition to the desire manifested by citizens of the state to have these reports, applications also come from sanitarians, boards of health, teachers, physicians, clergymen, lawyers, statisticians and philanthropists in other states, by reason of the general interest in the subjects treated. The edition of one thousand copies is, therefore, quite insufficient to meet the popular demand for these reports.

Work of the Board.

The special work accomplished by the board since its organization may be briefly stated in the following summary:

1. The inspection of state institutions.
2. The inspection of county almshouses and prisons.
3. The inspection of charitable institutions receiving state aid.
4. A special census of the insane population of the state in 1877, by personal visitations of the secretary of the board to the various institutions where they are confined.
5. A census of the idiotic and imbecile paupers in the state.
6. A census of the blind and deaf mutes in public institutions in the state.

7. The suppression of nuisances, by the exercise of *advisory powers*, in various localities.

8. The organization of local boards of health in most of the counties of the state, under the provisions of section 4, act of 1880, chapter 438.

9. The delivering of public lectures on hygiene, in many of the principal cities and towns of the state, by the secretary.

10. The investigation into the causes of the epidemic of diphtheria in Frederick City in January, 1882.

11. The investigation and "stamping out" of small pox in Charles county, by rigid isolation of cases and systematic vaccination.

12. The examination of various localities in the state, at the request of local authorities, physicians and prominent citizens, with reference to the existence of prevailing diseases and the best method of arresting the same.

13. The organization of sanitary conventions, to be held annually or semi-annually, in different sections of the state.

14. The collection of a library of reports, documents and scientific works upon the subjects within the peculiar sphere of the board.

15. The preparation of six extended reports on general and special sanitary subjects, for publication by the State, containing a very considerable fund of information and suggestion, statistical and otherwise.

16. The preparation, printing and distribution of forty or fifty thousand circulars on the following subjects, namely:

1. How to resuscitate persons supposed to be drowned.

2. Drainage, with suggestions as to the most fruitful source of typhoid fever.

3. Sanitary rules for the prevention of scarlet fever.

4. Prevention of diphtheria.

5. Sanitary precautions to prevent the spread of small pox.

6. Special instructions for disinfection.

7. Rules for the management of infants.

8. Rules for the management of children over two years of age.

Besides the labors above enumerated, a vast amount of routine work in the office of the board and elsewhere has been performed, in the way of correspondence, personal interviews, &c., which cannot be specified in detail. The correspondence of the secretary with the officials of institutions, boards of health and sanitarians in other states, and even with officials in Europe, particularly on the subject of statistics, and the work of the board, has been very extensive.

Powers and Purposes of the Board.

Under the acts of the legislature, as interpreted by Attorney General Gwinn, the board has no executive authority whatever, either to abate nuisances, or to act in any other capacity, except as investigators and advisors.

As was urged by our lamented president, the late Dr. E. Lloyd Howard, the abatement of special nuisances, and such like acts, should form no part of the duties of a State Board of Health. Its work should rather consist in aiding local boards; in collecting statistics of sanitary value; in making investigations in the causes of disease and death; in advising proper measures for the prevention and suppression of epidemics; in making inspection of jails, almshouses and other public institutions.

To carry out these purposes fully and systematically, it is essential that the board shall have the co-operation of local boards in at least each town and county in the state; and also that there shall be enacted a comprehensive and effective system for the collection of vital statistics. The board has, from the first, realized the need of these agencies, and has been unremitting in its efforts to secure them. With this view, papers have been submitted to each legislature since the organization of the board, detailing plans by which it was thought most feasible to collect the vital statistics of the state, and on which it was thought local boards could best be established effectually and economically. They have not been acted upon, and the work of the board has, in consequence, been greatly impeded and limited.

Vital Statistics.

Outside of the city of Baltimore, no vital statistics of the least value are collected; and yet a correct system for the collection and classification of the records of births, marriages and deaths, is the very groundwork of all public hygiene. "Vital registration is the account kept by the state with its population. By it she takes cognizance of every unit of its birth, of its issue and its death. The precise facts thus obtained bring to light the influences at war against human life, and point unerringly to the means for its protection. By the facts thus procured, and only by these, can the value of life be determined, or the value of applied means for its preservation and prolongation."

It has been estimated that at least *one-third of all the deaths which occur in the State of Maryland in a year are from disease that is of a preventable nature.* And yet with this enormous waste of life going on from year to year, we not only neglect to take proper steps towards checking it, but we have no means even of correctly estimating the amount of the loss.

Local Boards of Health.

The board has earnestly endeavored, under the provisions of section 4, act of 1880, chapter 438, to organize local health boards in the several counties and towns, by enlisting the co-operation and assistance of the more prominent physicians and citizens, but while they were almost unanimously earnest in their approval of the objects of the board, it soon became manifest that their efforts were of too unorganized a character to accomplish anything of permanent value. Even in the larger cities and towns, except Baltimore, we find no health boards—merely imperfectly constituted inefficient "committees on health," entirely incapable, as a general thing, of appreciating the plainest maxims of public hygiene, and which in the face of threatened or actual epidemic disease would be quite useless.

In view of these facts, it is specially recommended that some efficient code of public health laws be enacted so that each county, town or city in the state, may have its local health board to act in co-operation with the State Board of Health.

Inspection of Charitable and Penal Institutions.

The importance of systematic and periodical inspection of state and county institutions cannot be over estimated, but the value of these inspections would be greatly enhanced if the secretary of the board were clothed, to a limited extent, with power to correct such evils and abuses as may fall under his observation while making the inspections.

The last inspection of these institutions, was, under the order of Governor Hamilton, made by the secretary in the spring and summer of 1883, when nearly all the almshouses and jails in the state were carefully examined. The general improvement which has taken place in these institutions within the last few years, or since the report of the secretary in 1877, should be a source of congratulation to every citizen in the state. With few exceptions, the almshouses and jails were found very clean and comfortable, the inmates well clothed, well fed and happy. In some of the counties the almshouses have become almost self-sustaining, and are a credit to their respective counties, but to avoid making this report too long, a detailed description of the almshouses in each county must be omitted. It is but justice well deserved, however, to make special mention of the cleanly, thrifty and comfortable condition of the houses in Worcester, Wicomico, Somerset, Talbot, Queen Anne and Caroline counties. It has been impossible to complete the visitation of the counties in southern or western Maryland, on account of a severe spell of sickness, which confined the secretary to bed for upwards of three months, but it is scarcely to be doubted that the same improvement, so gratifyingly noted upon the Eastern Shore, will be found in every section of the state.

Types of Almshouses.

The almshouses in Maryland, as noticed in previous reports, are of several distinct types.

The most common type is that of a country farm house, corresponding in its general style to the average farm houses of the neighborhood in which it is situated, with, perhaps, a tendency to be a little below the average, in respect of convenience and comfort.

The Frederick County Almshouse illustrates another type. This almshouse, about a mile and a half from Frederick City, differs from the ordinary almshouses in this respect. The whole air of this establishment, the internal arrangements, the management and discipline, resemble those of a well organized, well kept hospital. A fine lawn stretches out in front of the building; the quarters for the colored inmates are some distance in the rear, and a well planned, and in every way comfortable, receptacle for the insane has been provided. The place exhibits, in its entire aspect, the marks of thorough oversight and intelligent care. It is a credit to the county and to the state.

A very favorable instance of another style of almshouse is to be seen in Washington county, near Hagerstown. It was built after plans of which the Secretary of the State Board of Health furnished the preliminary sketches, and although not built exactly in accordance with these plans, it is, nevertheless, very satisfactory. In this institution also, provision has been made for the care of the hopelessly insane, in the extremity of the building. The house is well warmed and ventilated; facilities are furnished for bathing, and in all respects what has been done deserves the highest praise.

In some of the counties—Howard and Calvert—there is no almshouse, and the paupers are boarded out.

Children in Almshouses.

The presence of children in almshouses is their saddest feature. What can be more dreary than the future prospects of a pauper child? All such should be provided with homes, if possible, outside of the almshouse, where they will be given every facility for obtaining the rudiments of an education, in the hope of lifting them out of their forlorn condition.

Registration of Paupers.

The registration of paupers, such as has been ordered by the general assemblies of Wisconsin and Illinois, is of great service, not simply as an aid to the collection of uniform and reliable information, but in securing a more trustworthy insight and control of the almshouses by county authorities.

Statistical Information Wanted.

With the view of securing data upon which to base an estimate of the per capita cost of the pauper population to the state annually, I addressed a circular-letter to the respective clerks of the county commissioners in each county in May, 1883, requesting them to fill up the following blanks, and provided stamped envelopes in which to return the same. To this request I received five responses only, four giving the information desired, and one *declining to do so unless I would send him ten dollars in advance to pay for his trouble and time.*

STATISTICAL TABLE, No. 1, *of County and Local Alms or Poor Houses of Maryland, as shown by Returns to Interrogatories of the Secretary of State Board of Health.*

LOCATION.	Amount levied by county for maintenance of paupers in 1882.	Amount realized from farm in 1882, from sale of produce, &c.	Amount paid for salary of keeper and farm labor in 1882.	Amount of physician's salary and cost of medicines in 1882.	Cost of improvements made in 1882.	Cost of maintaining paupers in the alms-house in 1882.	Cost of maintaining paupers out of the house in 1882.	Cost of cultivating farm, exclusive of labor, in 1882.	Number of paupers maintained in house in 1882.	Number of paupers boarded out in 1882.	Total number of deaths of paupers in 1882.
Baltimore City,											
Allegany County,											
Anne Arundel County,											
Baltimore "											
Calvert "											
Caroline "											
Carroll "											
Cecil "											
Charles "											
Dorchester "											
Frederick "											
Garrett "											
Harford "											
Howard "											
Kent "											
Montgomery "											
Prince George's "											
Queen Anne's "											
Somerset "											
St. Mary's "											
Talbot "											
Washington "											
Wicomico "											
Worcester "											

STATISTICAL TABLE. No. 2. *of County and Local Alms or Poor Houses of Maryland, as Presented in their Returns to Interrogatories of the Secretary of State Board of Health.*

LOCATION.	LAND.				BUILDINGS.					
	No. of Acres.	Cost.	How Paid.	Present Value.	When Erected.	Cost.	Funds Raised.	Estimated Value.	Value of Personal Property.	Capacity.
Baltimore City,										
Allegany County,										
Anne Arundel County,										
Baltimore "										
Calvert "										
Caroline, "										
Carroll, "										
Cecil, "										
Charles, "										
Dorchester "										
Frederick "										
Garrett "										
Harford "										
Howard "										
Kent "										
Montgomery "										
Prince George's "										
Queen Anne's "										
Somerset "										
St. Mary's "										
Talbot "										
Washington "										
Wicomico "										
Worcester "										

County Jails.

The county jails of Maryland, as of other states, are for the most part badly planned, if not badly built. Some of them are very insecure, and escapes are of frequent occurrence. Others are quite secure, but are wholly deficient in the essential conditions of health and life. They have ordinarily no sewerage; they are illy ventilated or not ventilated at all; they are imperfectly lighted; some of them are destitute of proper means of warming the air in winter, and scarcely any of them have any provision for bathing by the prisoners. Almost without exception these prisons are so constructed as to render the classification of prisoners impossible, and, consequently, the *accused* are indiscriminately placed with the *sentenced.* Witnesses, too, are frequently confined in the same apartments with prisoners. In some of the jails there is no means of separating the sexes except by cells opening into a common corridor. The jails are not always as neatly kept as they might be, and personal cleanliness on the part of the inmates is not sufficiently insisted upon. But in no instance has any evidence or intimation of cruelty to prisoners been found. As a rule they are well fed and kindly treated. In many counties they are fed from the jailer's own table, and in extreme cases clothing is furnished at public expense. The great curse and condemnation of the present system is *the association of the prisoners in idleness.* "Idleness in prison is a premium upon crime." Multitudes of men commit larceny every autumn simply to secure, free of cost to themselves, comfortable board and lodging, with congenial company, through the winter months. They do not dread the confinement and care nothing for the disgrace.

The cost to the counties for trial, and for protracted imprisonment of unconvicted persons, and of prisoners undergoing sentence for petty crimes, often committed with the view of securing quarters for the winter, is very great. The value of an article stolen may not be more than five dollars, yet the cost to the county for trial and imprisonment in such cases will sometimes amount to one hundred or two hundred dollars. Summary punishment at the "whipping-post" might diminish the evil, but a more humanitarian view of the case would suggest as a better method of dealing with minor offences—first, a speedy commitment by a justice of the peace; second, compulsory labor at the almshouse of the county, or in an intermediate grade of prison, to be known as "district prisons," where minor offenders, when convicted by a magistrate or otherwise, may be imprisoned at hard labor, instead of being confined in jail, after sentence, in idleness. The earnings of this class of prisoners, either on the farms of the county almshouses or in district prisons, to be provided by several counties conjointly, would not only defray the expenses of their own support, but would relieve the counties of at least a portion of the burthen of maintaining their pauper population.

State Institutions for Unfortunates.

It is impossible, for many reasons, to give the precise number of sufferers from the various forms of misfortune in the State of Maryland; but judging by the statistics of other states, wherein every superintendent of any public institution is required to prepare and transmit quarterly, to the State Board of Health, tabular statements of all admissions and applicants for admission, and discharges and absences of inmates, &c., the order stands, in respect of numerical prevalence, as follows:

Insanity—Idiocy—Blindness—Deafness.

The insane being the most numerous, and the deaf and dumb the least so. Insanity and idiocy are nearly coextensive, numerically, and both are far more prevalent than either deafness or blindness The question, however, is not as to the absolute magnitude of these evils, relatively to each other, but as to the amount of each which remains unrelieved.

There is no doubt that the least has been done for the relief of *idiocy*, principally because of an erroneous opinion which exists in the community that nothing can be done for this class of sufferers. According to the late census there are in the State of Maryland *one thousand three hundred and nineteen* of these unfortunates for whom no public provision has been made. The next greatest aggregate of unrelieved misfortune is among *the insane, of whom there are not less than one thousand eight hundred,* and of whom probably not more than one thousand can be accommodated in the public and private insane hospitals of the state, leaving at least eight hundred to be cared for in county almshouses, jails and private houses, or to wander over the face of the country. For these adequate provision should be made, either by increasing the accommodations of the present State Hospital, or by building a new hospital in a different locality.

The Maryland Hospital for the Insane.

The objections which have been suggested to increasing the capacity of the present State Hospital are:

1. That the attention to details in the care of the insane is all important, and it is believed by many that not more than three or four hundred inmates can be properly cared for in one establishment.
2. That the difficulty of sewering the present establishment is very great, and the purity of the atmosphere in the buildings must be impaired by the use of "earth closets."
3. That the water supply is insufficient and precarious, and experience teaches the impropriety of making large investments where any uncertainty, as to this point, exists.

These are matters, however, to be considered and decided by the intelligent board of managers of the institution, whose probity and business character are sufficient guarantees that they will make no recommendations which are not well considered and thoroughly judicious.

The supervision of the inmates by Dr. Gundry and its results, show that, in addition to a thorough acquaintance with the principles of medical science in their general application and an extraordinary knowledge of insanity, derived from long practical experience, he has a remarkable talent for managing such institutions.

Malarial Fevers.

Liebig says, in his letters on chemistry, (page 236): "In no case may we so securely reckon on the occurrence of epidemic diseases, as when a marshy surface has been dried up by continued heat, or when extensive inundations are followed by intense heat." In an appendix to the same treatise, he gives several examples of villages that were decimated by intermittent fever occasioned by flats contiguous to them being filled with water in the spring and autumn, and then partially drying up in the summer, thereby creating morasses abounding in the infusorial life characteristic of stagnant water. This was notably the case with Bailweiller and Feldkirch, villages of one thousand four hundred and forty-six, and five hundred inhabitants respectively, in the neighborhood of which it was found necessary to excavate certain fields to the depth of two or three feet in constructing the railway between Strasburg in Alsace-Loraine, and Balè in Switzerland. In 1843, previous to the excavations, of the one thousand four hundred and forty-six inhabitants in Bailweiller, only thirty-six were attacked with intermittent fever; subsequently one hundred and sixty-six cases occurred in 1844; seven hundred and forty-three in 1845, and one thousand one hundred and sixty-six in 1846, with a correspondingly increased mortality; and very much the same thing occurred in Feldkirch.

Wherever there is matter of animal or vegetable origin *in process of putrefactive change*, danger to human life is lurking in the water or floating in the surrounding air. *Where there is no decomposition, there is no fever;* hence, we may have marshy districts quite free from fever, although the forms of marsh vegetation, so far as these can be recognized, are all present. Putrefaction is, therefore, an essential factor in the production of malarial fevers. The exhalations arising from decayed *vegetable matter* in marshes, bogs, etc., contain a poison which produces, principally, intermittent fever or ague, and remittent or bilious fevers; but, the exhalations which are formed from the decay of *animal matter*, such as are formed in ill ventilated and crowded apartments, and which arise from putrefying excrementitious substances, contain a poison which produces diphtheria, scarlet fever, typhoid fever and dysenteries. When these poisons are carried to the lungs in the inspired air, or to the stomach in the water drank, they enter directly into the blood and produce disease, modified, as we have seen, according as the vegetable or animal matter predominates in the poison.

Effect of Malaria on Industrial Interests.

Every case of sickness and the loss of every life from preventable disease is a tax upon the material wealth of the state, besides being a great loss to the family in which they occur. It has been estimated that the industrial interests of Maryland are damaged every year to the extent of nearly one million of dollars by malaria alone, and this loss falls more heavily on the "Eastern Shore" and Southern Maryland than any other section of the state. This estimate is arrived at in two ways:

1. If we estimate the population of the state in round numbers at one million, we may safely reckon that two per cent. suffer annually with some form of malaria, and that one out of every fifty attacked dies from its effects. The lives of individuals represent a certain value as capital to be applied to the production of wealth. According to the best European calculations of values—the earnings and expenditures—the present worth of the excess of the former over the latter, for an unskilled laborer at twenty-five, is twelve hundred dollars ($1,200). That is, such a laborer at that age is worth so much to the body politic. This is the English and very nearly the German valuation. In this country wages are higher and earnings greater, and of course the annuity and its valuation are greater. This, too, is the esti-

mated value of an unskilled laborer who earns the lowest wages. The value of the skilled mechanic, the merchant, the professional man, whose earnings are larger, must be very much greater. It is at least safe to assume the European calculation of twelve hundred dollars as the average worth of men of all conditions and occupations in Maryland, and we may, therefore, approximate the annual cost of malaria to the state as follows:

Estimated number of malarial cases, including children	20,000
Cost of ten days' sickness of each one, including physicians' fees, medicines, &c., at $3.00 per day	$600,000 00
Loss of time from industrial pursuits of three-fifths the number attacked, twelve thousand, at $1.00 per day for ten days	120,000 00
Estimated number of victims, four hundred, of which two-fifths represent each a capital value of $1,200.00, or	192,000 00
Four hundred funerals, at an average cost of $25.00 each	10,000 00
Total loss	$922,000 00

2. If we count the number of deaths in a community for any given period, and multiply it by twenty, we shall have about the average total of sick persons for the period given. The United States Census of 1880 gives the total number of deaths due to malarial fevers in the proportion of about twenty-eight per thousand of all deaths from reported causes. The total number of deaths in Maryland for the year 1880, from all causes, may be set down in round numbers at thirty thousand, which, according to the above estimate of the census, would make the number of deaths from malarial fevers eight hundred and forty per annum. Now, if we multiply the number of deaths by twenty, we shall approximate the number of cases, which would be in this case about sixteen thousand eight hundred.

In the United States political economists have estimated the cash value of an able bodied, industrious, unskilled laborer, at one thousand six hundred dollars, and that the cash value of men, women and adolescents of both sexes above twelve years is one thousand dollars. We will, therefore, make the following calculation upon the United States basis of one thousand dollars as the cash value of each adult life to the body politic:

Number of cases of malarial fever in one year, based upon estimate of United States Census	16,800
Cost of ten days' sickness of each one, including physicians' fees, medicines, &c., at $3.00 per day.	$504,000 00
Loss of time from industrial pursuits, say of three-fifths of the number attacked (10,980), at $1.00 per day for ten days	109,800 00
Number of victims based upon estimate of United States Census, eight hundred and forty, of which two-fifths represent a capital value of $1,000.00	336,000 00
Eight hundred and forty funerals at an average cost of $25.00 each	21,000 00
Total loss	$970,800 00

At least one-third of *all the cases of sickness and of the deaths* that occur are preventable by proper sanitation, and it is believed that the expenditure of ten or fifteen thousand dollars annually in sanitary surveys and prophylactic measures would reduce the annual loss to the state from malarial fevers alone at least fifty per cent.

The science of medicine points out the fact and its consequences, and appeals to the civil administration of the state for an adequate remedy. In France the evil was first measured by a careful survey of all malarious districts to ascertain their dimensions, and to calculate the area subjected to the malign influences of this poison. Observation and experiment have established certain limits to the influence of malaria, but these are liable to variation by circumstances. Places at some distances, especially if situated upon an eminence, are sometimes affected with the same, if not greater intensity, than places in the vicinity. The distance to which malarial emanation may extend by gradual diffusion, has been observed to be from one thousand four hundred to one thousand six hundred feet in elevation, and from six hundred to one thousand feet in horizontal direction. But when winds are in operation, the extent to which the poison may be transmitted is not known, and instances are recorded of its being conveyed three or more miles. A survey of all malarious districts in the State of Maryland would form an initial point for any remedy that may be devised.

Remedies for Malaria.

In the secretary's report for 1880, a number of suggestions were made for ameliorating the poison of malaria, and there is reason to believe that such improvements in sanitary science may yet be effected, that malarial and miasmatic exhalations will be greatly reduced in frequency and violence, if not completely gotten rid of. It must, therefore, be a darling object with every true philanthropist anxious to promote the best interests of his fellow man, that some experiments commensurate with the importance of the subject should be set on foot to ascertain by what means malaria may be eradicated and the state thereby saved millions of dollars. For accomplishing so important an object, adequate appropriations should be made to enable the State Board of Health to institute thorough investigation into the subject. Such a work would require much time and a vast amount of patient and laborious research, and a considerable sum of money, but the expense involved is a mere trifle when contrasted with the beneficial results which will inevitably follow.

The Eucalyptus Tree and its value in Malaria.

The power exercised by the eucalyptus tree in preventing and destroying marsh fever is undoubtedly very great. Mr. Playfair, the British Consul in Algeria, reported to his government that the culture of this tree had been of remarkable efficacy in improving the sanitary condition of unhealthy districts. Maryland may be too far north of the natural *habitat* of this tree for its acclimatization; but experiments might be made and continued until they demonstrate the impossibility of this most useful tree being acclimated in this state. There is reason to think it could be successfully grown upon the Eastern Shore and parts of Southern Maryland. The pine, the balsam fir, the balm of Gilead, are among the trees which have lately attracted attention in this regard, "because their exhalations and the ozone are in some way beneficial in neutralizing malarial poison." Even "the sunflower" is said to possess a virtue worthy of trial in this respect.

Prof. Gubler bears testimony to this fact, that this so-called "fever tree," or "fever destroying tree," exercises extraordinary effects in cases of intermittent fever. He states that in marshy districts near eucalyptus forests the fever is practically unknown, and this state of things is attributed to the aromatic vapors which emanate from the tree, and the preservative powers of the branches and leaves which fall upon the marshy soil.

In 1871 Raveret-Wattel published a report in which he said: "Science is far from having said her last word respecting the part that may be played by these useful plants," meaning the eucalypti, and these words have since been verified in a singular manner. Endemic fevers in the most unhealthy part of Algeria have been perfectly annihilated by the groves of eucalyptus which were planted some years ago, and the anti-miasmatic power of the grown up tree has been fully established.

A case is cited of a farm situated twenty miles from Algiers, and notoriously known to possess a pestilential atmosphere, in which thirteen thousand trees were planted with the effect of absolutely stamping out the previous endemic fever.

A Dutch landed-proprietor also planted a number of eucalyptus trees on the banks of the Scheldt, where he owned some property in a very malarious district. The effect was that the particular spot was rendered quite salubrious, while the surrounding neighborhood remained as fever-stricken as originally.

Italy has also furnished its evidence upon this question. Dr. Fedeli alleges that wherever plantations of the eucalyptus existed, malaria is unknown, and where the malaria has been endemic, the cultivation of the tree suffices to mitigate in all cases, and in some instances to entirely remove, the disease.

It is of interest to note that the Italian government has supplied landlords with large quantities of strips of the tree for forming plantations in all malarious districts.

The instance of the wonderful hygienic properties of the eucalyptus, in overcoming the fever which once infested the Trappist Monastery at Tre Fontaine, near Rome, is too familiar to require repeating here.

Many other instances could be given of the unquestionable value of the eucalyptus in transforming unhealthy districts of marshy, uncultivated lands, into healthy, habitable spots—indeed, all quarters of the globe have furnished evidences of its sanitary value.

It is said that some species grow well in hot, and others in cold climates, and thus there are eucalypts to suit the tropics of India and the more temperate regions in America.

By the natural atmospheric oxidation of the oils of eucalyptus and the pine (turpentine), there is produced an almost illimitable amount of per oxide of hydrogen and camphoraceous matters which must, perforce, act according to their chemical natures upon the pestilence that may be floating in the air, and upon the animal and vegetable matters that may be rotting in the soil.

The governments of this and other states ought, therefore, never to lose sight of the value of the eucalyptus and pine. Valleys and swamps may, by their agency, be freed from malarial fever; and in the place of a poisonous atmosphere they substitute a state of balminess and purity at once luxurious and healthful.

The Marshy Districts of Maryland.

It is estimated that not less than five hundred thousand acres of marshy land exists in Maryland, poisoning the surrounding atmosphere with noxious exhalations. If these marshes were properly and completely drained, as Harlam lake in Holland, and a certain parish in the county of Fife,

Scotland, have been, we should soon have the pleasure of viewing luxuriant crops adorning the places where the eye has been accustomed to see stagnant water, and where noxious vapors, impregnated with disease and death, are now so usual.

There can be no doubt of the fact that when a section of country is liable to malaria, its mischievous effects may be materially diminished, if not completely gotten rid of, by agricultural improvements. This is not a mere theoretical assertion, for the advantages of such measures have been proved by experience in England, Scotland, Holland and France. Before the marshy districts in England were properly drained strangers rarely visited them, from the certainty of contracting ague. The inhabitants themselves of these districts were seldom exempted from that distressing complaint, and were, consequently, distinguished by an emaciated and jaundiced look. But, since the improvements which have been effected by drainage and agriculture, they have become as healthy as their neighbors. Holland has reclaimed by drainage upwards of one hundred thousand acres of the most fertile land in the world, and from being, as it were, a pestilential marsh, has become one of the healthiest countries in the world. This energetic people now have under consideration, if not actually under contract, the project of reclaiming, by drainage, five hundred thousand acres more of land from the Zuyder Zee.

The same results might confidently be relied on if the same improvements were introduced, by joint stock company or otherwise, into Maryland, and it would soon prove not only the means of converting the least valuable sections of the state into veritable "garden spots," but would, moreover, contribute effectually to the healthfulness of the sections referred to, and afford security to its inhabitants against disease.

These marshy lands, either covered constantly or intermittently with water, could, doubtless, be purchased at a mere trifle—say from ten cents to fifty cents per acre—and, when properly dyked and drained, would realize from fifty dollars to two hundred dollars per acre, according to circumstances. The taxable basis of the state would be thereby largely increased, and malaria, if not totally extirpated, would be greatly reduced in its violence in those counties which are, unfortunately, most afflicted with the disorder.

A Public Waste that Effects the Public Health.

Upwards of two millions of dollars annually leave the state for the payment of guanos and other fertilizers, which is about the amount thrown away in the sewage waste. The excretal product of each individual in the state, which is now absolutely lost, if properly preserved, would amount in actual value, to two dollars per individual per annum, and reckoning the population, in round numbers, at one million, the aggregate value of the material would be two million dollars, which, if applied to the lands instead of the guanos purchased, would save the state this amount annually. It is not only the waste which is to be deprecated, but the public health is imperiled and the public water courses are defiled by the present methods of treating sewage matter.

By the "water carriage" system, whether in large or small sewers, the fœcal matter is not only removed in contact with large bodies of water, which it contaminates, but also through conduits which must necessarily remain in open communication with the atmosphere, in order to give free scope to the daily fluctuations of the sewage liquid.

This is not only a *sanitary wrong* inimical to health, but a *financial wrong*, inimical to the agricultural and commercial interests of the country. No system of sewerage that discharges into rivers, bays or estuaries, sewage matter which is capable of being reduced to a storeable and marketable article of trade, like guano, should be approved.

The Sewerage of Maryland Cities and Towns.

We have seen that *sanitarily* and *financially* the "water-carriage" system of sewerage, even the so called SEPARATE WATER CARRIAGE SYSTEM, is a failure, and it would therefore be a decided mistake for any of our cities, towns or villages, to adopt it. "Fœcal matter in contact with water," says Prof. Müller, contaminates the water *without becoming itself less dangerous;* the water favors rather the process of putrid fermentation." This being the case, we by no means destroy the noxious properties of excretal sewage when we empty it into the nearest stream, but we "contaminate the water" often at the expense of the life and health of individuals who dwell near the stream, or of animals that drink, or fishes that breathe its polluted waters. If the city of Baltimore, with a population of nearly four hundred thousand, should adopt and execute any system of sewerage by which its immense volume of refuse matter would be discharged into the tidal waters of the Patapsco river, it would be not only at the risk of destroying the fish, and of polluting still further the harbor of the city, by the refluent action of the tides in bringing back the material, but also at the annual waste of nearly one million dollars in manurial matter, which it is entirely practicable to save and utilize.

In sanitary matters we have as much to *unlearn* as well as to *learn.* We have traveled in one groove so long that our vision is circumscribed by the two sides, and it seems that light can only reach us in the *one* direction in which it dawned upon our forefathers. Our heads have become so firmly packed with *false* doctrines that *facts* cannot be gotten into them. We seem to have gone *incurably mad on the water-carriage system,* to the exclusion not only of all other systems, but even of all ideas with respect to them. Let us emerge from the "rut" and stand upon high ground, that light may reach *from every direction.*

The Sanitary Convention.

With the view of awakening an interest in sanitary matters throughout the state, by bringing together for consultation all who felt an interest in public and private hygiene, and to diffuse, as far as practicable, among the people such information as would tend to secure exemption from avoidable causes of disease, the State Board of Health, by resolution passed in May, 1883, decided to hold conventions annually in various sections of the state, at which addresses and papers on subjects pertaining to the public health should be submitted, followed by the broadest latitude of discussion.

The first of these conventions was held in Baltimore on the 27th and 28th of November, 1883, and, though not numerously attended, proved to be a great success in point of the interest manifested and the value of the papers submitted. In what more humane and important work could men be engaged than that of promoting sanitation among the masses, of instructing and enlightening them as to the laws of health, and as to the duty and wisdom of removing those causes that scourge humanity with the miseries and afflictions of preventable diseases?

In inaugurating these conventions the State Board of Health sought the aid not only of the medical profession, but of the public generally, in its efforts to lessen human suffering, and to make men's lives healthier and happier. The object of the board has been and will be to bring cleanliness, cheerfulness, health and comfort to homes and institutions where, perchance, filth, disease and sorrow have held high carnival. What work is more philanthropic, or deserves greater sympathy, encouragement and approval at the hands of all classes of citizens? Yet comparatively a small proportion of the population manifests any interest in sanitary matters, such as inquiries into the purity of the air we breathe, the water we drink, the food we eat, or the effect of other influences by which we may be surrounded, and which are factors in the promotion or destruction of health and life.

While the convention, as before stated, may be regarded as a success, it is, nevertheless, evident that its success can only be considered comparative. The interest taken in the convention by the public was certainly not what it ought to have been. Here were matters discussed by experts relating to the public health, such as sewerage, water supply, malaria, local health organizations, quarantine, vaccination, contagious and infectious diseases, vital statistics, &c., and yet how many of our state and city officials, how many large property-owners, and others supposed to be specially interested in these things, were present? Here were discussed important questions relating to schools and education. How many of the boards of education and public school teachers of the city and state participated in the proceedings? Here were matters relating to private as well as public health—to the prevention of disease and the prolongation of human life—discussed by those who have made these questions their study, and how many of the community, whose pockets, whose comfort and whose lives are affected, left their business or their pleasure for a few hours to gain information or give the moral influence of their presence to the gatherings?

One gratifying feature in connection with the convention, however, was the readiness with which the medical profession took part in the promotion of its objects. The doctors make their living by attending sick people, and yet they freely came forward, and without pay or hope of reward did their utmost to devise measures to prevent people getting sick. It was an exhibition of unselfishness deserving of all acknowledgment.

It is to be hoped that the work of the sanitary convention just closed will be of lasting benefit. It will certainly strengthen the hands of the State Board of Health in a renewed effort to promote sanitary reform throughout the state, and in taking all measures that will advance the public health.

It is clear, that if proper sanitary precautions were taken by state and local authorities, half at least, of all the lives lost each year, and more than half the money expended in the care of sick people and the relief of consequent distress, might be saved. The protection of health and life is certainly as needful as the education of the mind and the defence of property, and the day is not far distant when the sanitation of the people will be placed on a thorough basis. Several important matters, such as the formation of effective local boards of health, the necessity of a proper registration of vital statistics, a law to regulate the practice of medicine in the state, etc., will be brought to the attention of the legislature, and if anything is accomplished in these particulars, the labors of the convention, a full report of which will be found below, will not have been in vain.

Respectfully submitted,

C. W. CHANCELLOR, M.D.,
Secretary

FIRST ANNUAL MEETING

OF THE

SANITARY CONVENTION

UNDER THE AUSPICES OF THE

STATE BOARD OF HEALTH.

HELD IN BALTIMORE, MD.,

November 27th and 28th, 1883.

Proceedings of the Sanitary Convention.

First Day—Morning Session.

The convention was called to order by the president, Prof. Richard McSherry.

In the absence of the permanent secretary, Dr. C. W. Chancellor, who was confined to his bed by sickness, Dr. G. Lane Taneyhill was, on motion of Dr. James A. Steuart, requested to act as secretary.

President McSherry opened the convention in the following short address:

GENTLEMEN: In calling this convention to order, I have in the first place to express my high appreciation of the honor of presiding over a body of men who represent so adequately the intelligence and worth of the people of Maryland. At the same time I may say, that not being experienced in the duties of a chairman, I must ask your patient forbearance.

In the second place, I have to regret, as we must all regret, the unavoidable absence of our able and accomplished permanent secretary, Dr. C. W. Chancellor, who, after most efficient labor in preparing materials for the action of the convention, is suffering with a severe attack of illness, which confines him to his own domicile.

We are assembled here, gentlemen, to consider some of the most momentous questions of the age. The subjects open to discussion touch all interests. We have before us such subject-matters as "ventilation; house-drainage and sewerage; distribution and purification of waters for domestic use; hygiene of public establishments, steamboats and railway cars; contagious and infectious diseases; injuries to health from overflowed lands and from mill-dams and other obstructions in water courses; school life and hygiene; causes of insanity; malaria; vaccination and vital statistics; sale of poisons; and laws regulating the practice of medicine and surgery."

We have two or three days for the consideration of these great matters, which will bear discussion for as many centuries. But the vastness of the subjects need not appal us. We may not exhaust them; we certainly cannot; but what we can do is to bring them in such form before the community as to enlist general attention, as much attention, for instance, as is given to party politics, and which merits a great deal more. Here is something not for a party, but for humanity at large; and of modern medicine, which comprises all of these subjects, it may be truly said: *nihil humani alienum.* Unthinking people underrate medicine when they suppose it to be merely the administration of drugs. The *materia medica* in its highest sense covers all that bears upon the physical interests of man. And man's physical interests are not confined either to his digestive organs or to the development of his muscle; but incidentally, with his brain and nervous system are involved a sound intellect and intelligence, the *mens sana in corpore sano;* and furthermore, his very morals are more or less involved. Morality is fostered and promoted by the agencies favored by medicine, as temperance, and a masterly control over the evil passions and propensities. Sound medicine herein corresponds with sound religion. It is not hereby asserted that the part of medicine which we call *hygiene* will take a man to heaven; it stops, indeed, with earth; but there is nothing equal to it in the temporal order so well calculated to make "life worth living." There is a very close alliance between good health and human happiness. Health, peace and competence, the poet tells us, without fiction, are among our prime necessities, and he properly adds, that health consists with temperance alone. And health is wealth, too; it is capital. The health of nations is the wealth of nations, or, according to the motto of the *Sanitarian*, "public health is public wealth." Muscle itself is a great desideratum, and though held in less esteem than brain, when you bring them together, they are in their combination powerful factors in success, whether in the arts of peace or the arts of war. According to Dr. Letheby, "the political influence of a nation is as much dependent on the muscular strength of the people as upon their intelligence and commercial activity."

The design of such conventions as this is to make men happier, healthier, wiser. It is to co-operate with medicine in its widest sense, not to supplant it. The physician here only co-operates with his fellow citizens in matters of common interest, involving the public weal as well as the welfare of individuals, the welfare of families, including *paterfamilias*, his good wife and their children, and even their children's children, from generation to generation.

Disease, like death, visits equally the huts of the poor and the mansions of the rich, the tenement-house and the palace. It flew out with other evils from Pandora's box, and cannot be returned. It is inevitable, but not all inevitable. Not more than a half of prevailing diseases come from Pandora. An eastern legend tells us that Death and Pestilence made a compact by which Pestilence had the right to enter a certain city and destroy forty thousand inhabitants. But eighty thousand were carried off, and Death charged his ally with a breach of contract. "Not so," said Pestilence; "I took but forty thousand; Panic took the rest." And so, if one-half of our diseases came from Pandora, the other half are products from other sources, from folly, vice and ignorance, and such are not inevitable. These can be arrested measurably, if not entirely. Prevention is better than cure, as primitive innocence is better than sin and repentance, a fact of which we have an illustrious but most unhappy example, which runs through the ages, in the history of Adam and Eve and all their progeny. Until they knew evil they were happy—and healthy! but what they lost has never been regained.

Prevention is the great aim of this, as of other sanitary conventions. We accept the inevitable, but we must and will contest the ground, step by step, and inch by inch, against all that form of evil which comes under the head of preventable diseases. Our design is to combat physical evils, in every shape, and to no small extent, all vice and immorality. We will canvass the means of obtaining for the people good food, pure air and pure water. Let us find, or at least seek for, the means of destroying the factors or the products of innumerable diseases. We may find it possible to drown some noxious micro-organisms under floods of water, and soap; to suffocate others with chlorine or in fumes of burning sulphur, and to poison other kinds with mercury and arsenic. We must attack our enemies, enemies as they are of the human race, in their lurking places, as in swamps and sewers. We should urge the use of fire to kill trichinæ in pork, to save the lives of the unconscious consumers. We should endeavor to bring the ever-spreading corrosions of what is called the "social evil" under sanitary law. It behooves us to search for agents capable of destroying the bacilli in tuberculous matter, and to arrest, if we can, the passage of such matter from tuberculous subjects to subjects not yet diseased, but only predisposed or vulnerable.

We have much else properly subject to our consideration and action, so much that I shall not trespass longer upon your time, but will now invite the convention (after hearing an address of welcome from his honor, Mayor Latrobe), to enter at once upon the important business for which we are here assembled.

Professor McSherry then introduced Mayor Latrobe, who spoke as follows:

MR. PRESIDENT AND GENTLEMEN: It affords me pleasure to welcome the members of the State Sanitary Convention to Baltimore. I am sure the result of your deliberations will be beneficial. No subject is more useful and interesting than that of personal and public hygiene. Upon it depends, in a great degree, the prosperity and happiness of a community. Although the prominence given to sanitary science by Southward Smith, Lyon Playfair and others, some thirty odd years ago, has led many to believe it to be of comparatively modern origin, there is abundant evidence in early history to show that the ancients regarded public health as a subject for state legislation. The oldest known code of laws—that of Moses—gives special directions in connection with the cleanliness of the persons and habitations of the people, and one of the greatest monuments of a former civilization is the remains of the Cloaca Maxima, which the Romans constructed for the drainage and sewerage of their city. The success resulting from a proper attention to public hygiene is shown by the reduction in the death rate of so great a metropolis as London, now regarded as one of the healthiest cities in the world. Here in Baltimore, with our surface drainage, abominable system of cess-pools and other nuisances, our health reports show a very small death rate. I attribute this in a measure to our abundant supply of good water, the rolling character of the ground upon which the city is built, aiding, as it does, the surface drainage, and enabling every heavy rain to thoroughly wash out the streets; the absence of tenement houses; the naturally healthy location of the most populous sections of the city, and last, but not least, the vigilance of our health department. With a proper system of sewerage for sewage matter (it is a question with me whether surface drainage for storm water is not really more conducive to public health), a more liberal use of our ample water supply, the introduction of public baths and the entire abolition of these sixty thousand sinks now honey-combing the surface ground of our city, I have no doubt our health department would guarantee to make Baltimore the healthiest city in the world. I refer to these matters incidentally in my remarks, as I see by the programme that many of them will be matters for discussion in your deliberations. It was with pleasure that I listened a few days since at the Johns Hopkins University to a lecture on the subject of sewerage as applicable to large cities. I believe the time has come when Baltimore must realize that a proper system of sewerage is necessary for the preservation of its public health; and I am sure that a people which had the courage to invest over nine million for the introduction of water will not be alarmed at the contemplation of the cost of a proper system of sewerage required to protect health, and which, if judiciously controlled, will be as self-sustaining as are our great water works. I am pleased to welcome you to Baltimore, and wish you success in your deliberations.

The first paper read was by Mr. Henry C. Hallowell of Montgomery county, Md., entitled:

The Necessity for Local Boards of Health.

Mr. Hallowell said: Some one has defined civilization as that condition of society in which individuals can co-operate. Certainly nothing more marks the progress of a people than assembling for consultation upon subjects of common interest. The *Agora* of the Greeks had their counterpart in the town halls of New England, where the embers of opposition to foreign rule were fanned into the revolutionary flame. At no period of the world's history has this tendency to meet for considering the condition of the various occupations of mankind and the influences that promote or retard individual and collective happiness and prosperity, been so conspicuous as now. Conventions are held to consider every imaginable topic. Not only do learned scientists meet to investigate the mysteries of nature in the remote realms of space, or amidst the almost infinitesimal atoms of the microscopic world; to discuss the intricate problems of social and political science, or the philological needs of a reform of language; but railroad conductors, provision dealers, ticket agents, mechanics, merchants and farmers, all hold annual meetings for considering their special wants and aims.

Apart from the immediate good derived in a practical form from the information imparted and the ideas gleaned in these assemblages, the mere coming together, the commingling of earnest men in a common cause, has a beneficial and elevating effect.

A still more enlightened state is reached when these assemblings are not to advance personal or class interests, but are *pro bono publico;* where the participants themselves are in no immediate need of the reforms advocated or in danger from the evils warned against, further than that, sooner or later, each must share indirectly in the prosperity or misery of the rest.

Such conventions as this mark a state of public interest in the common weal, which is most gratifying. Composed, for the most part, of earnest and busy men from various portions of the state, and of various occupations and pursuits, it has been called to consider subjects of the most vital importance, and upon which ignorance of the grossest character exists, such as might well humble the pride of those who boast of the enlightenment of the nineteenth century.

Dwellings are erected in row after row, where the only aim seems to be to obtain a maximum of space in a minimum of cost, and at the expense of sanitary needs, the future welfare of the wretched tenants being no factor in the case. Cities build sewers, open streets and make excavations with scarcely a thought as to the season and consequent deleterious effects upon the adjacent population. Permits are given for occupations and manufactures, whose noxious vapors and drainage contaminate both air and water, and render life a burden to many incapable of moving their household goods, frail and wretched as these may be.

Wealth, refinement and intelligence are no safe-guards against the insidious approaches of disease. In our cities, occupants of residences, compared with which many of the palaces of the old world are dingy and insignificant, have, from defective plumbing, found their decorated homes but gilded graves. Seekers for health at sea-side resorts have gone from sickness to death by the use of contaminated water and disease-infected ice.

The lovely summer homes of millionaires have in more than one instance been abodes of the grim spectre who only waited until the gay rooms were filled with festivities, and youth and loveliness, ere he launched the fatal dart that was to convert the house of feasting into a house of woe. Rye Beach, during the past summer, has sadly confirmed these statements.

But if such inroads of disease are made more conspicuous in cities and places of resort, from the greater number of victims the rural districts are far from being the blessed abodes of health that enthusiasts suppose. Bards have sung the praises of pure water and fresh air, and essayists have waxed eloquent over the primeval happiness of living near nature and receiving her blessings unimpaired. Yet prosy truth discloses the fact that it is not because of knowledge or care that the rate of mortality is not greater. Vitiated air, wretched diet, impure water, never-ceasing toil, exposure and hardship, claim their victims more frequently than statistics show, and would swell the list to vast proportions were it not for the pure, invigorating breezes and the enforced ventilation of country-built houses. Cowper, keen observer of nature that he was, says the peasant—

> "Dips his bowl into the *weedy ditch*,
> And, heavy laden, brings his beverage home,
> Far fetched and little worth."

Country villages in particular are sadly in need of sanitary information and regulations.

For a confirmation of these statements here made, I will give illustrations from my own county, Montgomery, one of the most healthful, naturally most beautiful, and destined to be one of the most fertile and populous in the state, having a population more than usually intelligent.

To a single pool of stagnant water, damned up by the embankment for a road constructed by the county commissioners, were attributed last year several deaths and forty cases of malarial fever. These, with ten more the present season, were all within three-quarters of a mile of the pond. Who can describe the long hours of mental and physical suffering, the desolated homes and depleted purses, resulting from such ignorance of hygienic laws. In another part of the county a dilapidated fish pond was a source of malarial fever that infected a neighboring hamlet and made life miserable to more than one. Diphtheria carried off victim after victim, one household losing four inmates within the short space of one week. Had there been a more widely diffused knowledge of the utmost care required with regard to everything connected with that dreaded scourge, some of the sufferers at least might have been saved.

Even where sickness and death have not resulted, many have dragged along a miserable, half sick, half well existence from want of attention to cleanliness in and about their homes, and to the necessity of an abundant supply of fresh air, pure water and nutricious, well-cooked food. Where health has not been impaired, comfort has often been destroyed from want of power to control surrondings. In one beautiful village a family had its summer pleasure ruined by the fumes from an adjacent stable, the piles of compost and excrements festering, through the long summer days, every breeze wafting odors, *not* from "araby the blest," through door and casement.

At a school building erected by men of more than average intelligence, the *lieux d'aisance*, as it is politely called in France, was placed within twelve yards of the door and windows of a dwelling on an adjacent lot, though there was abundance of space elsewhere, and had not the owner of the dwelling protested, the occupants would have found it well nigh uninhabitable.

The traveler on roads leading through beautiful scenery is suddenly assailed by smells from pig-stjes and other places from which the neighboring residents have no escape. Wells and springs are vitiated by surface and subterranean drainage. High weeds and decaying vegetable matter, neglected cellars and filthy barn-yards, all lower the health rate and cry loudly for some apostle of reform to preach a crusade in favor of greater care and increased knowledge.

What is the remedy? In cities and towns organized boards of health, sanitary inspectors and officials of various grades have, or are supposed to have, a supervision of the health of the people.

Even these are hampered by selfish interests, gross ignorance, unfriendly legislation and a want of power to act promptly and efficiently, and yet accomplish much good. In the country, however, we have to contend with these difficulties and more, and without redress. Who is there to draw attention to the commonest facts of hygienic science, to diffuse information, to warn against the approach of disease and epidemics, to take note of and action against selfishness, that in pursuit of its own ends, threatens to sacrifice the comfort and even the health of others. "What is everybody's business, is nobody's business." There is no remedy, as a general thing, for sanitary short-comings, and we are at the mercy of intentional and unintentional offenders against the laws of health. One may buy a lot in a village, beautify it and render it all that is desirable as an abode and as a refuge from the smells and ills of cities, and there is no power to prevent a bone or soap boiler, or fertilizer manufacturer, from entirely destroying his health and comfort, by the establishment on an immediately adjacent lot, of offensive works. In our county seat, now a pretty and growing village, one of our most prominent and law-abiding citizens was forced to take the law in his own hands and give the owner of a slaughter house warning that, if it was not removed, he would do it by force. Is this right? Should citizens be placed in situations so dangerous to peace and order.

If some wise laws were passed organizing county boards of health, and giving them duly guarded but necessary powers, not only would the members diffuse a vast amount of valuable information, and do very much towards spreading correct and much needed knowledge, but there would then be some central power to which appeals could be made for the redress of grievances, where information could be sought and given upon doubtful points, and it would be *somebody's* business to look after the health and consequent happiness of the community. Does not the state owe this much to its citizens? Do not the people see the necessity of such a body, properly organized and entrusted with proper powers. That it is feasible has been proved in Montgomery, and perhaps elsewhere. At the request of Dr. Chancellor, Dr. Jas. S. Martin invited some physicians and others to join in the organization of a county board of health, under the sanction of the State Board. We met and adopted the following plan: A president and secretary were chosen, and subsidiary boards composed of from five to seven gentlemen, including always several physicians, were organized in each election district. The local or subsidiary boards were to meet quarterly, and the members of these constituted the county board, which met annually, and could be called together at any time by its officers. The local boards were to have a general care of the health of the districts, diffuse information, and, if necessary, report to the president and secretary of the county board. At the annual meetings questions of interest were discussed, and an interest awakened in its objects and aims.

Unfortunately our people, intelligent and progressive as they are, were not quite ready to carry on the organization, being discouraged chiefly, I think, by the fact that we were only an advisory body, having no power to abate nuisances as the laws are at present. But even in its two or three years of existence it gave unmistakable proof of how useful such bodies may become. One way in which they can reach the people I will give: As president of our county board I prepared a lecture upon sanitary topics and matters bearing in various ways upon the health of individuals and communities, such as care about the drinking water, air, diet, cleanliness, &c., giving instances of the fatal results from neglecting these things, and also showing to how great a degree we can ourselves preserve the health and comfort of our bodies and conduce to length of days. This was delivered in most of the villages of the county, sixteen times in all. Now comes the interesting fact that, *not once* was it given without one or more persons coming to the lecture and thanking him for the facts mentioned, and pointing out the need of attention to some one of the requisites for health named in that particular locality. Information was sought, questions were asked, advice solicited as to location of drains and out buildings, and in many ways was it demonstrated that some central, advisory body was a need and an important factor in any progressive community. Letters were likewise frequently received by the president upon the same themes.

I will frankly confess that some of the subsidiary boards never met, but others did, and one of them never failed to hold its quarterly meeting. To this latter can be directly traced various warnings and papers that in all probability would never have reached the public but for the discussions there. Dr. William E. Magruder prepared a paper upon poisoning from the use of goods put up in cheap, or improperly soldered tin-cans, which has been widely noticed in prominent medical journals, but first of all was given, in substance, to the county press. Dr. Jas. S. Martin, in a well written article, drew attention to the probable approach of Asiatic cholera, and the consequent need of more than ordinary care as to the cleanliness of our surroundings, particularly in villages. Numerous communications were published by the president and secretary, some of which bore fruit in various places.

If efforts, crude as ours in Montgomery, have produced good results, what might we not expect if suitable laws were passed giving discretionary power to a properly organized board! The wisdom of this learned body can doubtless devise some plan that will meet with the approbation of our legislators, and be promptly adopted.

Power might be given to the county board of health to present as a nuisance to the judge of the circuit court residing in the county, anything believed, on investigation, to be detrimental to the public welfare. The judiciary, being removed from personal and local prejudices, may well be entrusted with such duties.

This is only a suggestion. Your wisdom can doubtless find some more effectual plan.

That some such system would tend to promote the comfort, prosperity and happiness of the people, there is not a shadow of doubt.

On motion, the paper was referred to the State Board of Health for publication.

Dr. Jackson Piper of Towsontown, then read the following paper on

The Sanitary Requirements of Baltimore County, in Relation to both City and County.

A friend of mine, a distinguished physician of this city, some years ago, had the effrontery to tell the writer that all zymotic or contagious diseases originated in the country, and were imported thence to the cities. I had so much confidence in the purity of country air, that I ridiculed the idea as preposterous, and boldly asserted the contrary. Since then his proposition has seemed not so monstrous; for while each suffers in this regard from the other, the sanitary regulations of the cities are so much better organized and enforced that, except in rare instances, these diseases are kept within bounds; while in our towns and villages fear alone, in most instances, is the controlling element which prevents their spread.

Medical literature is rich in statistics to prove that complete systems of sanitation have diminished epidemics, have controlled their progress, and have in a remarkable degree reduced mortalities. Dr. Pettenkofer, in his admirable illustration of the impurities which accumulate in porous cess-pits upon the air of a town and upon its drinking water, and the death rate of the population, has shown for periods of five years at Munich, that from 1852 to 1859, when there was absolutely no regulations for keeping the soil pure, the mortality from typhoid fever alone was 24.2 per cent. per 1,000,000 of inhabitants; and that from 1876 to 1880, when the sewerage was complete, the per centum of deaths was reduced to 8.7. Similarly, at Frankfort-on-the-Main, the deaths from typhoid fever were reduced from 8.7 to 2.4 per 10,000. At Dantzig and Hamburg the results were equally striking.

A move in the right direction for Baltimore county was made two years ago, by the state legislature enacting a sanitary law for Towson, Woodberry and Waverly, and their vicinities, under which law the writer holds an appointment.

While it is an excellent law, as far as it goes, its scope and power require enlarging, and an attempt to effect the needful changes will be made at the incoming session of the present legislature. This law provides that the sanitary inspectors of their respective districts shall make investigations and inquiries respecting causes of disease and mortalities; shall investigate all nuisances affecting health, and are äuthorized to go upon all premises or into any house, and under certain methods and penalties prescribed, to have removed nuisances detrimental to health.

In case of any epidemic, contagious or infectious disease, the county commissioners shall send one or all three of the inspectors to any portion of the county. The defects of this law are that no provision is made to furnish a regular system of garbage-carts; it gives no control over alleys, streets and other highways, to have the same graded, drained and paved and kept in order; to remove, relocate and reconstruct in improved methods objectionable privies, cess-pools, stables and wells; to prohibit pig-pens and slaughter-houses within town limits; to have collected in safe places for instant removal kitchen and other wastes or stagnant pools, or rank vegetation on public highways.

The city is mutually concerned with the county in the passage of a sanitary law that will afford protection to both. The large outlying towns that form an integral part of Baltimore, have a community of interests with the city. It will therefore be necessary, to a proper understanding of the subject, to give a cursory glance at these towns, their population, their topography, their insanitary condition and their diseases, and in order to arrive at some definite results as to the important question of a compulsory law for vaccination, it will be necessary to give the area in square miles of each district in the county and its population, so as to discuss the feasibility of such a law, its probable cost, the number of vaccine physicians required, their salaries and the amount of ground each physician can compass in the year. This question is beset with great difficulties. Some of the districts are small and densely populated, while others are large and sparsely settled. The figures are therefore given so that this convention, if it deems the subject of sufficient importance, shall have data from which intelligent conclusions can be drawn and an efficient law evolved. For this same reason the writer will give his own conclusions and a draft for such a law.

Commencing on the York road, about a mile and a half from the city, is Waverly, which now covers thirty acres of ground, that fifteen years ago were used as pastures. This town has a population of four thousand. Almost continuous with it are the towns of Oxford, Peabody Heights, Homestead, Friendship and Hampden, and there is altogether a population of twelve thousand within a circle whose diameter is three miles. The character of this country is low, and the drainage bad; the houses in the villages in many instances badly constructed, and the sinks also, and in close proximity to the wells; the water courses or streams tortuous and obstructed with offal from slaughter-houses, glue and hair factories, and these streams have, I believe, a common sewer in Jenkins run. Malarial and typhoid fevers, diphtheria and scarlet fever and other zymotic diseases prevail. The sanitary officer for this precinct, Dr. H. G. Prentiss, has been indefatigable in his efforts to abate these nuisances, and his reports show an improved health rate.

Four miles from the city is Govanstown, with a population of one thousand two hundred and fifty. The country here is higher and more rolling. The health of this town is generally good, though the same defects exist in foul water-closets, imperfect drains and badly located and con-structed wells.

Next comes Towson, with a population of one thousand five hundred. This town is five hundred feet above tide water, has a natural water shed, is healthy as to location, and is steadily improving in its sanitary aspect.

As an evidence of this, my report to the county commissioners shows, for the summer and fall ending November 1, 1882, thirty-seven cases of typhoid fever in town and county, with twelve deaths; seven cases of diphtheria, and three deaths, and other diseases prevalent. This year, 1883, there were nine cases of typhoid, and no deaths therefrom; six cases of diphtheria, and two deaths; one case of scarlet fever, which recovered; six cases of measles, and no deaths, and other diseases at their minimum, and but two deaths in the town, one of these being from old age.

Five miles from the city on the Franklin road, we have the picturesque village of Franklintown, with a population of three hundred, and in the midst of a fertile and populous region; then the thriving village of Wetherdsville, five miles distant, with a population of three hundred; Powhatan, four and a half miles, three hundred; Rockdale on the Liberty road, of two hundred; Elysville and Alberton, virtually one village, Pikesville on the Reisterstown road, and Woodberry on the Northern Central, a bustling manufacturing town of a thousand people, and the adjacent villages of Sweet Air, Hampden and Clipper Mills, aggregating six thousand people depending upon the mills and factories. The mill owners here have erected neat cottages, and due regard to sanitary arrangements have been made.

Under the intelligent administration of the sanitary inspector, Dr. R. B. Norment, pig-pens have been almost abolished, and the sinks and alleys kept clean.

Five miles from the city is Mount Washington, population one thousand.

The country about these towns is hilly and beautifully picturesque.

Calverton, on the Baltimore and Potomac railroad, has a population of four hundred, and extensive stock yards, where an immense traffic is carried on in cattle. Hookstown, one hundred; Clifton, five hundred, and Rockland, on the Falls road. Catonsville, six miles from the city, population one thousand six hundred, is located upon an elevated plateau five hundred and fifty feet above tide water, and enjoys a great reputation for salubrity. Carrolltown, three and a half miles distant, is a pleasant village, having a high location and surrounded with charitable and reformatory institutions. Irvington, one mile and a half, a development of city extension, is salubrious and rapidly growing in population and importance, is a suburban resort. Just east of the south-eastern limits of the city is the important village of Highlandtown, population six hundred and forty-four. The extensive breweries in the neighborhood furnish employment for a considerable number of people. That portion of Canton outside of the city limits has a population of two thousand and eighty-four, which is rapidly increasing because of the growth of the industries located along the wharves and railroads, the extension of the commerce of the port, and the movement of the people from the overcrowded streets across the city boundaries. Ten years ago the Canton Company owned nineteen thousand building lots, and the aggregate of all its properties and funds was six million, five hundred and fifty-six thousand, six hundred and twenty-eight dollars. Wharves have been built, elevators constructed, railroads find their tide-water termini, factories flourish, and enterprise in a thousand different employments, finds encouragement and compensation. The sanitary condition of Canton is, however, in a deplorable state. July 18, 1883, I was sent by the county commissioners to investigate nuisances complained of there. I found the alleys filthy, the stables and water closets uncared for, and a stream that passes through the town a common receptacle for the refuse of breweries and other manufactories. I served notices to clean up, and obtained from the commissioners a brigade of garbage carts. The villages of Gardenville, Laurance and Georgetown complete this long and tedious list.

The districts around and near Baltimore number six, and have an aggregate population of fifty-eight thousand four hundred and thirty-nine, which is nearly three times the population of the seven remaining districts, and are :

1st District area	........28.28 square miles.	Population	12,498
2d " "	.........44.79 " "	"	 3,706
3d " "	.........39.55 " "	"	 8,761
9th " "	.........38.90 " "	"	21,414
12th " "	.........85.72 " "	"	10,314
13th " "	.........13.86 " "	"	 3,314

The remaining seven contain:

4th District area	........57.58 square miles.	Population	 4,300
5th " "	....47.26 " "	"	 2,241
6th " "	.........36 65 " "	"	 2,326
7th " "	.........59.93 " "	"	 3,074
8th " "	.........62.86 " "	"	 6,000
10th " "	.........48.30 " "	"	 2,374
11th " "	.........66.30 " "	"	 4,581

Total area of Baltimore county, 630.98 square miles; total population, eighty-three thousand three hundred and thirty-four, of census of 1880.

These country towns have evils in common, the most objectionable of which, and the most difficult to deal with, being the water-closets. A shallow trench, box or barrel are the common methods of construction. The soil becomes saturated with the contents, which finally sink into the wells, or by evaporation pollute and poison the air. In my reports for Towson I have time and again urged the construction of vaults laid in stone or brick on the sides and bottom cemented throughout, so as to be perfectly water-tight, and made high enough above ground to prevent inflow of surface water; the house above having a chimney for ventilation, and their contents from time to time deodorized and disinfected with solutions of quicklime, chloride of lime or sulphate of iron. But few heed such suggestions, and the only way to effect a change is to make property-holders by law to so construct them. These vaults cost from ten to fifty dollars, according to size, and if there is any better or cheaper plan the writer should be glad to know it. Another fault is shallow wells and their proximity to stables and sinks. To remedy this I have recommended driven or bored wells. It seeme to me these two methods, in the absence of sewer drainage, the cost of which would make it impracticable in our county towns; if engrafted upon the present sanitary law, together with the suggestions referred to in the first part of this article, and the appointment of experienced and energetic officers, would vastly remedy the evils complained of. Until these results are attained we must expect to suffer from zymotic and other filth diseases.

Another matter of vital importance is a law for compulsory vaccination and revaccination. The writer was sent to investigate the presence of small pox in Canton on February 9, 10 and 11, 1883, a period of time when it was sensibly on the decrease in this city. He found on inquiry of the physicians practicing there (Drs. Williams, Warner and Norris), and from other sources, the existence of some two hundred cases in an area of a mile square, the houses not posted—many of the Germans refusing vaccination—the public schools in full operation, and convalescents and patients suffering from mild attacks of varioloid in actual attendance—no provision made to disinfect the houses and destroy the clothing; and a number of houses, the residents of which refused to employ physicians for fear they would be reported and sent to the hospital. I had put up while there seventy-five flags, which I carried with me, and was told afterwards by a magistrate that a number more were ordered and put up. If any town in the state requires an act of incorporation, a sanitary inspector and a compulsory law for vaccination, Canton is the place. A statement of these facts alone should arouse the citizens of Baltimore, as a matter of self-protection, to help us in the county, by besieging the members of the legislature for a compulsory law.

The vaccine law which now holds for the county is that all persons unable to pay shall, on application to any physician, be vaccinated at fifty cents per capita, to be paid by the county, and any physician refusing shall be fined five dollars for each and every offence. This does not reach the apathetic and indifferent, or those opposed to vaccination. This law subjects the county to great expense without corresponding benefit. Persons are vaccinated and revaccinated without system or method, and many possibly are revaccinated who do not require it. The county commissioners paid the past year the sum of three thousand five hundred and sixty-two dollars and seventy-five cents for vaccination. not a cent too much, provided it was judiciously expended. It is proposed by the writer to repeal this law and substitute for it a compulsory act.

SECTION 1. *Be it enacted by the General Assembly of Maryland*, That section eight of article twenty-fifth of the revised code of

Maryland, be and the same is hereby repealed, and the following sections be enacted in lieu thereof:

SECTION 1. *Be it enacted*, That the commissioners of Baltimore county shall appoint ...... number of competent practicing physicians, whose duty it shall be to visit each dwelling house, public and private school in the county, and vaccinate and revaccinate all persons requiring it; and it shall be the duty of the several vaccine physicians to keep a record of the names, ages, residences and time of vaccinating, whether the operation performed is primary or secondary, and if primary to have satisfactory evidence that it has properly taken.

SEC. 2. *Be it enacted*, That the county commissioners shall direct the county surveyor to cause to have made the metes and bounds of each precinct, and to have recorded the same in the offices of the said commissioners, to be furnished to each physician for his respective district or precinct to which he may be appointed; for which services the said surveyor shall be paid the sum of ...... dollars.

SEC. 3. *Be it enacted*, That the county shall be divided into ...... precincts, embracing ...... square miles to each precinct, and that the vaccine physician shall be a resident in the precinct to which he is appointed.

SEC. 4. *Be it enacted*, That each physician shall receive the sum of...... dollars per annum, to be paid quarterly, and that the salaries for districts Nos. ...... shall be ...... dollars, and for districts Nos. ...... shall be ...... dollars.

SEC. 5. *Be it enacted*, That before the said commissioners shall pay to each physician his quarter's salary, the said physician will be required, under oath, to say that he has visited one-fourth of the houses of his respective district, and vaccinated properly all therein requiring said operation, and that the said vaccine physician shall not receive his second quarter's salary until, as before required, he shall, under oath, &c., and so on until the close of the year, and shall, in addition, at each quarter produce his record books, which books shall be the property of the county commissioners at the expiration of his term of office, or on resignation or dismissal; said books to be used as reference by his successor.

SEC. 6. *Be it enacted*, That said physicians shall be appointed for a term of two years.

SEC. 7. *Be it enacted*, That it shall be the duty of all the vaccine physicians to sign in their respective precincts, upon proper evidence of vaccination, all certificates that may be required of them to enable the children to enter any of the public schools of the county, and that this duty shall be performed free of charge.

SEC. 8. *Be it enacted*, That any vaccine physician refusing to sign any certificate, as in accordance with preceding section, shall, upon sufficient evidence of the same, be dismissed by the county commissioners and another appointed in his place.

SEC. 9. *Be it enacted*, That it shall be the duty of each vaccine physician to keep a strict record of all births occurring in his respective precinct, and to vaccinate every infant before it completes its first year, and in case of small pox being near, to vaccinate it at once.

SEC. 10. *Be it enacted*, That it shall be the duty of all vaccine physicians to enforce a revaccination of every one at his or her twelfth year on which his or her birthday occurs, and so on every twelfth year that afterwards ensues, and that the evidence of the party so vaccinated, or the record books of previous physicians, may be used to establish the fact that such revaccination is required.

SEC. 11. *Be it enacted*, That it shall be the duty of the vaccine physicians, and other physicians in attendance, or of parties who may be cognizant of the fact, to report to the county commissioners all cases of varioloid or small pox that may come to their knowledge; and on said report being true the county commissioners shall empower the vaccine physicians, or the physicians in charge, to have removed, if practicable, such patients to a hospital made and provided for such patients by the commissioners; and, if not practicable, said physicians shall see to it that said patients and their attendants shall be kept in strict seclusion until the danger of contagion shall be pronounced by the said physicians to be over. A fine of ten dollars or more shall be paid for each and every offence by the party or parties to which this section refers.

SEC. 12. *Be it enacted*, That it shall be the duty of the vaccine physicians to visit such houses, and in convalescence to personally order the destruction of all clothing and furniture that may contain the contagious element, and to have thoroughly disinfected such houses infested with small pox.

SEC. 13. *Be it enacted*, That the county commissioners shall allow a fair compensation of all property so destroyed, under oath of parties to whom said property belongs, his or her heirs, in case of death.

SEC. 14. *Be it enacted*, That it shall be the duty of the county commissioners to provide good and efficient virus, at the county's expense, for the use of said vaccine physicians in the discharge of their duties.

SEC. 15. *Be it enacted*, That it shall be the duty of all physicians, and of parents when no physician is in attendance, to report to the vaccine physician any births occurring in said vaccine physician's precinct, on penalty of a fine not exceeding five dollars for each offence.

SEC. 16. *Be it enacted*, That any physician may take as evidence of vaccination any certificate to that effect given by the family physician, provided, on examination, such vaccination, at the proper time, is likely to be successful.

SEC. 17. *Be it enacted*, That all report of births and vaccinations performed by others shall be entered by the vaccine physician in his record book.

SEC. 18. *Be it enacted*, That any party or parties in person resisting or refusing to be vaccinated, or refusing vaccination for their children, shall be fined ten dollars for each offence, and shall be imprisoned until such fine shall be paid.

SEC. 19. *Be it enacted*, That the money required to carry this act into full effect shall be raised by the county commissioners by assessment on the entire county, as made and provided in the payment of other expenses of said county.

SEC. 20. *Be it enacted*, That any or all of the fines or penalties imposed by this act shall be recoverable in an action of debt in the name of the county commissioners, before any justice of the peace of Baltimore county, and the fines so recovered shall be applied by the county commissioners to the payment of the enforcement of this act; and, in case of imprisonment, any justice of the peace of Baltimore county, on complaint, shall issue his warrant for arrest of party or parties infringing said act, and cause his apprehension; and, on sufficient evidence, the said party or parties shall be remanded to jail to await the action of the grand jury.

In regard to the number of vaccine physicians required, taking, as a basis of calculation, the whole area of the county, and, allowing ten square miles for each precinct, it would give, with the increase of population since 1880, seventy-one vaccine physicians, and as the work in the more thickly settled portions of the county would be greater, on account of more houses to visit and more parties to vaccinate, it seems that a larger compensation should be allowed to physicians in these districts, and that the precincts of these populous districts should be less than ten square miles.

I have allowed for the large districts a salary of three hundred dollars per annum, and for the smaller populated districts one hundred and fifty dollars per annum. The whole expense of vaccinating the county at this calculation, amounts to twelve thousand eight hundred and fifty dollars, a large sum, but not too large for the work done.

As the work would be very onerous the first year, this amount would be required, and the expenses for the succeeding years might be reduced one half, which would call for some very material changes in the proposed law.

A great outcry will be raised by the taxpayers at such an expense, but the results to be obtained are fully commensurate with the outlay.

It is hoped that our legislature will be imbued with a spirit of liberality and broad statesman-like views on subjects so important and momentous to the people. Monarchial Europe has recognized the necessity and economy in the end of such measures. Who does not recognize that filth is a factor of crime, or that cleanliness conduces to virtue? Money so expended is money made, for just in the ratio that disease is lessened, so is pauperism; and with the abatement of both, will there be less of drunkenness and crime, and less occasion will there be to expend money in keeping up our courts, our jails, our almshouses, our insane asylums and our reformatory institutions. Moralists, political economists, philanthropists and physicians tell us this. And it is a proper and just demand that sanitary measures should be rigorously instituted and the money consideration thereof should be the least worthy of regard.

Discussion.

Dr. Leas said: "Mr. President, I have listened to that address with interest, because I am a resident of Baltimore county, and resident of that part of the county which has not received any attention on the part of the board of health. The proposition presented by the doctor is one worthy of the highest consideration. If he proposes to make the physicians sanitary inspectors as well as vaccine physicians, it would be well to give them fifty dollars a year more, and we could then reach some of the objects which are contemplated. Baltimore county would then be provided for in those respects in which she is so sadly wanting now. At present there are many sources of disease and many nuisances which, with proper attention, might be abated. Therefore, I would suggest that Dr. Piper insert in his paper a provision to make these vaccine physicians sanitary inspectors also."

DR. STEUART SAID: "It strikes me that a combination of these two propositions would be eminently efficient. Nothing is more important than a co-operation of the local boards of health with the State Board of Health, and through them to have the necessary measures inaugurated; for after all it is important that we should construct a form of machinery through which these sanitary measures can be carried out. Unless there is a plan organized by law, it will always be disregarded by the public, and never carry any weight with it. It merely illustrates the old saying of 'what is everybody's business is nobody's business.' Those who undertake these regulations should have the power to carry them out. There should be organized arrangements, such as the legal appointment of local boards of health, who should appoint the vaccine physicians and also have power to draw upon the county commissioners for the necessary expenses contingent thereon. We all know that there is a very close and niggardly feeling existing towards sanitary committees and physicians in the counties. I propose that there be a local board of health for every legislative district."

MR. HALLOWELL: "Is Dr. Piper willing to include that proposition in his board of health bill?"

DR. PIPER: "I am asked whether I accept the amendment of Dr. Steuart? I do not accept it, sir, for if we ask too much we are likely to get nothing. Give us what Mr. Hallowell has recommended—a vaccine physician in every district, and let there be one in Towsontown. I would like to accept Dr. Steuart's suggestion, but feel it is rather too weighty."

DR MCSHANE: "I endorse the proposition of Dr. Steuart, and

no other. Dr. Piper's provisions are for Baltimore county only, while those of Dr. Steuart are broader and more comprehensive, taking in the whole state."

Dr. Benson: "I endorse the propositions of Dr. Piper and Dr. Steuart. I will warn them against one thing, and that is in adding on fifty dollars per year for sanitary inspector. Fifty dollars per year is not enough. As you all well know, good work must be paid for. If you make it fifty dollars per month instead of fifty dollars per year, I will vote for it."

Dr. J. McShane: "On the matter of compensation, the proper way to act is to leave the counties to decide what it shall be."

Dr. Benson: "I would say nothing about the compensation in the bill particularly, but only wish to see that it be made a proper one. If we value the services of the sanitary inspector at fifty dollars per year, the citizens will not estimate it any higher."

Dr. Steuart: "I think it would be better to leave the question of compensation entirely out of the matter. We are willing to leave to the board of health the question of compensation. Dr. Piper has very carefully drawn up the law, and it would be very easy to include in it a law that local boards of health be established by the local authorities generally, and that they having local supervision, have the right to appoint vaccine physicians."

Dr. Morris: "One of the objects of this convention is to aid and strengthen the State Board of Health, which has vainly endeavored, time and again, to impress upon the legislature the importance and necessity of enacting certain sanitary laws. What more can it do? I think we should take the matter in hand, and not simply refer it to the state board, but appoint a committee from this convention to see the legislature, and urge the enactment of proper laws. I therefore move that the subjects suggested in both the papers of Mr. Hallowell and Dr. Piper, including the draft of a law by Dr. Piper, and the question of organizing county boards of health, be referred to a committee of three members of this convention, to be appointed by the president, to be designated "The Committee on Sanitary Legislation," which committee will co-operate with the State Board of Health, formulate the subjects, and present and urge upon the next legislature the adoption of the same."

Dr. Blake: "I listened with great satisfaction to the discussion that the vaccine physicians should be made sanitary inspectors. I last year had the pleasure of being a member of the city council. There were two physicians on that committee, and they all agreed that the vaccine physicians and sanitary inspectors' duties should be combined, and notwithstanding their reports, some untold efforts of outside parties weighed them down, and their effects were lost. I think there is not an intelligent physician here to-day but has seen the injurious effects of their loss. It is unreasonable to compromise the public health by putting it in the hands of those who know nothing of medicine. I don't propose to discuss what their salary will be, for that is a minor question when we consider the public health of the county."

Dr. Henkle: "The value and efficiency of a piece of machinery depends upon its simplicity. I am not sure whether I understand the gentleman's views upon this subject, but what I do know is that I understand my own views. Dr. Ohr of Allegany county took an earnest interest in getting the legislature to meet this question. I had the honor of co-operating with the doctor for some time. Now, if you wish a law to accomplish the purpose, you must, in the first place, make it very simple. Do not load it down with complications. I have seen very few attempts to organize local boards successful in counties. I am not positive, but I venture to say that of all the boards of health appointed in the counties, not one has ever had a meeting. But Dr. Johnson said we have to take the world as it is and not as it ought to be. I was very much struck by the bill of Dr. Piper. It is the most comprehensive presentation I have ever heard, and I would be glad to see some law based on that bill and made applicable to the whole state. But, gentlemen, let me say once more, you must make the machinery simple or you will be disappointed. I would authorize the county commissioners in all the counties in the state to appoint at least one capable physician in each legislative district, who should be vaccine physician and sanitary inspector. It would not cost a great deal, and much good would be effected. I think Dr. Morris' proposition is a proper one. I recommend that this convention should formulate a law that should be generally applied to the whole state."

Dr. Kemp: "What is the general scope of this convention? I did not intend to say a word, but as the discussion is taking a much larger latitude, it will involve a great many points that have not yet been brought before the convention. Dr. Henkle has made a very good remark, and that is, not to make the machinery too cumbersome or it will not work. Fifty years ago the health commissioners of Baltimore had a book, by turning to which you could find the number of the house you sought in any street, and there it could be seen what kind of a building it was, whether of wood, stone or brick, and it also embraced all other information that sanitary inspectors might wish to know. Gentlemen, that is the very information that the sanitary inspector wants, and which at the present time he has so much difficulty in getting. What took, thirty years ago, a vast amount of machinery to carry out, can be done at the present time with machinery of much simpler and less intricate kind. So I would endorse the idea of having as few as possible working, but those few must be hard workers, live men, and must derive the power from law to carry out what they deem proper. I do not know what the organization of boards of health may be, but I do know that there is not a board of health in the land that can meet the requirements that a few energetic, live men can."

Dr. Rohe: "I think the discussion has taken too wide a range. We should come back to the main point. I agree with Dr. Morris, that a committee on legislation should be properly selected and endowed by the convention, with the power to act in conjunction with the State Board of Health. I therefore call for the previous question on Dr. Morris' motion."

The call for the previous question was sustained, and Dr. Morris' motion was adopted by the convention without a dissenting voice.

Miscellaneous Business.

The following letter from Colonel Wm. Henry Legg, of Kent Island, was read, calling the attention of the convention to the fact that a disastrous epidemic of typhoid fever had occurred on that island in 1880, the cause of which, the writer thought, should be investigated:

Colonel Legg's Letter.

Kent Island, Md., November 22, 1883.

Dr. C. W. Chancellor, *Secretary State Board of Health:*

Dear Sir: Your invitation to attend the sanitary convention was received to-day. If I had the time, its acceptance would afford me great pleasure, and I am sure I should derive much valuable information, especially from hearing the discussion of the subject of "contagious and infectious diseases." There is one disease—typhoid fever—which I hope may be thoroughly discussed. About three years ago—summer of 1880—it visited this beautiful island, and in that season and the next almost decimated its population. The young and the healthy were mostly selected as its victims. There was scarcely a family it did not visit and take away some loved one, and some families it almost wholly destroyed. Had the small pox broken out and prevailed generally among us, it would not have been worse. The health of the island is generally good, and this year we again have had our usual good health. I am not a doctor, but "typoid" fever, as country people call it, is "catching," or infectious. Every physician should, when he has a case, guard the family and public against the infection by all known means. That is my opinion; take it for what it is worth! In this locality it has run its course and subsided. Some attributed it to the well water I am getting to be an old man, but nothing here ever occurred like it before, and we are drinking water out of the wells our fathers dug. So that theory won't do. Yours, very truly,

WILLIAM HENRY LEGG.

Note.

The above letter of Col. Legg is interesting. It is to be regretted that the secretary of the State Board of Health was not called upon *at the time* to investigate the cause of the fever. As the disease was so wide spread it was scarcely due to the well water, but was most probably the result of a polluted air. Where typhoid fever occurs in one or more families using water from the *same* well, it is wise to suspect that the water in that well is contaminated, and to have it chemically examined; but corrupted air may also become a prominent factor, if not a primary cause of the spread of the disease.

It is a matter of experience that during the decomposition of organic substances, whether vegetable or animal, aided by heat and moisture, and other peculiarities of climate, a poison may be generated which, when in a state of high concentration, is capable of producing the most fatal results by inspiration of the air in which it is diffused.

Experience also shows that this poison, even when it is largely diluted by admixture with atmospheric air, and when, consequently, it is unable to prove *suddenly* fatal, is still a fruitful source of sickness and mortality, partly in proportion to its intensity, and partly in proportion to the length of time and the constancy with which the body remains exposed to it. Facts without number, long observed, such as the great amount of sickness and mortality in marshy districts, the fevers, diphtherias and dysenteries incident to certain localities where the laws of nature have been violated and overthrown by neglect of sanitary precautions, sufficiently attest the presence in these localities of a deadly poison. But this poison is too subtle to be reduced to a tangible form. Even its existence is ascertainable only by its mortal influence on the human body; and although the induction commonly made as to its origin, namely, that it is the product of putrefying vegetable and animal matter, appeared inevitable, seeing that its virulence is always in proportion to the quantity of vegetable and animal matters present, and to the perfect combination of the circumstances favorable to their decomposition, still the opinion could only be regarded as an inference.

But modern science has recently succeeded in making a most important step in the elucidation of this subject. It has now been demonstrated by direct experiment that, in certain situations in which the air is loaded with poisonous exhalations, the poisonous matter consists of either vegetable or animal matters, or a combination of both substances in a high state of putrescency. This matter constitutes a deadly poison. A minute quantity of this poison, applied to an animal previously in sound health, will destroy life with the most intense symptoms of malignant fever. By varying the intensity and the dose of the poison thus generated it is possible to produce fever of almost any type, from a mild intermittent to a malignant yellow fever, and endowed with almost any degree of mortal power.

It is proved, further, that when the poison is diffused in the atmosphere or in the water-supply, and is transported to the lungs in the inspired air, or to the stomach in the water drank, it enters directly into the blood, and produces various diseases, the nature of which is materially modified, according as the vegetable or animal matter predominates in the poison.—C. W. C.

Letter from F. E. Davis, Architect.

BALTIMORE, November 27, 1883.

DR. C. W. CHANCELLOR, *Secretary State Board of Health:*

DEAR SIR: It would give me pleasure to have the members of the sanitary convention visit the prison department of the central police station house, North street near Lexington street, to inspect it as to the ventilation of the cells and the plumbing.

As the system is in some particulars at variance with accepted theories and practice on the subject, it would perhaps be interesting to note it and its workings.

Very respectfully, your obedient servant,

FRANK E. DAVIS, *Architect.*

On motion, the invitation of Mr. Davis was accepted.

The secretary announced the subjects of the papers which would be read at the evening session, and the convention adjourned to meet at 7:30 P. M.

First Day—Evening Session.

Dr. W. Stump Forwood read a paper on

Canning Houses and Their Relation to the Public Health.

The modern term "*canning*" signifies that process by which fruits and vegetables are preserved in tin vessels called cans, rendered air-tight by solder, after the expulsion of the air has been effected by means of heat, thus preserving these articles of food in nearly their natural state for an indefinite period of time.

This industry has been developed within a few years, having its origin in Harford county, beginning upon a very small scale. It was first introduced, we believe, by Mr. Baker, who began business by the use of an ordinary cook stove. He has since erected several canning factories that are operated by steam boilers upon a very large scale. And to supply material for their operation, he annually cultivates several hundred acres of sugar corn—confining his business to the canning of corn.

From Mr. Baker's small beginning years ago, the business has increased until the present year, 1883, when it is estimated there are five hundred canneries in operation in Harford county.

These preliminary statements regarding the origin and progress of the canning industry in our county are designed simply for the purpose of drawing your attention to the supposed pathological conditions to which canning factories give rise. The word "supposed" in this connection, is used advisedly, for investigations into the subject thus far have not been sufficiently accurate or positive in results to warrant us in assuming an absolute connection between cause and effect.

While peaches, apples, blackberries, green peas, beans, and more especially sugar-corn, are largely canned, the canning of *tomatoes* constitutes the chief staple of the industry in Harford county; and it is to the offensive effluvia arising from the offal of these articles that the origin of various diseases has been attributed.

The first canning houses were started in the vicinity of Aberdeen and Perryman's, and are more numerous in those neighborhoods at the present time than in other parts of the county. And it was in near proximity to these canneries where exceedingly offensive odors prevailed, and chiefly among those employed in conducting them, that a fearful epidemic of a lingering, malignant fever arose early in the autumn of 1881, and continued its ravages with great fatality until the supervention of the freezing weather of the ensuing winter.

So many good and well-known citizens were stricken with the disease in the vicinity of the canneries—and in some instances their entire families were likewise attacked—that a widespread alarm was occasioned throughout that section of the county. So far as we can learn from subsequent investigation, the majority of the cases thus occurring were enteric or typhoid fever; but owing to the fact that the majority of the cases prevailed in the immediate vicinity of the canning factories, it soon became to be known throughout the county, in the language of the laity, as "*canning house fever.*" This association of cause and effect was quite a logical inference on the part of the non-professional, when it is borne in mind that the odor arising from the decomposition of huge piles—dozens of cart loads—of tomato peelings that were allowed to ferment and decay at the doors of the canning houses. It even became a question with the medical profession, and it still has its advocates, whether this noisome material, constantly poisoning the atmosphere, did not generate a new disease of a typhoid or malarial character; or, at least, add malignancy to those hitherto more tractable maladies.

With a view to averting a like epidemic in the following "canning" season, as well as for general protection against preventable diseases, a county board of health was organized at Bel-Air, July 23, 1881, at which the following resolution was unanimously adopted :

"*Resolved*, That a committee, consisting of Drs. Lee, Forwood, Hayward, Kennedy and Chapman, be appointed to issue an address to the canners of Harford county, advising them in regard to the best means of disposing of the offal accumulating about their factories; and that the same be published in the county newspapers."

There were no canning houses located in the vicinity of Darlington, the place of your reporter's residence, at the time of the adoption of the foregoing resolution, and hence he could not appeal to his own observations for the information necessary for the instruction of the canners; but having been elected to the secretaryship of the board, and having accepted the appointment on the committee, he felt it a duty to prosecute the necessary investigations with all possible vigor and dispatch. He strenuously appealed, verbally and by letter, to the other members of the committee, the majority of whom were located near canneries, and also corresponded with many leading citizens in various parts of the county, who were engaged in the canning business, urging them to state the best and most practical means, in their judgment, for disposing of the offal so as to avoid *nuisance*, as well as sickness.

These efforts in the interests of the "public good," on the part of your reporter, after the expenditure of considerable time and some money, resulted fruitlessly, as might have been anticipated; for it is a universal law that valuable labor cannot be obtained without a corresponding valuable equivalent. The state did not propose to make any compensation to the board of health for their labors in preserving the public health. The secretary's efforts in procuring suitable reports from those qualified to make them, with the design of issuing an address to the canners in 1881, as to the proper disposition of their offal, having proved unavailing, the Medical Society of Harford, at its meeting held in Bel-Air on May 8, 1882, took up the subject that had been neglected by the board of health the previous year, and introduced the following resolution, offered by Dr. R. D. Lee, which was unanimously adopted:

WHEREAS many of the citizens of Harford county have become alarmed, in view of the frequent sickness and great mortality which has prevailed in the immediate vicinity of canning houses, and supposed to owe its origin to the offensive exhalations from their neglected offal; and observing with increased alarm the rapid multiplication of these establishments in all parts of the county, it becomes our duty as the guardians and conservators of the public health, to investigate the conditions which are supposed to jeopardize health and comfort, and suggest their remedy or removal. Therefore, be it

"*Resolved*, That the Medical Society of Harford County invite the county board of health, and our citizens generally, who may be connected with the canning interest, to co-operate in a joint meeting, to be held at the court house, Bel Air, on July 31, 1882, at 11 o'clock A. M., for the accomplishment of a common purpose, when it is hoped that the committee appointed last year will present their report upon the proper disposition of the offal matter about canneries, for the consideration and action of the said joint meeting."

It fell to the lot of the reporter to prepare the "*Address to the Canners*," which was presented to and accepted by that meeting held July 31, 1882. The delivery of the address was premised by the following remarks:

In presenting the following address to the canners, the secretary of both organizations takes occasion to say, that the member of the committee from Aberdeen, Dr. Kennedy, who has had considerable experience and opportunities for personal examination in regard to the odors and the diseases associated with canning houses, has furnished the secretary with the substantial points which constitute the foundation facts of this report.

In fact, the report is due to his interest and energy. The other members of the committee, much to our regret, have, in essential particulars, failed to co-operate with us in supplying the materials here presented; hence, the delay in the preparation of the address.

All members of the committee, however, who have had the opportunity of examining the report, now give it their endorsement.

These details are here presented for the purpose of showing the State Sanitary Convention the impediments to be overcome in the prosecution of sanitary work without moneyed compensation. We here see that in a county, composed of citizens of wealth, and of a high grade of intelligence, where an alarming epidemic was prevailing, that it required a committee of an organized board of health a period of more than a year to make their report upon the best means of staying the ravages of the prevailing diseases; and that finally the report was made through the agency of the *Medical Society*—prepared at last entirely by the labors of two members of the committee of five originally appointed for that purpose.

The special question is: "*Are Canning Factories, as at present conducted, prejudicial to the Public Health?*"

This is a question of very great importance to sanitarians generally, and to the citizens of Harford county especially; for these factories are now numerous throughout the county.

At the beginning of the present month, November, we received a letter from Dr. C. W. Chancellor, the secretary of the State Board of Health, calling our attention to this convention and its objects, and requesting for the occasion a presentation of our views on the "Effects of Canning Factories on the Public Health."

Feeling a deep interest in the subject, and having previously devoted considerable attention to it, we accepted the invitation; and with the view of obtaining as much information as possible, we addressed copies of the following letter and list of "Inquiries" to twelve of the medical gentlemen in the county, who we believed were located where they had the best opportunities for observing the relation between canning factories and the public health. The letter reads as follows:

"DARLINGTON, MD., Nov. 6, 1883.

"DEAR DOCTOR: Dr. Chancellor, the secretary of the 'State Sanitary Convention,' which will meet in Baltimore on the 27th and 28th of the present month, has requested your correspondent to deliver some remarks before that body upon the 'Effects of Canning Factories on the Public Health.'

"As the value of my statements to sanitarians will depend entirely upon their accuracy, I have determined, for purposes of corroboration, to ask you and a few other physicians in the county, who have had opportunities for observing the various types of disease that have prevailed in the vicinity of canning houses, and which were apparently modified by the effluvia arising therefrom, to favor me with your views in connection with the accompanying interrogations. Very truly, yours,

"W. STUMP FORWOOD."

The following are the "Inquiries as to the Effects of Decomposition of Canning House Offal upon the Public Health," which accompanied the foregoing letter:

"1. Have any cases of diseases been brought to your notice, which, in your judgment, originated from, or were aggravated by, the *effluvia* arising from the decomposition of neglected vegetable matter in and about canneries? If so, please state the *nature* of the disease; and whether, in your opinion, it *originated* in canning house effluvia, or simply derived increased virulence from its agency.

"2. If you have observed types of disease which appeared to be associated with canneries, and popularly known as "Canning House Fevers," please say what peculiarities have characterized their symptoms, course and pathology.

"3. Please state if enteric fever, dysentery, or any other disease, has prevailed in your practice to a greater extent in the vicinity of canning houses than elsewhere.

"4. Should these questions be answered in the negative, please state whether, in your opinion, the decomposition of vegetable matter about canning houses exercises any appreciable influence whatever upon the health of those exposed to the emanations arising therefrom.

"5. If it is believed that canning houses, as now conducted, affect injuriously the public health, please state what practical measures or precautions, in your opinion, may be successfully adopted for averting such results."

The first reply is from Dr. H. Clay Whiteford of Darlington, who, during the season just closed, has filled the office of inspector to thirty-one canneries. The duties of this office do not require him especially, though incidentally, to inspect canning houses and their surrounding as to their *sanitary condition*, but simply to inspect the *quality of the articles canned* by an association of canners, who place their goods upon the market under a common brand.

The inspector's duty is to see that no member of this association puts up an inferior article, and thus bring the brand of many of the most careful packers into disrepute.

Dr. Whiteford, under date of Nov. 10, 1883, says:

"DEAR DOCTOR: Yours of the 6th received and contents carefully noted.

"As we find our canning houses conducted now, I am of the opinion that they are not a special cause of disease more than is found around any farm-house in the country, if as much. You are well aware that in and around every barn you will find a yard for deposit of stable manure of various animals; a pig pen with its proportion of abominable filth; the chicken house; the out-of-door water-closet, etc. All of these places of deposit are ten-fold more at fault than the canning house. The owners of those places do not, except rarely, take any precautions against the foul stench arising therefrom. A few will throw some lime or plaster around, the majority neglect them entirely.

"During the past packing season, it has been my duty as inspector, to look after the quality of goods and the general cleanliness of thirty-one canning houses. While in this line of duty I have always kept before me the health of the people in and about the canneries, and I have found that the district over which I have traveled was singularly healthy, and has so remained up to this time. Surely, if the canning houses were a source of disease, and to such an extent as they have credit for being, we could not possibly have enjoyed such good health in the past season.

"During the summer of 1880 there was but one canning house in this neighborhood; and I never, during my professional career here, since 1869, had half as many cases of malaria and diseases of the same type, claimed by some to be the result of canning houses, as were presented in that season. Now clearly these cases were not the result of canning houses. If so, why should we have had such good health this year, when we have at least twenty-five of these factories within four miles of us? All this noise that we have heard so much of is thunder in the distance only. The alarm is false, and there is no doubt about it, the facts prove it. As sanitarians we would do most good by giving more attention to the depositories of decayed matter in and around each homestead, as referred to above, than to be charging all our troubles on the packing houses, which only run about forty or fifty days in the three hundred and sixty-five.

"But, dear doctor, do not understand me as excusing the canning houses from their full share of cause; they must take some of the responsibility.

"Just at this moment a few cases in point come to my mind. During the season of 1881, A. S. and R. M. began work in Whiteford and Hopkins' canning house. They were in poor physical condition, and both went on duty with *ague*. They worked hard night and day during the season, and without any medicine; one gained nineteen pounds, and the other twenty-four pounds in weight, and went home at the end of the season *entirely well.* Again this house employed foreign help, just from the lower counties of this state, where they had been engaged in picking strawberries. Several of them had had the malarial fever. * * * These people lived and slept throughout the season within two hundred feet of the packing house.

"In closing these remarks allow me to suggest that the constant volume of heated air arising from "process kettles," etc., may have a tendency to counteract or dissipate any evil gases that arise from decayed matter, as result from tomato peelings, corn husks, etc. This is only conjecture; but why the impunity, if there is a *cause* and that cause *inert?* Very truly,

"H. CLAY WHITEFORD, M.D.

The following is the answer made to our queries by Dr. P. Chapman of Perrymans:

"PERRYMANS, HARFORD CO., MD., Nov. 18, 1883.

"MY DEAR SIR: Your favor of the 6th inst. was duly received, and in reply I will state that I have given some thought to the subject of canneries and the diseases arising therefrom, and have come to the conclusion that many of our good citizens have gone to early graves in consequence of the *effluvia from canneries.* I believe they create the germ of *typical typhoid* or *enteric fever.* We have had, in my experience here of seven years, what Woodward and Flint term typho-malarial fever in the beginning; and as canneries increase I find they are intensifying the typho into a genuine typhoid fever. I have seen several in a family stricken down, and from no other cause, as far as I could learn, but the bad management of canning houses. Therefore I would suggest for the good of those engaged in the business, and for the good of their neighbors, that our representatives in the next legislature see that special legislation is enacted to prevent the evil arising from the same."

Dr. Chapman then proceeds to answer the questions *seriatim*, as follows:

"1. I am not prepared to say whether the typhoid germ originates directly *de novo* from any peculiar aspect given it by the microscope, from canneries. I am not a believer, to the full extent, in the assured germ, humoral or any other theory, as a specific cause of disease; but believe that the virulency of all diseases is increased in ratio with the intensity or multiplicity of *micrococci* or *bacteria* evolved from decaying animal or vegetable matter, sometimes resulting, from influences unknown, in contagious diseases; at one time in typhoid, at another in diphtheria, and at others in scarlet fever, etc.

"2. We have here a 'canning house fever,' which shows violent poisons, to be eliminated either from the bowels, by copious grumous hemorrhage—pre-eminently hemorrhagic in its character—nose, throat and I might add *the skin,* in the order named, showing the essentials of blood-poisoning. I have had no post-mortem.

"3. I certainly believe that *enteric* and *dysenteric* troubles are closely connected with canneries; and that the hemorrhagic type prevails especially in tomato canneries.

"4. I think they do; though this question has been answered in the above; and the next session of the legislature should not adjourn without having passed *special nuisance laws,* protecting innocent citizens against the more careless ones, who are indifferent to their own welfare, and care less for that of their neighbors.

"5. I now answer your last and most important question. I believe that the vast majority of our citizens engaged in canning are ready to act upon wise counsel; but some are thoughtless, others are ignorant of the sanitary precautions necessary to preserve themselves and neighbors from the injurious consequences of badly-kept canneries, and others—but few, it is to be hoped—care nothing for their own health or lives, or that of their fellow-citizens, so they themselves prosper in their business. I would therefore repeat that the next legislature should pass stringent laws regulating the canning business, a matter that concerns us all; certainly all my section of the country. The law should be executed by *paid officers*. A physician in each neighborhood should be appointed, whose duty it would be to inspect each and every cannery at least once weekly during the eight or ten weeks—from August 15th to October 30th—which constitute the canning season, with power to impose a special fine in case his rules are disregarded. And the magistrate should be empowered with authority to have the arrest made, and require the offender to pay the fine directly, without the delay which usually attends the formalities of the law and the courts.

"The sooner our people are brought to see the necessity of some legislation regulating this important and growing enterprise in our midst, the better will it be for their future health and welfare.

"Truly and respectfully yours,

"P. CHAPMAN, M. D."

Dr. W. W. Hopkins of Havre-de-Grace, takes the opposite view.

"HAVRE DE GRACE, November 9, 1885.

"DEAR DOCTOR: Yours of the 8th, making inquiry of me in regard to the deleterious effects of canning house offal, if any, upon the community in which I live and practice, must be answered by my saying that such is not my observation nor belief that it has had any other bad effect than that of being offensive to our sense of smell, when they are located in close proximity to the public roads. I am not inclined to the belief that decomposed vegetable matter will produce disease. We will have to search for the germ where most authorities think it is to be found, viz.: in cesspools, sewers, drains, etc.

"To produce enteric fever, whether such places must be further poisoned by having the specific germ—the dejections of a patient suffering with the disease—poured into them, may be questioned, doubtless; but the proof that such is the case is strong. I sometimes think that, to accuse the decomposition of vegetable matter of being a source of disease, is to imply that Providence made a mistake, as it is something that we could not be expected to get rid of. It always will be around and about us; we cannot run from it, nor drive it from us.

"The fever that prevailed with us in 1881, frequently termed 'canning house fever,' resembling, if not true typhoid fever, would, certainly, to some extent at least, have prevailed in the last two years, had canning houses been the cause.

"Yours truly, WM. W. HOPKINS."

As to the general decomposition of vegetable matter in nature, as referred to by Dr. Hopkins, as an evidence of its innocuousness, the analogy is not a correct one; for nature never disposes watery fruits, like tomatoes, in large masses, as are seen about canneries, where their fermentation would be offensive to the olfactories.

These heaps of offensive materials result not from nature, but from the artifice of man.

Dr. Scarboro of Dublin, writes:

"NOVEMBER 18, 1883.

"DEAR DOCTOR: In answer to inquiries, I must say that, very contrary to what I should have expected, I have never yet been able to trace any case of any kind of sickness to canning house influence.

"On the contrary, the negative testimony has all been the other way. I have known several instances where the canning houses were exceedingly offensive, and yet there was not a case of sickness anywhere in the vicinity more than usually occur.

"Many persons supposed that the malignant cases of malarial fever in the Galbreath family, two years ago, was caused by the canning house. But this could not have been, for the fever began before they had commenced canning; and the cannery was half a mile from the dwelling, with higher land intervening. What the cause was I do not know, but five persons who boarded in the house took the fever, while those who worked at the cannery and boarded elsewhere were exempt.

"I attended two girls with dysentery in the last summer, who had worked at canning; but I had other cases similar who had not been near any cannery.

"As I said before, this is very much contrary to what I should have expected.

"Now, although perhaps rather foreign to your inquiries, I must say that I believe that malarial fever and typho-malarial fever are caused more by the water drank than any other cause.

"A few years since, a very severe type of typho-malarial fever broke out at J. B. Scarboro's.

"His wife had it, and she insisted, from the first, that it was the *water* that caused her sickness. On taking the water out of the well, it was found to be in a very foul condition, there being several dead toads and rats in the well.

"But with all this, I think that strict regulations should be enforced in regard to the cleanliness of the canning houses; for, while it may not be possible to prove them to be the cause of sickness, they are in many cases a positive nuisance, and most offensive to their neighbors, and really to the traveling public.

"Very truly yours, etc.

"SILAS SCARBORO."

Feeling anxious to obtain all the information possible on this subject, we introduced it to the meeting of the Medical Society of Harford County, held on the 13th of the present month.

The remarks made on that occasion by Dr. J. T. Payne, who resides in the northern part of the county, were clear and practical. He said that, previous to his personal experience, he had been prejudiced against canning houses for sanitary reasons; but two years ago, before there was a canning house within five miles of his residence, a malignant type of low fever appeared, and pervaded the neighborhood generally, with very fatal results.

But there were no canning factories there then to take the blame. Since that year a number of canneries have been erected and operated in the same neighborhood, and yet no epidemic of any kind has since appeared. He had not seen any case of disease that he could attribute to canning house infection; but he strongly protested against the discomfort they occasioned the public through their offensive odors, and favored legislation for their abatement.

Not having any transcript of Dr. Payne's remarks, we have simply stated, in our own language, the chief points of his argument.

Dr. R. D. Lee of Bel-Air, remarked :

"I am convinced, from careful observation, that the effluvium arising from the decay of vegetable refuse from canning houses, during the summer and autumn, by infecting the air, is a fruitful source of diphtheria, dysentery, diarrhœa, etc., and a decided aggravation of fevers peculiar to paludal districts; tending to convert the simple autumnal intermittent into a remittent or continued fever, so well marked and characteristic as to acquire the name of typhoid-malarial, or 'canning house fever,' among the physicians practising in the belt of our county bordering on the bay and tributaries.

"Diphtheria, especially, has been frequent and violent wherever the canning houses have been numerously aggregated and proper cleanliness neglected.

"We say this without prejudice ; on the contrary, we are justly proud of our great industry, of which our county has been the great pioneer.

"There is a general complaint of the noxious gases emanating from these places, and the residents are anxious to have the nuisance abated."

Almost at the last moment, November 22, we received a reply from Dr. J. H. Kennedy of Aberdeen. As before stated in connection with Dr. Chapman's remarks, the views of Dr. Kennedy, who has also lived in the midst of the earliest and the most thickly located canneries, from their origin to the present day, are entitled to great weight ; for his opportunities for observation have perhaps been better than those of any other practitioner in the county.

Dr. Kennedy replied to our inquiries as follows :

"1. A number of cases have come under my notice, which were apparently due to the effects of canning house effluvia ; and many other cases were more or less modified by the same cause. As to the former class, they were principally typhoid ; and a few cases of a peculiar kind of unclassified fever, which I suppose might have been designated as '*canning house fever*.'

"Those which seemed to be only influenced by the poison atmosphere of canning houses were persons who suffered attacks of intermittent and remittent fevers only while exposed, and were curable only after having withdrawn from the source of infection.

"2. These cases referred to above as being unclassified, or canning house fever, differed from typhoid in many respects.

"For instance, the suddenness of onset and rise of temperature to one hundred and five degrees by the fifth day; and by the gradual or modified decline to normal, or below by the seventh day. There was no diarrhœa, tympanitis or eruption; nor dry, black or fissured tongue.

"A case in point, which I saw October 19, 1883, for the first time, was ushered in by a slight chill; with moist, coated tongue, constipated bowels, with intense pain in the head, the stomach and upper portion of the body generally—temperature one hundred and two degrees, and which continued to rise until the 24th, when it reached one hundred and five degrees; after which, by the eighth day, it fell to ninety-five degrees. The intense suffering, which was out of proportion to the symptoms, continued, and was of a nervous character, first in the stomach, then in the chest; and the head and spinal column would be successively affected; no vomiting; tongue clean and fiery red; delirium constant. No periodicity. Quinine useless. The temperature did not reach the normal point until the thirtieth day of the disease, when recovery slowly began taking place. The countenance was most haggard, and the complexion was of a ghastly hue throughout.

"I will sum up as follows: I have not changed my opinion, formed from the epidemic of 1881, and expressed in our address to the canners, although canning houses have increased in number, and cases of typhoid and other fevers have been fewer.

"The people in this portion of Harford county were thoroughly aroused by the epidemic of 1881, and very many of them have removed the greater portion of the offal from their canning houses, and instituted measures of purification, which, though defective and poorly enough carried out, have done wonders, as the olfactories of all exposed can attest. And again, we have not had a crop of fruit in either year since 1881, that offered such an amount of refuse matter around canning houses for putrefaction. Nor has there been in either year since then such continued elevation of temperature, favoring decomposition, as was maintained throughout that very long and very hot season.

"In conclusion, I do most defiantly maintain that the poisonous, *villainous odor* of a *filthy canning house* is lowering to vitality, and no more likely site could be found for discovering the germs of disease. I have never observed such cases of fever as I have described in malarious or other localities remote from canning houses. I have noted few or no cases of special disease about or connected with the houses that can corn exclusively, where the husks and cobs are removed, in which cases no unpleasant odor arises.

"When the winter is at all mild, as regards temperature, the heaps of tomato offal, frequently left about canning houses, emit their sickening odors throughout that season; and upon the opening of spring this filth acquires a new activity of offensiveness from the warm rays of the sun, and from some of the canning houses a disagreeable smell is distinctly perceptible throughout the year."

We have now given the "pros" and the "cons" of this question at considerable length.

And it will be seen that the gentlemen consulted differ materially and radically upon the main question, viz.: Do canning houses produce or aggravate disease?

As far as our personal observation goes, we do not feel warranted in attributing special diseases to canning houses. In the year 1881, we had charge of more cases of enteric fever than ever before in a single year, during thirty years practice. The majority of these cases were remote from, and beyond the influence of canneries. Within the two years that have since elapsed, at least twenty-five canneries have been erected within the circle comprising the bounds of the cases occurring in 1881, and yet not a single case of enteric fever or of any other disease that could be charged to canning houses has, during those two years, come under our notice.

Our correspondents, though perhaps not "known to fame," are all physicians of ability and experience, who are well known and highly respected in Harford county, where they possess the warm esteem and confidence of the large communities in which they respectively practice their profession; and while differing as to the etiology of disease, they all unite in *condemning the nuisance* resulting from the decomposition of the offal about canneries, which destroys the comfort of those who reside in the vicinity, and of those who travel the public roads.

They all suggest legislation for the abatement of this nuisance; and in this suggestion we unite most heartily. The outcry of our citizens generally against these insufferable odors is too loud and too unmistakably earnest to pass unheeded longer. Some positive steps for its suppression must be taken at once. And it now becomes the duty of this body to institute the proper initiatory proceedings for submission to the action of the approaching session of the legislature. To give a single instance from a non-professional source, to show the feelings of the people upon the subject of this nuisance, we transcribe the following letter, just received from a gentleman while writing upon the subject he speaks of:

"WEBSTER, MD., November 22, 1883.

"DEAR SIR: Seeing by the newspapers that you are to deliver an address before the State Board of Health, and knowing you are a friend of suffering humanity wherever found, and that you have the health of the public at heart, we beg you to pay a visit to the canning house of Evan Thompson. Said canning house is situated on the public highway, about one hundred and fifty yards from my dwelling, and about thirty feet from my spring-house. During every rain the filth backs into my spring-house, and I am unable to use the water for weeks; in fact, we have not used the water for drinking purposes all summer.

"Hoping to see you here soon, I am,

"Yours respectfully,

"G. W. PAUL."

This letter needs no comment, further than to say that it is the echo of views entertained by hundreds of others.

Legislation is required to compel the canners to exercise scrupulous care in the immediate removal of the offal from the canneries by water-tight carts to receive it, without allowing a particle or a drop of the liquid to fall upon the ground about the establishment. It is essential, for the avoidance of odor, that all of the offal should be carried away and scattered broadcast upon the fields of the adjoining farms, where the sun dries and harmlessly dissipates the moisture from the substances, and the residue afterwards unites fertility to the soil, and thus repays the labor of removal.

But it is useless to adopt laws without providing the means for their execution. Sanitarians, who render efficient service, must be paid for the same. Physicians, qualified for the duties of inspecting canning houses, and directing remedies for existing nuisances, and advising the best means of avoiding the same, cannot and will not leave their private practice, from which they derive their support, for the labors of a *public* office which they are asked to fill "without money and without price." However self-sacrificing human nature may have been in ancient times, their present necessities in the struggle for existence compels them to look for the *quid pro quo.*

It is the duty of the state to provide for the protection of the lives and the property of its citizens; and all who are interested in sanitary legislation—and who are not?—should unite in impressing upon our legislators, at the very beginning of the approaching session, the importance, yea, *the necessity*, of providing an ample fund, to be appropriated to the remuneration of those sanitary workers for the benefit of the state, in due proportion to the value of the services required and rendered. Until this is done, boards of health will only exist, if at all, in name.

In the purely sanitary consideration of this subject, it is only necessary to ascertain to what extent pure air may be admixed with extremely offensive odors, containing nitrogen and sulphuretted hydrogen, and inhaled habitually without inducing deleterious effects upon the health. And we must bear in mind that the sense of smell, like that of taste, and the other senses, is a sentinel that stands to guard the system against the assaults of invisible foes.

If it can be proven that animal life may be maintained indefinitely in such an atmosphere—the ordinary canning house atmosphere—the next question that logically presents itself is: What right has any man, or number of men, for purely selfish purposes, to so befoul with irrespirable stench the pure air of heaven, as to destroy the pleasure and comfort of his fellow-men—depriving them of that one blessing which we have always been taught to believe was designed to be "free, alike to the rich and poor?" Upon this point we ask your most serious consideration. As we said before, while we are not prepared to prove this decaying matter to be a factor of disease, *we unhesitatingly declare that canning houses, as now conducted, are unmitigated nuisances!*

Dr. Forwood conclnded his able paper by saying:

"The legislature should pass a bill providing for the pay of agents to guard the public health, and that a part of their duty should be to enforce such restrictions as the State Board of Health may impose for the abatement of nuisances caused by canning houses."

Discussion.

DR. BENSON: "This is the best dissertation on the canning house fever I have ever heard. I would move the thanks of the convention be tendered to Dr. Forwood for his careful investigations."

The motion was unanimously adopted.

DR. ROBERT MORRISON: "I would suggest as a cause for the propagation of disease from the masses of decaying vegetable matter around canning houses, that if there is anything in the germ theory, cannot the mosquitos and flies generated by this decaying matter be the carriers of the germs of disease?"

DR. ROHE: "I have been much instructed by this interesting paper, and am glad that the thanks of the convention were offered to Dr. Forwood for it; but I gain from it the one prominent idea, which is an old and well settled one, that "doctors disagree;" and the question arises, is it the province of this convention to take any action on this matter, with a view to influence legislation, when we are forced to acknowledge that we cannot prove that the evil really exists."

DR. LEAS: "What does Dr. Forwood desire?"

DR. FORWOOD: "I did not propose to offer any resolution on this subject, but only suggestions. We have a great nuisance at our doors, and we would have it removed. I thought this would be the best place to make the move."

DR. MCSHANE: "I understand that a committee on legislation, to co-operate with the State Board of Health, will be appointed by the president of this convention. I move that this paper be referred to them for action."

DR. STEUART: "The aim of this convention will fall short of its purpose if we fail to get the opinions of the gentlemen present upon just such subjects as that before us now. We are endeavoring to mould public opinion, and I think this convention should express itself and be recorded on this point."

DR. MORRIS: "Dr. Chancellor told me a short time ago that he believed the outbreak of diphtheria in Frederick was in a measure caused by canning factories. I am convinced that the epidemic, two years ago, in the fourteenth ward, was caused by decaying refuse of fish. But while this is true, I do not think we have any right to ask legislation on this subject until something much more definite than at present exists has been proved."

The paper was then referred to the State Board of Health and the Committee on Legislation.

An interesting paper, by W. C. VanBibber, M. D., was next read, on

Malaria or Bad Air.

The subject of malaria is an extensive one. In this paper it will be divided into that malaria which is found in dwellings, showing its effects in domestic life; and into that malaria which spreads over wide districts of country, and shows its effects among the inhabitants of those districts. There are general principles and laws which govern the atmosphere everywhere, whether it is good or bad, and these, it will be seen, have something to do with the question of malaria; but an attempt will be made in this paper to arrive at some conclusions concerning the impurities of the air immediately within the jurisdiction of this State Board of Health.

The meaning conveyed by the word malaria amongst physicians, as well as with the public, has recently undergone some change. Whereas, formerly, the word was kept within the meaning of its derivatives, now, it is not used to express a cause, but as a name of a disease, and that disease is the most prevalent, and may be said to be, the most fashionable one of the day. At the same time it is used as a prefix or adjective, as malario-typhoid or typho-malarial, with the intention to qualify the supposed influence which it exerts on all other diseases, more or less, according to its own peculiar laws. Within my own recollection the word was once more restricted in its application. Less than twenty years ago it was never used in connection with a case of disease which originated, and was treated, in the hilly portion of this state. How different is it now? At present there are cases of disease, found in every locality throughout the state, in what should be well appointed towns, as well as in the country, which are termed malaria, or malarial fever, and for which no other adequate cause or classified name can be found. This is so generally the case, that physicians have been charged by the public with having hobbies, and with using the word malaria as an expression to cover or conceal their ignorance of some unknown cause for those effects which they evidently see before them. This is a serious charge against physicians, and is one which should be explained. If there is any foundation for this charge, one of three things must be true. Either it must be admitted, that formerly, it was a mistake to restrict the meaning of the word, or that at present, the habits of building and living, are so changed, as to render the extended meaning of it necessary; or else, the physicians must declare that there is an error now in attributing prevailing symptoms to this cause, and calling the disease "malaria." It may be a difficult thing to show which one of these propositions should be accepted, and this difficulty is to be regretted. It would certainly be an interesting and profitable line of inquiry to pursue, to point out the changes which have been made in the personal habits of the people of this state, and to trace the effect of such changes in the resulting health. Changes have been made in the way of warming and ventilating houses, both in town and country. Change in industries, as Dr. Forwood has told us, in the style of living, in the habits as to hours, and in many other ways, all of which might produce that peculiar cachexia which is now called by our physicians and people "malaria." This word has been mentioned as a substantive name of a disease in every paper read before this assembly. A resemblance may be traced in the disease thus named, and an attempted description of real malaria, which will be given further on in this paper; but whether they both depend upon malaria, or bad air, is the point to be determined. It cannot be expected to determine such a point in a paper like this, except by inference. The object here now is to point out where contaminated air may reasonably be expected, and to classify the causes of its contamination. The theories concerning the essence or active principle of malaria are too well known to be recited, and therefore its supposed chemistry or composition will not be discussed. With each one of the sources of malaria as they are mentioned in this paper, so far as it is possible, some remedial means intended for general or popular use, will be suggested.

The malaria found in houses, both in public buildings, and in private dwellings, large and small, called more properly contaminated house-air, and which shows its effects in domestic life, has many sources. In this city the most serious source is from the cesspools, but this will be mentioned separately. Excluding this, for both city and country, the want of ventilation may be regarded as the next most important. Building houses without fire-places is becoming each year more common. Entire rows of "speculation" houses are built without fire-places, and otherwise badly planned in regard to ventilation. A large majority of the public buildings, churches, court houses, halls and school houses in the city and country are said to be badly ventilated. A fire place, with a thirteen inch flue in the clear, should be built upon each floor of every dwelling. The Academy of Music, the Natatorium, the Normal School, a few of the public schools in this city, and other buildings also, are completely ventilated, and prove that imperfect ventilation is not a necessity, but results entirely from carelessness. Wet, damp and unclean cellars produce in-door malaria, which permeates most dangerously the entire house. Building houses upon bad ground is another source of malaria within doors, and want of house cleanliness is another. These will all be remedied, one after another, as the bad effects from them are practically demonstrated to the inhabitants; but it is particularly necessary to mention them, in order to keep their importance before the people.

The malaria which is found, and has its origin, outside of dwellings, may be divided into that which is peculiar to cities and large towns, and that which spreads over wider districts. The atmosphere of a city is more readily contaminated than the same area of country land, because the walls and yard enclosures prevent the air from moving through a city with the same freedom of natural currents which it does in the country; when air is partially stagnated, it may be more easily contaminated. The air of a city is deteriorated by the radiation of heat from walls and pavements in summer, and is contaminated from the exhalations from gutters, butcheries and refuse manufacturing products at all times. The air of this city in particular is further contaminated by the exhalations from the earth itself, which holds gases of many kinds in its pores, and is constantly exhaling them into the air which we breathe; particularly is this the case in summer, and more particularly when the earth is dug up in large areas in warm weather. Dr. McShane, of this city, has particularly studied this point, and will give some of his conclusions to the convention. The negligent fitting of gas pipes, permitting leaks, so saturates the earth in many places with burning gas, that some of the finest trees have been killed. All these are undoubtedly sources of malaria. Can they be remedied? Hard as the problem may seem, it would be by no means impossible, provided our citizens would lend a more determined hand in the matter.

To lessen the deteriorating quality of the air from heat radiation, I have elsewhere advised the more general planting of trees and the construction of gardens on the tops of back-buildings, stables, low ware houses, &c., for which kind of building the hills of this city offer peculiar facilities. The variety of trees make a difference, and there is a choice of selection from a considerable number of species The maple and linden are the kinds most generally selected here, and they are beautiful. The worst city trees, in general use for the streets, are the ash and white mulberry. The most beautiful, in my judgment, are the alanthus, or trees of heaven, and the horse chestnut. The alanthus has been unfortunately discarded from the streets of our city for years, on account of a peculiar aroma from the male tree during two weeks in the month of July. There are certain individuals who say that this aroma gives them headaches. I think in most cases it is purely an imagination concerning the headaches; and it is well known that the female alanthus tree, which is more beautiful than the male, exhales no aroma. The female alanthus is the most beautiful tree suited to our climate that can adorn a city.

For the bad air, and the disease conveying properties of city air, there is one and only one remedy; this is cleanliness. The leaders of government, and the instructors on health, must combine to patiently educate the public how to be clean, and to show them the necessity for it. If the earth in the city exhales bad gases, it is because noxious and putrescent matters are laid beneath it. Can the present state of this evil be remedied in the great city of this state? On account of its geographical situation and its topography, Baltimore should be an exceptionally healthy city. It is in a temperate climate; in a sheltered position; has an abundant market, from land and sea; most of the luxuries of the table are abundant and cheap; a profusion of water, moderate prices for fuel, and every kind of social and agreeable recreation for its citizens. For its topography; it is situated upon hills, from which a grade could have been originally established to deep water, by filling up the intervening hollows, which would have made its surface drainage better than it is now. Much could be done in this way yet by filling up the "submerged district" or "meadow," and draining over its surface to deep water. Yet notwithstanding these advantages, compared with other cities, Baltimore is not an exceptionally healthy city. The published death rate is 18.3 per thousand, and the appearance of its inhabitants do not make it remarkable in respect to health. Why is this so?

I believe that besides the sources of malaria already mentioned, there are two other sources to be discussed, which are worse than all the rest combined. I mean the malaria emanating from the cess-pools and the sewers. Of my own personal knowledge, I can testify, that the Harford run and the Pearl street sewers emit nauseous and even deadly miasms. But the cess-pools are admitted by all persons to be the greatest nuisance which we have. It is an increasing nuisance, for, if bad now, what will it become in the course of time? There are now in Baltimore from fifty-four thousand to sixty thousand houses, and the same number of sinks upon an area of nine thousand six hundred acres. In some places the earth is thickly studded with them. These discharge their gases, at all levels, into the air. To remedy this, I have an idea, and the spirit moves me to proclaim it. The matter is of such paramount importance that it should not be evaded. I know full well the difficulty and the almost hopelessness of the subject. Although I believe you will listen to me with reluctance, and although my mind shrinks from the task, yet I will begin it from a standpoint which may merit both consideration and calculation. The difficulty of the entire subject is owing more to its unpleasant nature, and to a natural loathing from its consideration, than from any real difficulty of bulk or weight, when taken from inventive, engineering or industrial standpoints.

Physiology teaches that an average adult weighing one hundred and forty pounds, requires, in round numbers, about two and a half pounds of solid and three pints or pounds of liquid nourishment in twenty-four hours. From this he passes about two pounds of liquid and less than one-half a pound of solid excreta daily. Is it impossible to remove this, or at least a greater portion of the solid matter? Ask those who know the price of labor if it need be so exceedingly expensive as to condemn it from this item alone. But it requires custom and time to familiarize a population with the idea of a removal of this matter, and it requires the ingenuity of man to collect the material, and after these are overcome then the difficulty will no longer be great. The weight or bulk of the material to be moved is comparatively small. It is for this reason that I believe the best closet has not yet been invented, because, when it is perfected, it will have for its chief object the removal of at least the daily one-half pound per adult capita of solid excreta. Let any one make the calculation for all ages of inhabitants for a city the size of Baltimore. The end of the best calculation I can make for this entire removal brings the expense down to the one-third of a cent daily for each individual.

It would indeed be a wondrous boon to this city, and to the inhabitants of all the cities of the earth, if this one problem could be solved on the basis of complete removal of solid human excreta. When the small quantity to be removed is known and carefully considered, I trust the day is not distant when it will be accomplished. I have an unfailing confidence in the inventive ingenuity of the free-born American citizen. Does any man believe that the system now in use here is the best that can be devised? It is the truth to say that numberless of our citizens are afraid of their own homes. For one, I feel that when the subject is seriously undertaken with further knowledge and different calculations from those which have maintained heretofore, something more, something different, something better may be done. And to encourage us in this belief, after this paper was written, the *Sanitarian* of the 22d of November, *received to-day*, contains a paper upon "the treatment and utilization of town refuse," by John Collins, F. C. S., F. G. S. L., from which it appears that the town of Bolton, in Scotland, having one hundred and six thousand inhabitants, remove this kind of refuse. Mr. Collins says: "It does not pay expenses, of course, but it costs less than any other plan in operation on a similar scale." He does not give the minutia of the manner of collecting the excreta, but makes these suggestive remarks: "The collection and scavenging are mainly effected at night, and by means of closed carts of excellent design. There are a few water closets, but the *newer* cottage property are provided with 'pails.' These are roughly assorted on loading," &c. This looks as if the elaborate arrangements now in use here would some day or other be substituted by pails or some sufficiently ingenious contrivance to remove and utilize the solid excreta. Where men are crowded together, as in cities, it is necessary to remove the solid excreta daily, and not to hide it forever. I believe it will be easy enough to make way with the liquid excreta, which is easily chemically neutralized.

The last source of malaria to be mentioned is that which affects the inhabitants of the low lands, or the cretaceous, the tertiary and the post tertiary lands, of this state. It is known to us as that malaria which pervades large districts of territory. Its essence is not known. From the earliest days of medicine it has been supposed to produce ague-and-fever. Elsewhere, in a report upon the drinking waters of Maryland, I have spoken of the investigations of others in seeking for the cause of ague-and-fever in the drinking waters of the flat lands. This is an interesting subject; but as it is yet undetermined concerning the water, it is fair at present to hold that if ague-and-fever is conveyed into the human system through the air, that this is the great and prevalent out of doors malaria of which this State Board of Health has charge. We have all seen type cases of long continued or chronic ague-and-fever which have originated in this state. Let us suppose one particular case of an adult, who has had the disease since childhood, and he will present upon examination these prominent appearances and symptoms. In figure he may be taller than the average height, gaunt, thin and bony; with a muddy, ugly complexion, without tint or color; awkward in motion, slow in speech and action; slow in cerebration, ignorant, superstitious, untidy; always thinking of himself and his diseases; will talk by the hour of his chills and fevers, when they come on and when they pass off; will take any quantity of quinine, blue-mass, calomel, cholagogue or any advertised remedy; but is so fond of his home and neighbors in like affliction, that he will never leave it, or them. A most prominent symptom of his malady is that he will take no advice, and refuses to appreciate anything like advancement. Should this adult die suddenly, or, as often happens, die from some intercurrent disease, as pneumonia, the skilled pathologist will pronounce his liver different from the physiological liver in color, consistence and size. His spleen will be found large, soft and pulpy, and his blood changed in color and in microscopic appearance.

This type case of old-fashioned malaria, with some sectional differences, has been found in all parts of the world, between certain parallels of latitude, wherever our navies have gone. It is common on both the east and west coasts of North and South America, and in the adjacent islands; on the coasts of Africa, Asia, and on the shores of the Mediterranean Sea, and also in the river bottoms and swamplands of these several continents. This is the wide-spread out-of-doors malaria, well-known in medical as well as general literature. For its habitat and gravity in our own state and country one can consult the map issued by the census bureau in 1870. If this is a fair description of the disease in question, however imperfectly it is drawn, and if this board of health has even indirect charge or self-imposed responsibility concerning those suffering with this affection, is it not an interesting theme to them? Is it not a pleasant duty to promulgate knowledge, and ways and means by which these terrible sufferers may be relieved, if it is possible? To relieve them would be even more than equal to the work of Jenner, or like the rite of Apotheosis amongst the ancients.

Whether this disease comes from a malaria over the land or from germs in the water, the best means that I know to prevent ague-and-fever (nothing need be said here of its cure), are these: Temperance in eating and drinking, and avoiding during summer entire suits of linen clothes as a summer wear; drying the air of a sleeping room by fire, night and morning; building dwelling houses above the earth, in order to give an air circulation between the earth and the house; avoiding the night air out of doors in certain places; filtering and boiling drinking water; cleanliness about houses and yards; drainage from the premises; high trimming of trees around houses on sides facing healthy localities; and the removal of all stagnant waters from the neighborhood of dwellings. In a report made to this board of health in 1878, I suggested sprays of carbolic acid to be industriously applied during three months in the year in the houses where chills are known to prevail. All these means are easily enough carried out, and if they will prevent this terrible disease, are fully worth the trouble they will give.

I must be permitted to say here that it is not derogatory to the medical profession, as a body, that they cannot positively assert what is the peculiar principle or essence in the air, if it is in the air at all, by which fever-and-ague is conveyed into the human system. On the contrary, it is a credit to the profession, as a body, that, notwithstanding previous disappointments, many of its members are still diligently searching to find this unknown cause; and who will doubt that, in time, it will not be discovered?

In this paper I have endeavored to be practical in what suggestions were made. It was prepared with the hope that it might prove useful in calling the attention of some of our citizens to points which may not have occurred to them amidst their own special labors and occupations. By this I thought to fulfill the wishes of the board, who invited me to prepare it. I have not entered into the theories, the philosophy, or the science of causes, of malaria. I have not attempted to describe the micro-orgasms, which are supposed to produce it, because I had nothing to add, from my own researches, to what is already known on the subject, and in this case it is better to leave such discussions to the universities, where they properly belong.

Discussion.

Dr. Morris moved the thanks of the convention to Dr. VanBibber, and the reference of his paper to the State Board of Health for publication.

Motion unanimously adopted.

Dr. Taneyhill, secretary, suggested that all delegates and members from foreign parts, who desire copies of the proceedings of the convention, will obtain them by leaving their names and addresses with him.

DR. PIPER: "I suppose all the papers and proceedings will be published. I am sure the public will be much benefitted by reading them. Malaria comes from one of two causes, either vegetable decomposition or animal decomposition. It is either typhoid or malarial fever. I believe as strongly as Dr. Forwood does not that there can be a fever which will be a mixture of the two."

Dr. Morris: "The investigation of these subjects is the duty and purpose of the State Board of Health."*

Dr. Ward: "I have observed a curious fact which rather seems to negative the theory that most fevers to which our people are subject are the result of decaying animal or vegetable matter, and that, in consequence, they usually come in the fall of the year. This season there has been more sickness than I have ever known, but it occurred in the early part of the summer, when everything was in luxuriant growth and there was no decay, and not in the autumn, as formerly."

Mr. Hallowell related an incident indicating a cause of malaria. He said:

"In the summer of last year my ice house burned down. The heat melted the ice; the water was filled with charred wood; my well was thirty feet distant, but its water became dark and tasted of the burnt wood so that we could not use it for some time. In another instance I knew of a well polluted by the presence of water which had percolated through the soil for a distance of one hundred and fifty feet. In speaking of earth closets, I would say that I have one in my house which is frequently, in case of sickness, used in the room of the invalid, and there is absolutely no odor, and it is altogether very satisfactory. I don't see why this system should not be in use generally."

Dr. Rohe: "I have listened with great interest to Dr. Van Bibber's paper, but I do wish he would change the title of it. We as physicians are accustomed to associate with this word a definite disease. Now, Dr. VanBibber does not mean to attribute this disease to the causes of which he speaks. I would suggest 'bad air' as a substitute for the present title."

Dr. Steuart: "With the earth closet I have had much experience. My father was the means of having it introduced into the Maryland Hospital for the Insane. Thousands of dollars had been spent in vain endeavors to obtain a satisfactory water closet system, when the earth system was adopted, and has been in perfectly

---

* The question referred to was elaborately discussed in the special report of the secretary of the State Board of Health on the epidemic of diphtheria in Frederick City, and is again alluded to in the report of the secretary contained in this volume.—C. W. C.

successful operation for many years. I myself have used for several years one in my own house with perfect satisfaction. For country houses I think it is perfect. Any farmer can use it with the least trouble to himself. All physicians know that one of the causes of ill health among females in the country is to the bad and inconvenient arrangements of this kind which they have to submit to. We, as a convention, could not do better than recommend this system to the public."

DR. PIPER: "You cannot get one person in twenty to do the thing properly. The evils of overflowing pits, troughs, &c., are proof of this. My plan would be to make a vault air and water tight, into this put all the excreta, and have it removed at regular intervals and by the proper means. And this can only be done in the counties, as it is done in the cities, by legislation."

DR. MCSHANE: "I would suggest to Dr. Piper that the pits in Baltimore are the greatest evils which the board of health has to contend with. No vault ever made will hold excreta for any length of time. It must be removed before it has undergone decomposition, and this can only be done by water carriage. I have seen the best constructed wells after a time become porous, and as a result the soil surrounding it becomes as foul as the contents of the well itself. Wells are of no use at all: they are only storehouses of disease."

MR. HALLOWELL: "I have recently, in one of the journals found Dr. McShane's statement corroborated. The author states that the best wells are of no use. Nothing will hold the fœcal matter."

DR. BELL: "I will relate a very interesting fact, which occurred within my own knowledge, relative to wells. In many places in the city of Brooklyn the grade of the streets has been much raised, causing the lots on either side oftentimes to be deep ponds, in which water accumulates and much filth is dumped. Adjoining one of these ponds was a well which the poor people used, and to which they attributed some special virtue. The authorities became conscious of the evil of allowing these ponds to stand, and, in consequence, they were filled up. No sooner was the pond adjoining this pump filled than the pump went dry. It is interesting to seek the source of supply to that well and the character of the water."

Dr. McSherry: "I would like to ask whether ashes are as good a deodorizer as earth for earth closets."

Dr. Bell: "It is generally conceded that earth is better than ashes. The permeability of soils has been calculated to be five feet in surface and one in depth, but this differs somewhat with the character of the soil."

Dr. Piper: "I am much interested in this matter. The law as it stands at present is not sufficient. Property-holders should be made to build their privies in such a way as to accomplish the best result. In my opinion, a properly built vault will accomplish the purpose. I ask—' How shall I, as representative of the county board of health in Towsontown, act in this matter?' "

Dr. Leas: "As Dr. Piper is seeking information with reference to legislation, I would advise him in no case to urge a law requiring wells to be sunk. In regard to coal ashes, they have been demonstrated to be a good deodorizer. The city some time ago made an effort to use its ashes for this purpose. I have an arrangement which answers well. I have a box under the seat which is on a sled. I use ashes as a deodorizer. When this box becomes full, I hitch a horse to it, and haul it away, clean it and return it."

Dr. Steuart: "I would say one word. Dr. Piper suggests great difficulty in getting the people in the country to use the earth closets properly. I think he exaggerates this difficulty; it is not so hard as he imagines. I have seen it used very often, with great comfort and ease. The digging of wells is the worst plan that can possibly be adopted. No well can be built which will hold the excreta. I have seen hundreds of instances in Baltimore where the soil around the well was almost solid excreta. Some years ago a basement on South street near Baltimore was dug out, and almost all the earth dug from under the cellar floor was as foul as excreta, and the bricks of the basement were thoroughly saturated with it."

Dr. Benson: "It is utterly impossible to make any wells perfectly tight. When, however, it is necessary to make a sink, the best that I have seen is an oil hogshead, sunk about half its depth in the earth, and emptied at regular intervals. I am, however, entirely in favor of water sewerage."

Dr. McShane: "I have a privy arrangement that would answer well in the country. It consists of two barrels. The barrels can be put under the holes, and, when full, hauled away and emptied. Earth or ashes should always be used."

Dr. Piper: "The great difficulty I meet with is to get the people to do anything. I would like some of these gentlemen to inform me with reference to the result of experiments with artesian wells as a means of getting pure water."

Adjourned at 10.30.

Second Day—Morning Session.

Wednesday, 28th November, 1883.

The increasing interest in the deliberations of the convention was evidenced by an increased attendance. All seemed to take a deep interest in the proceedings.

In the absence of the president, Prof. McSherry, the first vice-president, Mr. Henry C. Hallowell, occupied the chair, with Dr. Rohé and Mr. A. R. Carter acting secretaries.

Vice-President Hallowell announced that the regular order of business would be proceeded with.

Dr. A. N. Bell, of Brooklyn, N. Y., editor of the *Sanitarian*, took the floor, and in a very able manner addressed the meeting as follows on the question:

What Shall Be Done with the Sewage?

The most important question that can engage the attention of sanitarians at the present day is—What shall be done with the sewage? If there is any truth in the germ theory—a theory which, it is safe to say, is the accepted doctrine of the most advanced investigators everywhere—most of the sewerage in vogue requires important modifications or abandonment; for it is quite certain that sewers, as now commonly constructed and appointed—of porous material, large size, with surface ventilation, subject to the retention of sewage in process of putrefaction, and depositing their contents at the margins of water courses which wash the shores of populous places—are better calculated to promote disease than to prevent it.

The absolute necessity of the prompt removal of sewage is no longer a question; all civilized communities recognize it. The innate abhorrence of matter so offensive to the senses is unquestionably based upon the danger of its presence, a natural recognition, shared even by many animals, which bury their excrements or otherwise remove them out of their sight and smell. If nature thus makes known her invisible laws by instinct, where reason cannot discern them, it is surely the unmistakable inference that the excreta of all carnivorous animals, those which practice the instinct of getting rid of it at least, and of human beings, should be speedily removed, if not, indeed, put into the ground, as the most effectual of all means of removal, and the most certain of all means of restoring to the earth that which has been taken from it for the support of nutrition.

We have no need, in this connection, to go into an elaborate discussion of the special fitness of the soil for the accomplishment of this purpose. It will suffice to state, briefly, the composition of human excreta, and the explicit conclusions based upon the fundamental laws of national economy.

Taking the results of a number of analyses sufficiently complete to give a fair average, the mean amount of human excrement per individual, during twenty-four hours, in ounces is 50.18, 4.17 ounces fæces and 46.01 ounces urine. (In detail, of dry substances, 2.716 ounces; mineral matter, 0.643; carbon, 0.982; nitrogen, 0.531; phosphates, 0.257.)

In a mixed population, according to Dr. Parkes, the actual amounts voided are considerably less than this average, or not more than two and a half ounces of fæcal matter and forty ounces of urine daily, for every individual; an estimate which gives twenty-five tons solid fæces and ninety-one thousand two hundred and fifty gallons of urine for every one thousand inhabitants. It is hardly necessary to state that of the composition as above given, nitrogen and the phosphates are the very things most needful for plants. To estimate the value of these substances, it has been calculated that the average amount of ammonia—representing the nitrogen in that form—discharged annually by one person, taking the average of both sexes and of all ages, is about thirteen pounds, and the money value of the total constituents of the excreta is, in urine, about one dollar and seventy-five cents; and in fæces about thirty cents, or one-sixth as much only as the urine; the total value being about two dollars for every individual. Apropos to this estimate Professor Thudichum remarks:

"1. The basis of human life, the very root of society, is the capacity to produce food in such quantities that a surplus of it may be exchanged for commodities resulting from the labors of other people unable to produce food.

"2. This capacity to produce food must be rendered permanent by a strict observance of the laws of nature regulating vegetable life, the knowledge of which is the basis of agricultural science.

"3. The first and most important of these laws is that we must return to the soil the mineral ingredients we have taken from it in gathering our crops. The atmosphere furnishes the nutritious elements, and the soil the minerals, out of which vegetable fibres, vessels and structures containing food are built up. Without these mineral ingredients no harvest can properly flourish.

"4. These mineral ingredients are continually ejected from human beings and animals in their excrements; by returning which to the soil we furnish it with building materials for new crops, at the same time keeping pure the atmosphere we breathe and the water we drink, and thus preventing epidemics and (premature) death."*

But I would not divert attention from the main issue.

However essential agriculture may be to the welfare of man, as related to our present purpose, it is of secondary importance. If, however, the safest, the most efficient and most economical way of excreta disposal is also the most promotive of agriculture, as we believe it is, so much the better.

But the art of sanitation has not kept pace with science in this regard. Valuable as the constituents of excreta have been shown to be, the means of utilizing them are yet far from having been rendered thoroughly practicable. Considered in its most comprehensive aspect, sewage, as we have to deal with it, is polluted water. Reference is here made, of course, to the sewage of populous communities under the most universally preferred means of sewage—water carriage. As thus presented, sewage consists of a specially offensive portion, excrementitious matter discharged from water closets, privies and gully holes; kitchen slops, containing vegetable and animal washings and other refuse; soapsuds and dirt from the laundry; drainage from stables, barnyards and

*Grundlagen der öffentlichen Gesundheitspflege in Stadten. Frankfurt, 1865.

slaughter houses; and ground surface washings and filth in various proportions. According to an average of the gross amount, based upon the most reliable English statistics, one hundred thousand gallons contain about seventy gallons, or one part in one thousand three hundred of substances in solution; forty gallons, or one part in two thousand five hundred of suspended matter—a little more than one-half of this matter being mineral and the remainder organic matter. Now, how to separate and utilize this one part of plant food in one hundred thousand parts of sewage, consistent with practical economy, we have not yet learned, and until we have, we must continue to bend our efforts wholly for the protection of the public health, by the disposal of sewage in all its forms as completely and expeditiously as possible, regardless of side issues and ulterior benefits.

Water carriage as at present practiced is divisible into two kinds, the combined and separate systems, both dependent upon the ultimate disposal of the sewage, whether directly into the sea, tidal water, inland river or lake, or to the soil, both systems being alike subject to modifications suitable to the circumstances, independent of or in combination with means for separating the solid portion of the sewage from the liquid.

The *Combined* system consists of a single line of street sewers, sufficiently large to receive all storm water, provided for by basins at the street corners, all waste water and drainage from manufactories, stables, abattoirs, etc., together with the house sewage and the roof and yard waters. Hence, the mains in large cities are frequently great tunnels from six to fifteen feet in diameter. Being commonly constructed of brick or other porous material, their walls are saturated with filth in constant process of putrefaction, and incessantly giving off foul emanations.

With capacity adapted to the amount of rainfall in the heaviest storms, they are flushed only at such times, when they run nearly full. Other times, and especially in time of drought, they contain comparatively little sewage, but are full of gas constantly seeking the easiest means of escape, whether in or outside our houses; and on the setting in of a storm, by the pressure of water, the ordinary traps to house fixtures are a well nigh useless appendage. Ostensibly to prevent the escape of sewer gas under such circumstances, many contrivances have been adopted for deodorization and ventilation, but in view of the now generally accepted theory of the germ origin of disease, and that sewer air is a prolific source of disease germs, such sewers are deservedly looked upon as dangerous to the public health. They should be discarded—wholly converted to the purposes to which they are only suited, storm water conduits, but with such additions as will also drain and cleanse the soil. Thus converted, they would constitute the first part of—

The *Separate* system. This consists of two parts: first, that which has already been indicated, to drain the soil and carry off all surface waste and storm waters; and second, a small, non-absorbent and impervious pipe system of only sufficient calibre to carry excreta and house water, and without surface ventilation or other opening (except for light and hand-holes in case of obstruction), ventilation being accomplished by the open ends, of full calibre, of every house-drain connection extending above the roof. Flushing is provided for in this system by means of syphon flush-tanks at such intervals and distances as to effectually prevent the retention of any sewage long enough for putrefaction to take place.

In cities of fifty thousand population or less, with favorable surface—as in the case of Memphis—this, the *second part* only of the separate system, may be laid in conjunction with surface drainage.

But in cities of larger population the separate system comprehends a separate line of pipe of sufficient calibre, with subsoil-yard branches and street gutter connections at such intervals as may be required to carry off all subsoil, storm and surface-waste water.

A modification of, or rather improvement upon the separate system, as hitherto practiced, has recently been invented under the name of the—

"*West*" system—that which is now constructing at Atlantic City and Coney Island. It is essentially a small pipe system, adapted to the carriage of excreta and house water exclusively. It begins with a large well sunk to a proper depth, according to the estimated amount of sewerage to be dealt with. This well is made thoroughly impervious to both air and water. From near the bottom of the well the main sewer ascends toward the surface with a gradient of not less than ten feet to the mile. With this main all necessary laterals and branches with co-ordinate gradient unite. All corners or turns are made with a bend and a V, so that there is no chance for any excrement to lodge, but to run smoothly to the well. The diameter of the pipes run from six-inch, which is used for connections, to twenty-four inch, which is used for the main sewers. The pipes being small, at all times nearly full, and having sufficient incline, the sewage runs with great rapidity, carrying everything before it; and being at once pumped from the well before putrefaction sets in, there can be no sewer gas. Besides, all house connections are continued to the top of the house and a few feet above, as a means of ventilation, and to keep all smell from the house.

In the well one or two powerful pumps are placed, of sufficient capacity to raise and force one thousand or two thousand gallons of sewage per minute upon filtering beds located at places devoid of possible nuisance. Here the liquid sewage is at once filtered through a mass of deodorizing and antiseptic material, and discharged into the sea or a water-course; or, if this delivery be objectionable or unavailable—as in inland towns—the filtered liquid is utilized for agricultural purposes, by irrigation; meanwhile the suspended matters are simultaneously converted into "bromo guano," and made merchantable to farmers.

While this system has special advantages for small towns, where storm-waters can be taken care of on the surface, it is also adaptable, by multiplication of centres of operation, to even the largest cities, in conjunction with a storm-water system, or to those cities which have dangerous systems fit for storm-water only, and to which they should be diverted; and to outlying districts of cities already sewered, not easily accessible by other means, except at great cost.

Moreover, in cities only partially sewered, or where more expensive and less efficient sewerage has been undertaken and suspended, sewers already laid—with a gradient of not less than ten feet to the mile—may be utilized in the adoption of this system in the interest of public health, efficiency, speedy completion and economy.

Shone's *Pneumatic* system, by means of *sewage ejectors* operated by engine-power to force the sewage through pipes over rising ground, has found favorable application in some English cities. It is more economical than deep cuts, and applicable as a remedy in overcoming the sluggish flow in sewers with insufficient gradient. For operation on a large scale, it contemplates the discharge of the sewage by gravitation into large collection stations, similar to the wells in the West system, according to the size and contour of the town. Into these the *ejectors* are placed, and the sewage forced to the outlet. This system evidently possesses some advantages, but as compared with the West system, is more complicated, more costly and less complete.

The Lieurner *Pneumatic* system is a still more complicated method, which has met with favor in a few Dutch cities. It comprehends air-tight iron tanks under the streets, connected by means of iron pipes, with water closets of special construction, and is operated by a powerful steam-power air pump. It pretends to deal with excreta *only*, a limitation which virtually excludes it from general adoption or favorable consideration. It fulfills no condition which cannot be more economically and effectually conducted by other means sufficiently described.*

Of the rest, the various pail, bucket and earth systems, for small towns, little need be said. They are greatly inferior to the "West" system, for manifest reasons. They make no provision for the disposal of kitchen-sink and other waste waters of the household, scarcely less dangerous than excreta, and of which the amount is rarely less than twenty gallons daily for every household. The dry earth system, to take care of fæces and urine alone, requires at least four pounds of dry earth or ashes daily for every individual, an amount which renders the system burthensome even for schools and public institutions, and for towns wholly impracticable. Besides, all these makeshifts are based upon the dangerous principle that excrementitious matters may be retained about the premises, provided they are deodorized, subject to convenience for removal, based upon the fallacy that deodorization and disinfection mean the same thing. That dry earth speedily deodorizes excrementitious matter is common knowledge, but there is no evidence whatever that it disinfects it. On the contrary, it is well known that earth thus surcharged, on becoming moist, is offensive in consequence of the putrefaction which is then set up, leaving the inference pretty clear that, even when dry, material which it has deprived of odor may be, not-

*For description of this system in detail—illustrated—see THE SANITARIAN, vol. VII, p. 396, *et seq.*

withstanding, in the highest degree infectious. Indeed, some of the most malignant of infectious diseases, cholera for example, are spread with the greatest facility when the material holding the seeds or germs is in a perfectly dry state. This is probably equally true with regard to typhoid fever and diphtheria.

Safety in the use of the dry earth system, essentially consists in the same practice as the "West" system: the prompt disposal of the material (the earth) which retains the excreta, before putrefaction takes place. Distributed in the soil the gaseous emanations and soluble parts suitable for plant food are thus effectually disposed of, and the residue returned to its original elements by the process of oxidation. The cardinal doctrine of all systems should be—

Ultimate removal before putrefaction—this is the danger signal, but, unfortunately, not always easily discernible; consequently, any system which fosters it requires the utmost degree of watchfulness.

Of the various means adopted for the storage of excreta, or for its removal from one place to another out of sight and smell, from time to time, to enumerate them is to condemn them. Everybody knows the danger of food and drink poisoned with excrementitious matter. Loaded cess-pools and privy vaults, as ordinarily constructed, in proximity to wells, springs and dairies, are a perpetual source of such danger; and to such an extent as to leave no room for doubt, that not less than one hundred thousand persons are killed annually in the United States, by filth poisoning thus propagated. The only tolerable cess-pool system is that which may be used in conjunction with subsoil distribution through open-jointed drain tiles. As thus adapted, with impervious walls, and both cess-pools and drains sufficiently distant from the domicile and water supply, cess-pools may be used with a minimum of danger. In reply to the question likely to arise: At what distance from a well would it be safe to place a privy vault or cess-pool? The greater the better; but ordinary soils have a lateral drainage area equal to five feet for every one foot of depth—that is to say, a well twenty feet deep is ordinarily the receptacle of any soluble matter in the soil water for a distance of one hundred feet in all directions. Under some circumstances—such as subsoil currents in certain directions, the danger distance is much greater.

Of privy vaults, if they *must* be used, it will suffice to say the walls should be made impervious, and disinfectants so freely used as to prevent putrefaction during the intervals—which should never be long—between removals of contents, and excavators used for emptying them. To render the walls of cess-pools and vaults impervious, the inner courses of brick should be laid up with tongs—each brick being dipped into a boiling hot mixture of coal tar and asphalt. But for the single domicile, a better way is not to have a vault, but a tight box or pail, to use dry earth or ashes as a deodorant, and the same care in regard to prompt removal as required for the earth closets.

Discussion.

DR. MORRIS: "I would move that the thanks of the convention be tendered to Dr. Bell for his valuable paper, and he be requested to write out the incomplete part and furnish it to the State Board of Health for publication."

Motion adopted.

DR. LEAS: "This is one of the subjects which has puzzled all men for many years. It is pressing itself upon us every day. The time is not far distant when Baltimore will be compelled to do something. What shall be done with the excremental matter? Here two difficulties present themselves: First, the cost; and, second, what shall be done with the large mass taken away? I think it will have to be taken away at night, and, possibly, the city tunneled for this purpose. I want to look at the matter from an agricultural standpoint. If a farmer can manure his land once in five years he will do well. If he has one hundred acres he must manure twenty acres per year. The city of Baltimore will supply, from the half-pound per head, manure enough for twenty acres every day. Three hundred and sixty-five times twenty gives the capacity per year. On this land seventy-three thousand barrels of corn could be raised, worth two hundred and nineteen thousand dollars. The authorities of Baltimore do not take sufficient interest in this matter. I tried some time since to get some street manure for my farm, but could not get it. It has been a practice here to fill up lots in the city with street scraping. This cannot fail to breed disease."

DR. MCSHANE: "In the city of Baltimore the value at present placed upon excrementitious matter is very low. Contracts are made for the removal of night soil, and this is sold to farmers. Of that which is taken away, only twenty per cent. is solid, and hence of any value at all. All has undergone putrefaction, and hence is not a good fertilizer. The farmers in the twelfth district, where most of it is used, have come to this conclusion. It can only be used to advantage in a *fresh state*. The garbage, however, has been made of some value. As some aspersions have been cast upon the Board of Health, I would say it is not a legislative body; it can do nothing more than the law allows."

DR. STEUART: "I must take issue with Dr. Bell on the usefulness of excrement, which has undergone putrefaction. Excrement must be broken up into its constituents before the plants can use it."

DR. BENSON: "I agree with Dr. Steuart perfectly. This matter is not useless. The more thorough the decomposition the better. The earth has to reduce it to its elements before the plant can use it."

DR. MILLER OF ST. MICHAEL'S: "We have used it for twenty years; we find that it acts equally well in any stage of decomposition."

Note by the Secretary of the State Board of Health.

[The high agricultural value of fæcal matter as a manure cannot be doubted. It contains all the ingredients required for the production of human food, viz., nitrogen, phosphoric acid and potash, and if the matter is collected and reduced to poudrette before these ingredients are impaired *by decomposition or superfluous water*, there seems to be no doubt that it will be found *as valuable as guano or any known fertilizer.* The fertilizing elements must, however, be retained *in statu quo* until such time as they may be required in the growth of the plant. This may be readily accomplished by the timely addition of a small quantity of sulphuric acid to fix the ammonia, and the subsequent drying of the material, after which it may be stored without detriment for a long period. The disappointment hitherto experienced in the manurial value of fæcal sewage has arisen from the fact that the matter used has remained in privy pits or earth closets until its most valuable ingredient, nitrogen, has been converted into nitrate of ammonia, which rapidly evaporates and is lost; or the fæcal matter may be so diluted by water, "which," Prof. Miller says, "favors putrefactive fermentation," as to render it valueless.]

DR. LEECH: "At Bay View almshouse, some time ago, we had an epidemic. The result of our investigation was that it was caused by the use of night soil, in the crude state, on the ground in which the vegetables used were grown. They gave evidence, when cooked of the manure, proving that it had not been properly decomposed."

Dr. St. George W. Teackle then read a paper entitled:

A Healthy, Easy and Economical Method of Protecting Suburban and Country Residents from the Dangers and Discomforts caused by the Gases given off from Decomposing Human Excreta and Household Slops.

The able paper of Dr. Piper of yesterday suggested to me that my personal experience with dry earth as a disinfectant might prove of interest to those residing in the counties.

The principle is not new, but heretofore it has been considered so expensive and troublesome, as to be almost abandoned; and when I first commenced to investigate it (last spring) I myself was very much discouraged by the high price of the patented machines, and the liability of some of them to get out of order, but satisfied that the principle was a good one, I adopted the following plan of using dry earth in both the closets, and also as a disinfectant and deodorizer of the household slops. The earth closet consisted of a box made of one and a half inch white pine board, three feet long, two feet wide and eighteen inches deep, a little wider at the top than at the bottom. This I had lined with galvanized sheet iron (but ordinary tin or good coating of gas-tar will answer as well). This box was made to slide under the closet seat close up to the under side to prevent any urine from getting outside of the box; a box or small keg for dry sifted earth or coal ashes in one corner of the closet, and a tin flour scoop, completed the outfit, the whole cost of which did not exceed two dollars and a half.

The only directions necessary being to throw in a scoopful of earth after using. The results were as follows: No smell whatever, though the closet was next to the summer kitchen, and within eight feet of the dwelling. When the box became filled it was placed upon a wheelbarrow, carried about two hundred feet from the house, its contents dumped in a heap, and covered with a few shovels of earth. The box was then replaced in the closet. This plan of getting rid of the contents of the box, which to my surprise was not at all odorous, and of course is only suited to places of three acres and more; but where the lots are small there would be no difficulty in getting the nearest market gardener or florist to attend to the whole trouble of removal for the fertilizing property of its contents; and just here I would remark that night soil, when treated in this way, is not dangerous to raise vegetables with, but when used in a crude state it is very dangerous; and from my experience with an epidemic at Bayview Asylum some four years ago, which was directly traceable to the too free use of the same on the farm, ought to be prevented by legislation. Last week I had the pile, resulting from the dumpings of the box, removed to compost with the stable manure, and it was absolutely free from any disagreeable odor, and no trace of any fæcal matter could be discovered.

To get rid of the household slops, I used the following plan: I took an ordinary sugar hogshead, bored a number of auger holes in the bottom, and sunk it about half its depth in a corner of the stable yard (about one hundred feet from the kitchen). The hogshead was filled with dry earth, gravel and a small amount of lime on top; a movable top of flooring (tongue and groove), with a hole in the middle, eighteen inches square, with a board funnel and hinge top, was made to fit rather tightly. All the slops for three months were poured down the funnel, and at the end of that time there was no perceptible odor. The contents of the hogshead I have since had emptied on the compost heap, and it closely resembled that from the earth closet, and the ground under the hogshead seemed pure and free from odor.

I relate these facts, not as a discovery, but from a desire to make known to those living in the counties the availability, practical results and comfort of utilizing dry earth as a deodorizer and disinfectant at mere nominal cost and trouble.

Discussion.

DR. BLAKE: "One of the most vital questions for us to consider is, 'How shall we get the public aroused to the importance of this subject?' It must be done by the press. The press has done very little for us in this direction. If we are to adopt such a system as that suggested by Dr. Bell, how shall we persuade the people to favor it? I do not think that a distribution of our proceedings will do enough. We should use the newspapers."

DR. ROHE: "I believe that example is more valuable than precept. Col. Waring gives examples of having used earth from a closet several times without any evil result. In Europe, in France and Germany particularly, the population is much more dense than here, and land more valuable; the use of fertilizers more necessary. After hundreds of years of experiment excremental matter has not been found to be effectual for the purpose of enriching the soil to any extent."

DR. STEUART: "I think Dr. Blake is wrong to condemn the press for not more fully reporting our proceedings. I think they have been very liberal to us."

DR. BLAKE: "I had no intention of casting any aspersions upon the press. I do not and have not expected them to do more than they have done. What I meant to say is that the best means of reaching the people is through the press, rather than by the distribution of pamphlets."

DR. BELL: "I regret that this discussion has taken an agricultural turn instead of being confined to public health. The best English authorities state that, as a fertilizer, earth closet dirt is of little use, only so good as ordinary garden soil. What I meant to say, when speaking before, was that for a plant to use excremental matter, putrefaction must take place in the ground, at the roots of the plant, and not before it gets to the plant."

DR. PIPER: "I move that Dr. Teackle's paper be printed as a part of the proceedings."

Adopted.

DR. BLAKE: "Dr. Teackle said that his hogshead must be perforated in the bottom. This would allow the liquid to percolate through the soil into any source of drinking water which might be near. How will Dr. Teackle get over this difficulty?"

DR. TEACKLE: "I have no difficulty to remove. When the liquid comes out of the hogshead it is so thoroughly filtered as to be perfectly pure. When I took up the hogshead and examined the earth beneath, it was in the same condition as when the barrel was first sunk."

MR. HALLOWELL: "We country people have many ways at our command by which we can get rid of these evils, but the question that stares you medical men in the face is, how will you get rid of the terrible evil that exists in the city?"

Dr. Benson read a paper on *Vaccination*, prepared by Dr. Wells, of Chelsea, Massachusetts.*

Discussion.

DR. MILLER: "A curious case came under my observation some time ago. I was called to see a patient. I found that he had a bad case of small pox. I found in the house a boy of ten, who had never been vaccinated. I vaccinated him at once on both arms. This vaccination took on one arm, but not on the other. A few days afterwards the boy developed a case of varioloid on the side on which the vaccination had not taken, and the disease was entirely confined to this side."

Second Day—Afternoon Session.

Hon. Eli J. Henkle opened the session with—

The Late Small Pox Epidemic.

The presence of small pox is just cause of alarm, no matter when or where it makes its appearance.

Contagious in the highest degree; loathsome beyond all the ills that flesh is heir to, and fatal to the extent of destroying from thirty to fifty per cent. of its unprotected victims, and mutilating for life all who survive, it has been truthfully termed "the most terrible of the messengers of death."

Very naturally, therefore, and very properly, the prevalence of this fearful pestilence, in an epidemic form in many sections of our country during the past three years, has awakened in the

*This paper has not been handed to the secretary.

minds of the public and the medical profession the most anxious thought and careful investigation.

My purpose in the present paper is to present concisely, as correct an account of the origin, progress, extent and decline of the late epidemic as the material at hand will supply, and also to offer such suggestions for its prevention in the future as the painful experience of the past has plainly indicated.

The first alarming outbreak of the late epidemic was in Philadelphia in 1881. One thousand three hundred and thirty-six deaths are reported there for that year, and, estimating the whole number of cases from the number of deaths, there must have been, at the usual death ratio, over five thousand cases of the disease there during the year. The death rate was 1.57 to the one thousand of population.

From this centre, and doubtless from others also, it extended in 1882, by the thoroughfares of public travel, until it invaded even the remoter sections of the country, and in several of our larger cities the mortality was truly appalling. Without enumerating the hundreds who died in the smaller towns and rural districts, there were, during 1882, nearly four thousand deaths in six of our chief cities, viz.:

In Richmond	96
In Pittsburgh	300
In New Orleans	415
In Baltimore	551
In Cincinnati	1249
In Chicago	1292

In New Orleans there were eight hundred and fifty deaths for the first five months of the present year, and though now nearly subdued, the last monthly statement shows that the disease still lingers in that city.

The death rate in the cities above-named, was, in

Baltimore	1 death to 741 of population, or 1.35 to the 1,000
Richmond	1 death to 708 of population, or 1.40 to the 1,000
Pittsburgh	1 death to 566 of population, or 1.76 to the 1,000
New Orleans	1 death to 538 of population, or 1.85 to the 1,000
Chicago	1 death to 434 of population, or 2.30 to the 1,000
Cincinnati	1 death to 224 of population, or 4.46 to the 1,000

These figures are taken from the official reports, and by comparison it appears that in the six cities where the mortality was greatest, the death rate was lowest in Baltimore and highest in Cincinnati.

The fact that the death rate was higher in Richmond, Pittsburgh, New Orleans, Chicago and Cincinnati than in Baltimore has a special significance, since during the prevalence of the epidemic Baltimore was characterized as "a doomed city," and her commercial rivals industriously created an impression upon the public mind that the scourge was more terrible here than in any city in the Union. A gentleman in Washington, just from Cincinnati, gravely inquired if it would be safe for him to bring his wife to Baltimore to do some shopping. He seemed quite oblivious to the fact that the mortality from small pox was, at that very time, more than three times as great in his own city, where he felt perfectly safe, as in the city of Baltimore that he so much dreaded.

But notwithstanding the fact that we suffered less, in proportion to population, than other cities, we cannot close our eyes to the fact that it was indeed a great calamity to our people and a loss that figures never can express. No attempt should be made to extenuate its horrors and no effort spared to prevent its recurrence.

The battle is over for the present, and the victory won. The enemy has been routed from his strongholds and driven quite beyond our borders.

The assiduous, faithful and skillful application of the means of resistance, when placed fully at the command of your Health Commissioner, enabled him, by the aid of his faithful assistants, within the short space of a few months, to utterly stamp out of existence the last vistage of the pestilence, and now there has not been a single case of small pox in Baltimore for five months.

And now it becomes our duty to call a council of war, study the lessons of the recent conflict, and adopt the best means of defense against a renewed attack of the enemy.

The old adage "in times of peace prepare for war," is quite as applicable to the prevention of disease as to resisting the invasions of a foreign foe.

The late epidemic furnishes much material of interest to the statistician and sanitarian, the study and preservation of which may be useful in the future.

The statistics and analysis which I have prepared cover the

entire period from the beginning to the end of the epidemic, viz.: From January 1st, 1882, to July 1st, 1883, a term of eighteen months.

As appears by the records of the Health Department, the whole number of cases was four thousand nine hundred and thirty-nine; of deaths, one thousand one hundred and sixty-eight. The proportion of deaths to the whole number of cases was 1 to 4.2; a fraction less than one-fourth of all the cases died. There was one case to eighty-two of our total estimated population, and one death for every three hundred and fifty.

It is of interest to note the sections of the city that suffered most, and those that had least of the disease: It was most fatal in the second, first, fifteenth and sixth wards, in the order in which I have named them. The deaths were three hundred in the second, two hundred and twelve in the first, one hundred and nineteen in the fifteenth and ninety-five in the sixth. No ward escaped entirely from the dreadful scourge. The eleventh, twelfth, tenth, eighth, fourteenth and nineteenth had the least, however. The deaths were in the eleventh and twelfth, three each; in the tenth, five; and in the eighth, fourteenth and nineteenth, six each. It was most fatal in those sections where the population live in crowded apartments, and under circumstances that render protection from the spread of contagious diseases of any kind most difficult.

Of the colored population there were two hundred and ninety deaths; of the white population, eight hundred and seventy-eight. It was more fatal among the negroes than among the whites, the proportion being one death to two hundred and five of the negro, and one to three hundred and ninety of white population. This difference is easily accounted for by their general habits of living and greater neglect of vaccination and revaccination. The great mortality in certain wards affords a valuable lesson of warning as to the points where the greatest vigilance should be exercised to guard against a recurrence of the disease.

Tabulated forms will be published in the next annual report of the Health Department giving in detail all the facts on this important subject. I wish only to call attention to the most salient points without wearying you with an array of figures. One fact of interest is the disparity between the number of adults and minors who died of the disease; two hundred and twenty-five adults, nine hundred and forty-three minors, more than four times as many of the latter as of the former.

The aggregate adult and minor populations are about equal in number, yet there were three thousand two hundred and ninety-seven cases among minors, against one thousand six hundred and forty-two among adults, a little more than two to one; and of deaths nine hundred and forty-three minors to two hundred and twenty-five adults, more than four to one.

The difference in number may be partly accounted for by the larger proportion of minors that were not vaccinated, but the difference is by no means sufficient to account for all of it. The public schools I believe are the centres from which contagious diseases are spread among our children more generally than by any other means. Investigations into the avenues by which diphtheria is disseminated among the children of cities has pointed to the public schools as the most probable media of its dissemination, since the disease is always, or nearly always, least prevalent during the summer vacations. For like reasons small pox would readily spread among the children of a school, should one or more of the scholars be suffering from its incipient fever. In winter, when the disease mostly prevails, the school rooms are heated by stoves or furnaces, and there is little or no ventilation, conditions most favorable to the propagation of contagion. Would it not be wise during the prevalence of an epidemic to close the schools in infected districts?

Another point worthy of note is the fact that of adults there were many more deaths among males than females. Of two hundred and twenty-five deaths of adults, there were one hundred and forty-five males and eighty females. More than eighty per cent. more men than women died, and the proportion of those who took the disease was about the same. This may be explained by the fact that the daily vocations of men bring them into more frequent and promiscuous intercourse with the various classes of people, and consequently they are more likely to encounter those having the disease.

Probably, too, the dread of being mutilated by the pits and scars, which so sadly and frequently disfigure the fairest features, urges the sex to a stricter observance of the precaution to be frequently vaccinated. It is an historical fact that women more willingly than men submitted to vaccination when its protecting power was but imperfectly established and its pernicious effects boldly asserted.

Since the first of January, a year ago, four thousand nine hundred and thirty-nine of our population were stricken down by this horridly loathsome pestilence, and one thousand one hundred and sixty-eight were hurriedly consigned to the grave. None can weigh or measure the cost of this carnival of death. The pangs of pain and wild delirium of the doomed victims. The want, the sufferings, the destitution, the heart-aches and the desolated homes beggar description and defy human computation. I shall make no such absurd effort.

Taking a cold, calculating estimate of its consequences, let us see how the account stands viewed purely in a dollar and cent light. It has cost the taxpayers of the city largely over one hundred thousand dollars to pay for the furniture, clothing and bedding destroyed, and for removing and burying the dead. This does not include the cost of extra vaccine physicians or expenses at the hospital, and a hundred other items. This was a direct outlay of money from the city treasury, which we all helped to pay. Not an indirect or supposed loss, but so many dollars directly taken from the pockets of taxpayers. But this sum, large as it is, does not represent the tenth part of the loss or injury really sustained by the city. Every life lost that might have been saved, is a direct loss to our industrial resources, wealth and prosperity. Students of this subject agree that every needless death represents a loss to the community of not less than one thousand dollars. One thousand one hundred and sixty-eight deaths, then, represent a loss to the material wealth and prosperity of the city of one million one hundred and sixty-eight thousand dollars.

Now add to these sums the immense loss that all know our commercial and mercantile interests suffered, and we have a faint idea, taking the most sordid view of the subject, of the cost to our city of the late epidemic of small pox.

The all important and practical question is, "What are we going to do about it?"

There is but one answer to this question, and that answer is already on the lips of every intelligent, unprejudiced person. Vaccination! thorough, efficient, systematic vaccination repeated with sufficient frequency to keep every individual protected from the contagion.

Contagious, loathsome and fatal as it is, and a terror wherever it appears, it is the most *avoidable* of all contagious diseases. Vaccination is the proudest achievement of science over a deadly foe, and by its faithful performance we are enabled to stay its onward march with absolute certainty, and say to the fell destroyer, "thus far shalt thou go and no farther."

To you intelligent and experienced physicians and sanitarians there is nothing new in this declaration. It is an old, old story, and too well-established to admit of doubt or require demonstration.

But well-established truths lose nothing of their value by repetition, and it is the duty of the physician and the philanthropist to keep them constantly before the public, to the end that they may be convinced, as we are, and especially that those in authority, our law-makers, and those appointed to execute the laws, may be awakened to a full appreciation of the remedy, and supply the means for its efficient application.

Proofs of the efficacy of thorough vaccination, as a protection against the ravages of small pox, are superabundant in the literature of the profession.

Imperfectly as it has been enforced in our city, from the lack of adequate appropriations to secure thorough work, the statistics of the late epidemic show its power to protect the lives of the people. Over twenty-nine per cent of those who had never been vaccinated died. Only a fraction over eleven per cent. of those who had at some time been vaccinated died. Doubtless in most of these the vaccination was done so long prior to the attack that protection had ceased. There is no evidence that any one took the disease after successful revaccination.

Prof. S. E. Chaillé, of New Orleans, in an admirable paper recently published on the "prevention of small pox," quoting from the highest official English authority, says: "Revaccination, once properly and successfully performed, *does not appear ever to require repetition.* The nurses and servants of the small pox hospital, when they enter the service, are invariably revaccinated, and it is never afterwards repeated; and, so perfect is the protection, that, though the nurses live in the closest and most constant attendance on small pox patients, and are in various ways exposed to special chances of infection, during an experience of thirty-four years small pox has never affected any one of these nurses or servants."

Infants and young children are specially subject to the disease. Of the four thousand nine hundred and thirty-nine cases, one thousand four hundred and fifty-nine were under five years of age, and four hundred and thirty-three died. Seventy-three of these are reported as having been vaccinated, and three hundred and sixty not vaccinated. Forty-four per cent. of the unvaccinated died, and twelve and four-tenths per cent. of the vaccinated. The evidence is by no means satisfactory that those vaccinations had taken.

Persistent vaccination and revaccination will prevent it, and will stamp it out wherever it prevails, beyond question.

So soon as the authorities supplied the means, and the Commissioner of Health was clothed with full power to proceed efficiently, an army of supernumerary vaccine physicians was sent out into the highways, courts and alleys to vaccinate all who were not protected, and the pestilence retreated from one section to another until it entirely disappeared.

Now we don't want it to come back any more, and we know it can be kept away by prompt, judicious effort. See what has been done in Boston. In 1873 they had three hundred and two deaths from small pox. They determined to stop it at once. The means were promptly supplied, and here is what the board of health of that city say in their last report: "During the last ten years the board of health has had absolute control of the means necessary for the suppression or prevention of an epidemic of small pox in this city. We possess the means for the most prompt isolation, disinfection and vaccination, and these three measures are enforced in every instance. The result has been very satisfactory, beyond the occurrence of an isolated case here and there, which has been introduced from abroad. Business has not been disturbed by the prevalence of this dreaded disease, the loss by death has been very small, and the expense to the city trifling. The number of deaths for the nine years since 1873 were: in 1874, two; 1875, one; 1876, two; 1877, four; 1878, none; 1879, none; 1880, one; 1881, six; 1882, eight."

Twenty-four deaths in nine years. Less than three a year. We had more deaths from small pox in one day during the late epidemic than Boston has had in nine years. Instances of the kind might be furnished almost without number. In all cases where the proper means have been applied, the same satisfactory results have been realized.

Prof. Chaillé has crystallized the whole argument into one short sentence. When speaking of the epidemic then raging in New Orleans, he said : " Give any man of sense requisite power for one month, and at its end there need not be a yellow flag left to affright the timid nor a small pox hospital to pay tribute to."

How can full protection be best secured ? And what is required in addition to present provisions to make security certain ? Frequent, thorough inspections and vaccinating and re-vaccinating every unprotected individual, so that every system is proof against the contagion, *will ensure* safety.

To accomplish this, the work must be done *systematically* and *consecutively*. From house to house, from street to street, from alley to alley, from court to court. Not visiting promiscuously, as convenience may suit ; a few visits on this street to-day and a few on another to-morrow, but working consecutively on each street or alley until it is completed ; then on another and another, until all are done, always beginning first on those thoroughfares where the disease is most likely to break out. Do this every year, and we are safe. But ten doctors, at three hundred dollars a year, cannot do it. The city has been paying three thousand dollars annually for our protection. Each physician had forty thousand people to inspect and vaccinate, and he had to do it for twenty-five dollars a month. It was impossible and absurd. They did all they could to avert the pestilence, but it came, and we have paid the price of our parsimony, the lives of one thousand one hundred and sixty-eight people, and more than one hundred thousand dollars in money direct. There should be at least one physician to each ward, at a salary of at least five hundred dollars. Twenty thousand people and four thousand families are quite enough for one man. Twelve and a half cents per family will pay five hundred dollars in each ward. Certainly this is cheap enough. The extra cost of the late epidemic would have paid one physician for each ward five hundred dollars a year for ten years.

There is no other safety. We want the service of active, intelligent, faithful physicians, and we want them to do a great deal of work, and do it well. You cannot get such service by the present arrangement.

True economy, as well as humanity, requires that we should imitate the course of Boston and other cities, and give our citizens the protection they are justly entitled to, and which can be supplied at so small a cost.

On motion, the paper was referred for publication.

Discussion.

Dr. Piper: "I believe and I think there is no doubt that the cause of the wide spread of small pox during the late epidemic was the attendance of children upon the public schools, coming from homes where the disease existed. This has been a great evil, and will continue to be so unless some means is taken to stop it. I know that many children do go to the schools unvaccinated. I further know that under the present system no effectual protection can be secured. A child is vaccinated and immediately given a certificate; it goes to school and no one takes the trouble to see whether the vaccination has taken or not. I think that the vaccine physicians should be required by law to visit every case after vaccination and see its condition, and that no certificates should be given until after the vaccination has taken or been repeatedly tried."

Dr. John Morris of Baltimore, read a paper entitled:

*Etiology of Baltimore Catarrh.

At the last meeting of the Medical and Chirurgical Faculty of Maryland, a very interesting paper was read by Dr. John N. Mackenzie of Baltimore, on nasal catarrh and its rational treatment. The form of catarrh, so graphically described in this paper by Dr. Mackenzie, prevails to some extent in various parts of this country, but its very general prevalence in Baltimore has led me to term it *Catarrhus Baltimoriensis*, or Baltimore Catarrh; and I propose to offer some suggestions in regard to its etiology, and to point out the local conditions which I believe are potential in its production.

---

*Abstract of a paper read before the American Public Health Association, Detroit, Michigan, November 14th, 1883.

The pathology and treatment of nasal catarrh will not be discussed in this paper, but it may not be out of place to describe briefly the character and lesions of the disease. As described by Dr. Mackenzie, and his description corresponds with my own experience, it consists essentially in the first stage in a localized injection and swelling of the mucous membrane, which of course involves an increased irritability, not only of the mucous membranes, but of the erectile tissue which is found on the inferior, middle and turbinated bones, and on the septum. With this hyperœmia is usually associated, catarrh of the pharynx and collections of mucous in the different orifices of the eustachian tubes. As the disease progresses the patient suffers from difficulty of breathing, on account of the accumulation of mucous in the nose and throat. Owing to these accumulations the breath is rendered offensive; and if the trouble advances to the chronic state, termed ozœna, it becomes peculiarly fœted. Deafness frequently supervenes, and is one to the extension of the disease to the eustachian tubê and middle ear and pthisis, in consequence of its invasion of the larynx and bronchi. Nasal catarrh is aggravated by conditions of the atmosphere, and its symptoms are particularly severe during the winter and spring months. Heredity seems to play an important part in its etiology, inasmuch as the lymphatic, scrofulous and syphilitic, invariably suffer from its ravages.

The great prevalence of this disease in Baltimore is very remarkable. If I may be allowed to form a judgment from the statistics furnished me by the principals of the public schools, and from inquiries among my medical friends, there are at least twenty-five thousand, or one in fifteen of the population, sufferers from nasal catarrh. The disease does not prevail to any extent in the counties of Maryland, or even in Baltimore county, which immediately adjoins the city, and which is subject to the same climatic and meteorological conditions as the city. Therefore it is fair to presume that it must have its origin in special local conditions. It has been generally supposed by authors, who have written on the subject, that nasal catarrh is due to certain peculiarities of climate or soil, or to the presence of dust in the atmosphere containing irritating particles. The muco pharynx being a *cul de sac*, and out of the direct line of the respiratory tract; it is supposed likely to form a lodging place or nidus for these particles. Dr. Morell Mackenzie of London, who recently visited this country, delivered a lecture a few weeks ago at the London Hospital Medical College on catarrh of the naso-pharynx, or American type of post nasal catarrh, which has been published in the British Medical Journal. His views in regard to the etiology of the disease, though given at some length, are indefinite, and not at all satisfactory. On account of the great amount of dust to be met with everywhere in America, he says: "The universal prevalence of catarrh is, indeed, fully explained by the abundance of dust both in the country and in the cities. Owing to the immense size of the country, and its sparse rural population, the country roads have not, as a rule, been properly made, and, except in some of the older states, are merely the original prairie tracks. In the cities, notwithstanding the magnificence of the public buildings, the splendor of many of the private houses and the beauty of the parks, the pavement is generally worse than it is in the most neglected cities of Europe, such indeed as are only to be found in Spain or Turkey. It must be recollected also that whilst in the decayed towns of the old world there is very little movement, in the American cities there is a ceaseless activity and an abundance of traffic. Hence the dust is set in motion in the one case, but not in the other. The character of the dust, of course, varies greatly according to locality. In some parts it is a fine sand, in others an alkaline powder, whilst in the cities it is made up of every conceivable abomination; among which, however, decomposing animal and vegetable matters are not the least imitating elements. An idea may perhaps be formed of the state of the atmosphere, from a consideration of the fact that in many cities the functions of the scavenger are quite unknown."

This statement of Dr. Morrell Mackenzie, which is, I think, greatly overdrawn, and the causes which he mentions as originating nasal catarrh, do not apply to the city of Baltimore. The city is comparatively free of dust as well as smoke, for the marble buildings retain their purity and whiteness in a very marked degree; indeed, I do not believe that dust alone will produce post nasal catarrh. It must be dust or air, surcharged with decomposing animal or vegetable matter. The trádes, too, that are supposed to cause catarrhal affections, such as knife grinding, stone cutting, diamond polishing, etc., are not carried on to any extent. Therefore, in endeavoring to ascertain the causes of the unusual prevalence of post nasal catarrh within its bounds, we must look for such local conditions and surroundings as would be likely to originate the trouble. My own judgment is, that nasal catarrh in Baltimore has its origin in the character of the house-air breathed during the winter and spring months, by a large majority of the citizens. Forty years ago this disease was almost unknown. At that time the houses were heated by stoves and open fire places. About the year 1846, a stove was introduced in the city, called the Latrobe stove, and at present more than one-half the houses of the city are heated by this stove, or modifications of it. These modifications are termed, the "Feinour Stove," the "Baltimore Heater," "Fire Place Stove," "Gem Stove," etc., etc. Mr. Latrobe's invention is a fire-place stove, set in the lower story, and designed to heat the upper rooms of the house, and, as originally used, was not injurious in its effects on the health of the people. Mr. Latrobe himself, in a letter to Dr. Chew VanBibber, gives a description of his invention, which will best explain its character. He says, "The invention originated in the objection made to having a radiator with a cylindrical fire-pot and lateral drums with return flues, on a *parlor* hearth. The stove was then set back into the fire-place, and the fire-board placed above it in the flue. The great loss of heat suggested the next step, which was to make the drums correspond with the sides of the fire-place, leaving a space of a couple of inches, between which space, the fire-board in front and an iron flange in the rear, converted into a channel-way, into which the external air (introduced through a hole in the hearth, communicating with the outside of the building by a wooden trough), entered and passed over the top of the stove and between it and the fire-board in the chimney, into the room, *moderately* heated by its contact with the sheet iron surfaces of the stove, which was no longer objected to as a piece of furniture, and which art made ornamental, while the appearance of the fire through the mica of the fire-door, made it cheerful. The great merit of the stove, in connection with *hygiene*, consisted in the great volume of outside air, moderately heated, thrown through the large opening in the hearth from a correspondingly large trough, into the apartment. The moisture in the air was not dried up, and no evaporating vessel was required. From the space between the top of the stove and the fire-board in the chimney, pipes were employed to conduct the heated air into an upper chamber of the house. This was the original Latrobe stove. Subsequently, in order to render the stove portable, it was made of cast iron in various shapes, and while the principle was not changed, its availability to heat upper chambers was increased, by depriving it of its original features of *air in large volumes and surfaces moderately heated.* In its new shape it has many names, such as Baltimore Heater, Fire Place Stove, etc."

The Latrobe stove, now in general use, is of an entirely different design from that described by Mr. Latrobe. It is made of cast iron, and the flue-board is placed in the second story, the smoke pipe entering into the chimney above it. A pipe conveys the heated air to the third story. There is no wooden box with a trough for cold air leading from the yard to the hearth, but the air for heating is obtained entirely from the cellar. Now let me ask what kind of cellars do we find, as a rule, in Baltimore, and what is the character of the air circulating in them? In an article on the Local Causes of Insanitation in Baltimore, published some years ago, I stated that no cellars in the world are constructed in a worse manner than those of Baltimore. The prerequisites of a good cellar, cleanliness, dryness, light and ventilation, are almost entirely wanting; and owing to the singular nature of the subsoil of the city, they become receptacles of noxious gases. The formation of this subsoil is peculiar. At some distance below tide level, extending under the city, there is a thick stratum of clay; upon this bed of clay there rests a stratum of very course gravel, overlaid in the higher parts of the town with a heavy deposit of sand. There are about forty thousand privies and wells in the city, and the contents of these permeate the stratum of sand just described to reach the bed of clay beneath in which they are permanently retained. In consequence of this between five and six of the nine thousand acres, constituting the area of the city, are surcharged with fœcal matter, emanations from which continually rise to the surface to poison the atmosphere. It is no unusual thing in tearing down old buildings to find the walls saturated with this filth, which is carried up from the soil by capillary attraction. There is another cause which adds very much to the impurity of cellar air in Baltimore. It has been the custom for many years in the city to fill up low lying lots and beds of streets with garbage and refuse, and all manner of rotten and rotting material. This is a permanent evil, for the processes of decay are ever going on, provided the necessary elements of heat and moisture are brought into action. Of course cellars dug in these lots must necessarily be the foci of noxious and irritating gases. Combined with the emanations of the soil just described, these gases inevitably render the air in the lower portion of the houses impure and unfit for respiration. Cellar air at best is unsuited for the purposes of life. An inferior order of animal life, says a writer on the subject, is justly and properly associated with the air of cellars; such animals as lizards, snakes, snails, turtles and toads. It is fair to presume then that the heated air breathed by a large number of the citizens of Baltimore, during the winter and spring months, is laden with bacteria, the outgrowth of animal and vegetable decomposition.* It has been argued that the air of furnaces, as well as heated air and steam, is a fruitful cause of catarrh; but if furnaces are properly furnished with a supply of fresh, pure air, they cannot prove a source of trouble; and hot air in itself will not produce catarrh, for houses in Germany and Russia are heated by it, and post-nasal catarrh is not common in those countries.

It therefore follows that there must be some peculiar characteristic in the air, breathed by the people of Baltimore, to cause such a general prevalence of catarrh; and in the absence of all other possible factors, I am constrained to believe that this characteristic is the presence of bacteria or other morbific germs in the house air of the city. As a proof of this, during the present summer the streets have been dug up at different points for purposes of city improvement, and Dr. McShane, the Assistant Health Officer, has made coarse analyses of the soil of these different points, and in every instance it was found to contain a large amount of nitrogenous matter. If my theory be correct, the remedy for this great evil is in the hands of the citizens themselves. The abolition of the whole abominable privy and well system, and the introduction of proper sewerage is the simple and easily provided remedy.

Referred to State Board of Health for publication.

---

* The subsoil of Baltimore is also saturated with hydrogen and carbonic oxide gas, consequent upon leakages in the gas pipes. This condition is no doubt a blessing in disguise, for these gases may have a destructive influence on the poisonous germs of the decomposing matter.

Dr. Jas. F. McShane, Assistant Health Commissioner of Baltimore, next read a paper on:

Vital Statistics.

It is one of the highest duties governments owe their people to collect and diffuse knowledge; more particularly that knowledge which will protect its citizens from the ravages of disease. No greater economy can be practised than the protection of the public health, nor can the material interests of a state or municipality be better promoted than by the collection, compilation and study of statistics which shall discover the causes of deaths, particularly from preventable diseases, and devise means for their removal and control.

Vital statistics are acknowledged by sanitarians as the foundation for sanitary work; and such statistics are absolutely necessary for reference in studying methods by which disease can be prevented. For an intelligent study of the prevention of death from any cause or disease, we must make the necessary inquiries as to mode of living, age, sex, occupation, time (of year), overwork, indulgence in injurious foods and drinks, privations and all the controllable errors of social life. Every contribution to sanitary science has had for its basis the patient accumulation of facts, their collation, classification, comparison and grouping. Thus the recognized basis of sanitary science is statistics of sickness, of death, of meteorological and other surroundings.

Statistics concerning the sickness of individuals is no less necessary than the reports of the number, time and causes of death, because there is evidently more sickness which does not result in death, but which it is important to prevent, if possible; consequently it is no less necessary to report cases of sickness than those of death. Physicians should aid in every possible way the regularly constituted authorities in their efforts to ascertain the existence of communicable diseases, so as to enable them to direct their efforts and attention to the necessary restriction and prevention of such diseases. A system of prompt and regular reports of sickness is essential, in order to obtain an exact knowledge on the subject, so that all the facts can be systematically arranged and compiled, and thus enable the people to be informed themselves as to the conditions under which sickness may or may not occur. In the compilation of statistics it is essential to obtain facts from every possible source, in order to adopt the best methods for the prevention of sickness and deaths. It is a matter of regret that in this state no provision is made for the proper collection and preservation of vital statistics, and every effort should be made by the State Board of Health, at the coming session of the legislature, to have the necessary enactments made to provide means for a proper system of the registration of births, deaths and marriages. By the law establishing the State Board of Health (passed in 1874), said board was directed to take cognizance of the interests of health and life among the people generally; they shall make sanitary investigations and inquiries respecting the causes of diseases—especially epidemics—the sources of mortality and the effects of localities, employments, conditions and circumstances on the public health; and they shall gather such information, in respect to these matters as they may deem proper; *they shall devise some scheme whereby medical and vital statistics of sanitary* value may be obtained, and act as an advisory board to the state in all hygienic and medical matters; they shall make special inspections of public hospitals, prisons, asylums and other institutions when directed by the governor or the legislature, and shall at each regular session of the legislature submit a full report of their acts, investigations and discoveries, with such suggestions as they may deem proper· It is evident, from the above synopsis of the law directing the establishment of the State Board of Health, that its duties are not only to report their acts, investigations and discoveries, but shall devise means whereby medical and *vital statistics* of sanitary value may be obtained; and until accurate registration of vital statistics is thoroughly carried out, it will be impossible to have an efficient system of state preventive medicine. I would suggest that the state board, in its next annual report, urge upon the legislature the importance and necessity for the enactment of proper laws providing for a systematic registration of vital statistics; and it should also be the duty of every individual interested in the well-being of this state not to let an opportunity pass, either in public or private; impress upon legislators the duty of dealing generously upon a subject fraught with so much good, and so vital to the health and happiness of every inhabitant. The State Board of Health would increase its usefulness by the dissemination of the knowledge gathered from a proper registration of vital statistics

The state should do away with the present penurious method of dealing with public health matters, as the information now gleaned and published is of little benefit, because it is imparted to but few, whereas it should be scattered broadcast among the people.

Discussion.

Dr. Ward moved that the paper be referred to the State Board of Health for publication.

Adopted.

Dr. Morris: "It would be worth while to say that for many years the State of Maryland paid the secretary of the senate one thousand dollars a year for collecting vital statistics, but no work was ever done. This office, however, has been abolished."

Dr. McShane: "One thousand dollars is totally insufficient for the registration of vital statistics for the city of Baltimore, to say nothing of the state at large. It is not only an important but an immense work."

Miscellaneous Business.

Dr. James A. Steuart offered the following preamble and resolution, which was adopted and referred to a special committee consisting of Dr. Jas. A. Steuart, Dr. J. Pembroke Thom, John P. Poe, Esq., of Baltimore; Dr. George W. Bishop, of Worcester county, and Henry C. Hollowell, of Montgomery county.

Whereas the urgent necessity for a law regulating the practice of medicine in the State of Maryland has for a long time painfully impressed itself upon the minds, not only of all respectable practitioners of medicine of every school of practice, but also upon all thoughtful and fair-minded citizens of the state. And as all, who have taken a sufficient interest in this important subject to inform themselves, are aware, many of our sister states have long ago passed laws regulating the practice of medicine, the result of which has proved the wisdom of such action, it is, therefore, proposed to this convention as an entering wedge to the future consideration of the subject, the following resolution:

Resolved, That a committee of five, consisting of three practitioners of medicine of the State of Maryland and two non-medical citizens, be appointed by the president of this convention to consider the subject above-named, with the view of bringing it to the attention of the legislature of Maryland at its next biennial session, and to urge the passage of such a law as the wisdom of that august body may approve.

The following letter from T. Alex. Seth was read and referred to the legislative committee:

MARYLAND LIVE-STOCK BREEDERS' ASSOCIATION,
BALTIMORE, November 28, 1883.

DR. RICHARD M. McSHERRY,
President Sanitary Convention.

DEAR SIR: At the request of several of the members of our association, I desire to call the attention of the body over which you preside to the enclosed copy of a bill which our association proposes presenting to the next legislature and hopes to have a law.

While the prime object of this bill is to prevent the spread of infectious diseases among our valuable herds, it must, if passed, materially aid the sanitary department of the state.

It is a fact well known to your profession and to many others, that much diseased meat is sold for consumption in our large cities, as also the fact that tuberculosis is a disease very prevalent among the dairy herds of the vicinity of Baltimore, and whether or not this dreadful disease is communicable from the bovine to the human race through the consumption of milk, is probably better known to your profession than to us. This is only one of many diseases that might, by a proper system of inspection, be eradicated.

We hope for the countenance and assistance of your honorable body in our efforts to have this or some similar bill made law.

I am, sir, with great respect, your obd't serv't,

T. ALEX. SETH, *Sec'y.*

An Act to Prevent the Spread of Infectious or Contagious Diseases among the Live-Stock of this State.

SECTION 1. *Be it enacted by the General Assembly of Maryland,* That it shall be the duty of the governor of the state to take measures to promptly suppress any contagious or infectious disease which may make its appearance among the live-stock of this state, and to prevent it from spreading.

SEC. 2. *And be it enacted*, That for such purpose the governor shall appoint one chief veterinary inspector, who shall be a graduate in good standing of some recognized school of veterinary medicine, at a salary in the discretion of the governor and his traveling expenses, who shall hold his office at the pleasure of the governor, whose duty it shall be to visit the stables of the city and counties wherever he has reason to believe contagious or infectious diseases may exist, and he may visit any such stable at any such hour of the day between sunrise and sunset, and shall have power, with the consent of the governor, to order all animals which have been exposed to contagion or infection to be secluded in such manner as the nature thereof may, in his judgment, render necessary, to prevent the spreading of such disease; to order that any premises, farm or farms, stables or railway cars where such disease exist, or has existed, be put in quarantine, so that no domestic animal shall be removed from or brought to the premises or places so quarantined until the same shall have been properly disinfected; to prescribe such regulations as he may judge necessary or expedient to prevent infection or contagion being communicated in any way from the places so quarantined; to call upon all sheriffs and deputy sheriffs, constables, policemen, or any officers of the state, the city of Baltimore, or of any county, for information and assistance to carry out and enforce the provisions of such orders and regulations; to prescribe regulations for the destruction of animals affected with infectious and contagious diseases, and for the proper destruction of their hides and carcasses, and of all objects which might carry infection or contagion; provided that no animal shall be destroyed unless first examined by such veterinary inspector or one of his assistants; to prescribe regulations for the disinfection of all premises, buildings and railway cars, and of all objects from which or by which infection or contagion may take place or be conveyed; to alter and modify from time to time, as he may deem expedient, the terms of all such orders and regulations, and to cancel or withdraw the same at any time; to order all or any animals coming into the state to be detained at any place or places for the purpose of inspection and examination; provided that animals coming from a neighboring state that have been quarantined and discharged shall not be subject to the provisions of this act; and it shall be the duty of all sheriffs and deputy sheriffs, constables, policemen, or other officers of the state, city of Baltimore or counties, to obey and observe all orders and instructions which they may receive from the said veterinary inspector in the enforcement of the provisions of this act.

SEC. 3. *And be it enacted*, That any person who shall transgress the terms or requirements of any order or regulation issued and prescribed by the said veterinary inspector, with the consent of the governor, under the authority of this act, or shall refuse to said veterinary inspector or his assistants access to his or their premises, farms or stables, or shall conceal the fact that contagious or infectious disease exists on his premises, shall be deemed guilty of a misdemeanor.

SEC. 4. *And be it enacted*, That any person who shall sell or otherwise dispose of an animal which he knows or has reason to believe is affected by any contagious or infectious disease, or has been exposed to the same, or shall permit the same to pass over or upon any public highway, street, lane or alley of this state, shall, on conviction thereof, be fined not less than fifty nor more than one hundred dollars for each animal.

SEC. 5. *And be it enacted*, That in the event of any building or buildings, sheds or stables being reported to the governor by said inspector as being incapable of proper disinfection, it shall be his duty to have such premises appraised, in a similar manner as prescribed in the succeeding section for appraisement of diseased animals, and destroyed.

SEC. 6. *And be it enacted*, That in the event of its being deemed necessary by the said veterinary inspector to prevent the spread of contagion or infection, to cause any animal or animals diseased to be slaughtered, the value of such animal or animals shall be fairly appraised by two appraisers, one of which to be appointed by the owner of said animal or animals, the other by said veterinary inspector, or in case the said owner shall neglect or refuse to name such appraiser, then by two appraisers to be appointed by said veterinary inspector, who, in case of disagreement, shall call in a third, which said appraisement shall be returned to the comptroller by said veterinary inspector, and the comptroller shall forthwith issue his warrant to the treasurer for the one-half of the amount of the appraisement of such animals as shall have been slaughtered, in favor of the said owner or owners.

SEC. 7. *And be it enacted,* That in the event of the outbreak of an epidemic of contagious and infectious diseases among the live-stock of this state, it shall be the duty of the governor to appoint such assistants to said inspector as may be necessary to promptly suppress such epidemic and to fix their pay.

SEC. 8. *And be it enacted,* That all the necessary expenses incurred under the direction of by the authority of the governor in carrying out the provisions of this act, including the salary and traveling expenses of said veterinary inspector, shall be paid by the treasurer out of any moneys not otherwise appropriated, and upon the warrant of the comptroller on being certified as correct by the governor.

SEC. 9. *And be it enacted,* That all acts or parts of acts inconsistent herewith be and the same are hereby repealed.

The following letters were also read :

NORTHERN CENTRAL RAILWAY COMPANY,
BALTIMORE, November 21st, 1883.

CHAS. W. CHANCELLOR, M.D.,
Secretary State Board of Health.

DEAR SIR: In reply to your favor of the 1st inst., addressed to Mr. Geo. B. Roberts, president, and referred to this office for attention, I beg to say that we shall be glad to comply with your request, and our surgeon, Thos. S. Latimer, M.D., will represent our company at your convention.

I am, very respectfully, yours,
GEO. C. WILKINS, *General Agent.*

MERCHANTS AND MANUFACTURERS ASSOCIATION,
BALTIMORE, November 22, 1883.

C. W. CHANCELLOR, M.D.,
Secretary State Board of Health, Baltimore.

DEAR SIR: In order that it may clearly appear to the three gentlemen, Dr. J. H. Grimes, Dr H M. Wilson and Mr. J. F. Supplee, who are appointed to represent this association in the State Sanitary Convention, what is the nature of the matters to be treated upon, you will please send to this office three (3) copies of the circular forwarded by you to H. C. Smith, president, that they may accompany notification of said appointment.

Truly yours,
J R. BLAND, *Secretary,* per CHASE.

Evening Session—November 28.

The first paper read was by Dr. Walter Wyman of the U. S. Marine Hospital Service, Baltimore, on:

Quarantine.

The effort of this paper will be to give a review of the quarantine situation during the season just ended, to explain the facilities possessed by the Treasury Department for managing National Quarantines, and the relation of the general government to local authorities in quarantine matters.

The quarantine season of 1883 has come to a close, but the present period should be considered as one of armistice, during which it behooves the conservators of the public health to study well the situation and to review the action of the *last* with special reference to the next campaign.

It was with no slight feeling of concern that reports were received early during the past summer announcing an epidemic of cholera in Egypt, and of yellow fever at Vera Cruz, Havana and other ports having intimate commercial relations with the United States.

With regard to cholera, the march of which through Egypt was marked by great mortality, and caused widespread alarm throughout *Europe*, the United States had also just cause for apprehension when it became known that vessels laden with cotten rags, purchased in Egypt long after the cholera was epidemic, had succeeded in getting to sea before effective quarantine had been established, and were already on their way to this country, via Liverpool and London, the rags being intended for use in paper mills chiefly in New England. Inquiry revealed the fact that six thousand tons of Egyptian rags are annually imported for this purpose.

I do not know that Baltimore has any direct commerce with Egypt, but she has a great commerce with British ports, and when, in the latter part of July, reports were current that these were infected with the Egyptian plague, or more correctly, cholera, the daily papers sounded a reasonable note of warning, and began the discussion of preventive measures. Fortunately, however, the report of cholera at the London docks proved untrue, and was caused by a misunderstanding of the English nomenclature, which gives the term of cholera, or simple cholera, to the disease known on this side of the Atlantic as cholera morbus.

But in Cairo there were reported two hundred deaths a day. The disease also appeared in Beirut, Syria, and the American Consul at this port gave notice that rags and wool were being shipped from infected Syrian ports, via Liverpool, to the United States; that the rags were collected from the poorest classes, and likely to be infected. Cholera was also epidemic at Swatow, China, and prevailed also at Shanghai.

In the meantime, however, a greater cause for alarm was the prevalence of yellow fever in the cities of the Spanish Main, particularly in Havana and Vera Cruz, the latter a city of twenty-three thousand inhabitants—a nidus of infection—with which the United States has greater commercial relations than has any other power, and whose shipping, usually more exempt than the city, was this year unusually infected. Of Havana, it may also be said, that to-day there is more shipping infected than has been the case at any corresponding period in many previous years.

From these infected ports vessels containing the dread disease began in July to make their appearance in American harbors. July 6th, 1883, there arrived in New York from Havana the steamship "City of Puebla," and the bark "Helen Sands," both carrying yellow fever on board. July 24th the British steamer Andean arrived at Newport News with several cases, one of which soon proved fatal.

July 28th the steamer "Californian," from Vera Cruz, with four cases of yellow fever, and having lost as many during the voyage, appeared in Chesapeake bay, and was stopped by the Baltimore city quarantine.

Later, in August, the British steamship "Buteshire," from Vera Cruz, with a record of fifteen cases of yellow fever while *en voyage*, was placed in quarantine at the capes.

Previous to this Pensacola was crowded with yellow fever vessels, all of which were quarantined, and infected vessels were also intercepted at Brunswick, Georgia; Galveston, Texas; Pascagoula, Mississippi; Mobile, Alabama; and at the Mississippi river station; while many being forewarned before nearing their ports of destination were received for treatment at the gulf quarantine at Ship Island.

On August 12th yellow fever invaded the Pensacola navy yard, and soon became epidemic in the naval reservation, the last case occurring October 12th.

In the navy yard proper there were fifteen cases and six deaths, while in the villages of the naval reservation there were one hundred and fifty-two cases and twenty-seven deaths, the total cases being one hundred and sixty-seven, and total deaths thirty-three, in a population of one thousand three hundred and thirty-eight. I am sure I will be pardoned for the digression in mentioning that among the victims of the disease was the lamented United States Naval Surgeon, Alfred M. Owen, whose self-sacrifice, devotion, unhappy fate, and untimely end, must fill with sorrow the hearts of those familiar with his history, and should cause his name to be deeply engraved in the affectionate remembrance of our profession.

The origin of this epidemic of yellow fever in the government reservation at Warrenton and Wolsey—the naval reservation—is still involved in doubt.

Later, in September, yellow fever raged in many of the Mexican cities on the Pacific coast, and was especially severe in Guyamus, Hemocilla, Mazatlan, Manzanilla and Atlata, and as might be expected, it was carried to San Francisco about the last of September, on the steamer "Newbern," and again October 19th, on the steamer "Granada," and within a few days two additional cases have been reported from the marine hospital at San Francisco.

Early in October a disease said to be yellow fever and marked by great mortality was reported at Brewton, Alabama, and while its origin is still in doubt, it is possible that the infection may be traced to the Pensacola navy yard.

Thus during the past season the situation has been briefly as follows: Cholera in China, Egypt and Syria, seriously threatening an approach to our shores; yellow fever raging in Mexico, Central and South America and in the West Indies, and actually knocking at the portals of New York, Philadelphia, Baltimore, Mobile, Pensacola, New Orleans, Galveston and San Francisco, and, finally, a serious epidemic of yellow fever in the Pensacola naval reservation, probably originating there, and from thence threatening the interior. It would seem that the danger to the country has been greater than the immunity which we enjoyed permits us to realize.

Before describing the various measures of defence which were adopted, it is now pertinent to recall the action of the last Congress, appropriating the sum of one hundred thousand dollars in case of threatened or actual epidemic to be used by the President in aid of state and local boards or otherwise, in his discretion, and for maintaining quarantine at points of danger.

The President, acting in his discretion, decided to use this appropriation through the agency of the Treasury Department, to whose medical bureau—the Marine Hospital Service—the expenditure of the fund was intrusted.

It was not until July that this decision was made, and in the meantime the only other power in quarantine matters, viz., that of the National Board of Health, had expired by limitation June 3rd. There was scarcely time for the new quarantine force to take possession of the various establishments and survey the field when a demand was made for immediate activity.

To meet the danger incurred from the importation of Egyptian rags, the collectors of customs were ordered to refuse them entry until the municipal health authorities at the port of entry gave the collector a written certificate that in their opinion no danger was to be apprehended from allowing the discharge of the cargo—thus placing the responsibility on the municipal authorities.

In Boston harbor, several cargoes of rags were thus withheld from entry by the collector, necessitating their discharge on Galloups Island, where, under the supervision of the Boston board of health the rags have been stored for disinfection and fumigation, and will be admitted to pratique when this process has been completed.

The surgeon general has recommended to several of the paper manufacturers, owning paper stock in Egypt, awaiting transportation to this country, to have the rags immersed in vats of chloride of lime before shipment.

With regard to yellow fever, the operations of the Marine Hospital Service began at Pensacola (the city), where, as early as April, 1883, the surgeon general, acting under direction of the president, after personal visitation, caused a house to house inspection to be made. Later a maritime quarantine was established and maintained by this service by the request of the governor of the state, and August 20th the same service took charge of the sanitary cordon placed around the naval reservation—a cordon employing forty-tive guards, and maintained, with the co-operation of the Board of Health of Pensacola, until October 31st. No disease got through the line.

At the gulf quarantine, Ship Island, Mississippi (which is the quarantine refuge for New Orleans and cities of the gulf), the service on July 6th assumed control and performed the labor of holding and disinfecting infected vessels; nineteen vessels with yellow fever on board being thus treated at this station.

It should be borne in mind that the administration of this station was rendered doubly difficult by reason of its proximity to the commerce fleet, which visits Mississippi Sound annually for cargoes of lumber. Although the island is fifteen miles from the shore, the channel runs alongside of it. For this and other reasons Ship Island, though long used for quarantine, is not recommended by the surgeon general in his last report for the permanent gulf quarantine station.

Concerning the Cape Charles quarantine, it will be more convenient to speak presently; but in reviewing the quarantine service in general, it is safe to say that at no period in the history of the United States have so many different ports been threatened with the inroad of yellow fever, and it is pleasant to add that at no time has the management of infected vessels been more successful.

In concluding this account of defensive measure, mention should not be forgotten of the appointment by the Marine Hospital Service of sanitary inspectors in Havana, Vera Cruz, London, Liverpool, and, finally, in Arizona Territory, where, in conjunction with the California board of health, they operated to prevent the inroad of yellow fever from Mexico. And even though it be but a passing notice, the scope of this paper preventing statements in detail, yet tribute must be paid to the great activity and efficiency of the local boards of health, particularly those of Baltimore, Pensacola and of the state board of Louisiana.

Of all the defensive measures enumerated above, there was none of greater interest to Baltimore and the State of Maryland, also to Virginia and the District of Columbia, than the quarantine established at Cape Charles.

Cape Charles Quarantine.

Chesapeake bay, two hundred and fifty odd miles in length, with a width reaching to forty miles, has residing upon its shores and the shores of its tributaries a population of over two millions of people.

The territory which it drains is one which in the past has been subject to frequent epidemic visitation from foreign ports, and its only quarantine stations have been heretofore the one at Craney Island, near Norfolk, and the Baltimore quarantine. Access to this great bay and its adjacent territory from foreign ports can be had at one point only—a channel but ten miles in width between capes Charles and Henry.

It would seem that if there had been designed a fertile region dependent on an ocean commerce, with special reference to its protection from imported disease, its physical configuration could not have been better made.

Cape Charles may be made a quarantine Gibraltar to protect Chesapeake bay from pestilential invasion.

The first vessel, with yellow fever, to appear at this point was the steamer Andean at Newport News, on July 24th. Her sick were at once removed to the hospital barge "Selden," the vessel placed in quarantine, and the United States revenue cutter "Ewing" ordered to ply between the capes, intercept foreign vessels, and cause those with sickness on board to anchor and await medical inspection.

The alarm caused by this first visitation, and the difficulty of locating a quarantine which would not itself become a source of danger, induced Surgeon General Hamilton, of the Marine Hospital Service, to call together a conference of the health authorities of localities interested, which conference met at the Hygeia Hotel, Point Comfort, July 27th, and was attended by Dr. Hamilton and the boards of health or their representatives, of Baltimore, Washington, Richmond, Petersburg, Ocean View, Hampton, Newport News and Norfolk.

By this convention it was determined—

First. That a national quarantine should be established at the capes, and

Second. That the quarantine station should be at Fisherman's Island, in close proximity to Cape Charles.

Authority for a national quarantine "at points of danger" already existed by virtue of the appropriation act of the last Congress; but it should be noted that this quarantine was established by the expressed request of local boards, including that of Baltimore.

The question of precise location was one which gave rise to much discussion. Craney Island was considered too near to Norfolk. Lynn Haven Bay afforded too little protection in rough weather, and was too near the regular course of incoming vessels, and Willoughby's Cove, while naturally well-adapted for quarantine purposes, was objected to by the proprietors of adjacent hotels.

Fisherman's Island, the site finally selected, and which may possibly become a permanent national quarantine station, is a small island, a mile and a quarter in length by a quarter of a mile in width, situated at the southern extremity of Cape Charles, entirely remote from all population.

In the North Channel, which lies between the island and what is known as the Inner Middle Ground, the largest steamers can be safely anchored. This channel is in fact "a natural quarantine anchorage," and is as near the regular ship channel as prudence would allow infected vessels to be anchored. Only the infected vessels are required to enter this channel, all vessels being boarded in their usual course, and if healthy, allowed to proceed without delay. If infected, however, the sick are removed to the island and the vessel fumigated and disinfected in the anchorage.

So important is this station now considered that the government has leased the island; by means of a driven well has secured an ample supply of good water for vessels, and the surgeon general, in his last report, recommends an appropriation of fifty thousand dollars for the erection of hospital buildings (twenty thousand dollars), a wharf (twenty thousand dollars), and disinfecting warehouses (ten thousand dollars).

From Surgeon P. H. Bailhache in charge, I learn that sixty-seven vessels were spoken, thirty-eight inspected and twenty fumigated, at this station, during the quarantine period which ended October 15th.

The Cape Charles quarantine was not intended to supersede or supplant the excellent quarantine of Baltimore, or that of Norfolk, but was rather an advanced out post for these two cities, *and a regular* quarantine for other cities on the bay and its tributaries; and a station morever to which infected vessels might be sent for disinfection and fumigation by the local quarantine physicians when they so desired. As I have shown, it was under the management of the Marine Hospital Service; and in fact all the national quarantines of the past two years have been practically controlled by this service, which may point with satisfaction to its successful efforts during the Mexican-Texas epidemic of 1882, and the Florida epidemic of the present year.

It may be of interest to describe at this point the peculiar and ample facilities for this work possessed by the Treasury Department, of which the Marine Hospital Service is a bureau. It will be seen that the Secretary of the Treasury, as one responsible head, has at his command organized resources which give him the most ample power.

Facilities of the Treasury Department for Managing National Quarantines.

First may be mentioned the COLLECTORS OF CUSTOMS, under the immediate control of the Secretary, from whom reliable *information* may be obtained at any time. There are collectors at every port of entry in the United States, who, from the nature of their office, become thoroughly acquainted with every vessel and every cargo arriving from a foreign port. They have also by law the power of search and detention of vessels, a power exercised at least twice in the furtherance of quarantine during the past season—once at Boston and once at Baltimore. Besides being representative citizens they are sworn officers, and are to be relied on both for information and execution of the laws.

Second may be mentioned the REVENUE CUTTER SERVICE, a bureau of the Treasury Department, in active operation since 1790, its chief object being the enforcement of customs regulations and prevention of smuggling. It is the coast guard of the United States. This service has about forty vessels, mostly steamers, plying along the coast from Maine to Alaska, with jurisdiction extending twelve miles from shore. It is officered by men whose seamanship is unsurpassed, and whose knowledge of the coast is thorough and practical. It has its own cadet school at New Bedford, Mass., where its officers are given a liberal education and special training. It is in fact a small navy, and is made by law a part of the naval force in time of war. This naval force is at all times under the command of the Secretary of the Treasury, and to illustrate its availability in assisting national quarantine, it may be mentioned that during the past season the revenue cutters in the gulf were instructed to cruise along the coast and warn vessels hailing from Hávana and Vera Cruz against entering any port of the

United States during quarantine season until after being duly examined by the United States quarantine officer at Ship Island, and no vessel from the ports named escaped their vigilance after the receipt of this order.

During the season of 1882, when the Marine Hospital Service took charge of quarantine at Brownsville, Texas, it was found that all ordinary lines of travel to that city had been closed, but the Revenue Cutter McLean, at Galveston, was placed under orders and carried without delay the medical supplies, nurses and surgeon in charge to the infected city.

And when the arrival of yellow fever at Newport News, the past season, made desirable a patrol between Capes Charles and Henry to examine incoming vessels, the revenue cutter Ewing was ordered to this duty, and as its ordinary cruising ground already covered this locality, it involved no additional expense and no change in the character of the duties of its officers.

Another—the medical bureau of the Treasury Department—is the MARINE HOSPITAL SERVICE, whose surgeon general is the chief adviser of the Secretary in all medical and sanitary affairs.

It is to the surgeon general of this service that the conception and execution of national quarantine matters are confided; but his acts are under the seal and sanction of the Secretary, and his more important ones are done with the personal knowledge of the latter.

The marine hospital service is essentially a civil service, organized as early as 1798, reorganized in 1871, and has for its primary object the health interest of sailors and the ships in which they sail. As sailors in times of epidemic form so large a proportion of its victims, and are so intimately connected with shipping and commerce, it seems but a natural part of the work of this service to engage in quarantine labor. Though its ordinary fund is contributed by the sailors themselves, the general government aids in various ways, providing much of the machinery for its conduct, donating the land for its hospitals, the hospitals themselves, and much of the amount required to keep them in repair. The government can therefore in equity use this service for such advisory labor as it may require, but its expenditures in time of epidemics are made wholly from the epidemic fund.

This service has physicians in every large, and many of the smaller ports of the country; one hundred and sixty in all. Its corps of medical officers, appointed after examination, have a business training, which connection with the treasury department makes necessary and thorough. Accustomed as they are to the transaction of public business—acquainted, per force, with navigation laws and laws pertaining to public health, and by specific orders with the various local health regulations—they are immediately available at all times, and competent to be entrusted with the details of quarantine management.

The COAST SURVEY, another bureau of the Treasury Department, furnishes accurate charts to enable vessels to approach any of the quarantine stations without danger, taking frequent soundings for the purpose of furnishing information of recent changes in the channels. Thus, when it was charged by interested parties that the water was of insufficient depth near Cape Charles quarantine, and the bottom not good for holding, the contrary was promptly proven by the record of work previously done by this bureau.

The LIGHT-HOUSE ESTABLISHMENT, with its vessels and facilities for bouying channels, furnishing signal lights, etc., is also a part of the Treasury Department, and was called into service at Ship Island, where it buoyed out the channel, furnished stationary lights and aided in the maintenance of quarantine. It also buoyed the channels for the Cape Charles quarantine.

Thus with the collectors as reliable business agents, the revenue cutter service as a naval force, and a corps of specially trained physicians, assisted by other divisions, and all under one head, does the Treasury Department find itself already well equipped, without additional legislation for the control of national quarantines.

We come now to consider the position of the government toward the states in matters of quarantine.

Local and National Quarantine.

The proper relation which should exist between state and local authorities and the central government in this regard is a problem which as early as 1796, and at several later periods, became the subject of debate in Congress, and is one which at the present day may be said to be still sub judice. It is not my purpose to discuss this subject in a controversial manner, but it may be of interest, and will assist in its intelligent comprehension, if we take a brief historical review of this relation as it has actually existed from time to time, and note what changes it has undergone.

It is a matter of history that several of the independent colonies, long before the formation of the Federal Union, had their own separate quarantine laws. Massachusetts, for example, enacted a quarantine law as early as 1648; South Carolina in 1698; Pennsylvania in 1700; Rhode Island in 1711, and New York in 1755. And in the earlier days of the Union, notably in 1793-4-5, state and local quarantines were established independently of one another and without aid from the general government.

The first recorded effort to obtain the aid of the United States in the matter of quarantine was made by the merchants and other inhabitants of Baltimore, who presented December 16th, 1790, a petition to Congress, praying that a health officer might be established, or other provision made by law for protecting them from infectious and epidemic diseases brought by passengers and others arriving from a foreign country. In reply to this petition a committee was appointed to bring in a bill to establish health officers in the principal ports of the Union, but this committee never made a report.

About three and a half years later, viz., June 9th, 1794, Congress approved an act of the Legislature of Maryland, levying a duty on vessels to pay the expenses of its health officer and quarantine establishment, which act was subsequently repealed, and was only intended to continue in force during that session.

The first resolution in Congress, looking to the establishment of national quarantines, was offered by the Hon. Samuel Smith, of Maryland, in the Fourth Congress, April 28th, 1796, and was as follows: "Resolved, that the President of the United States be authorized to direct such quarantines to be performed on all vessels from foreign countries arriving at the ports of the United States, as he shall judge necessary." From this and the records of the debates, it appears that the representative from Maryland was an earnest advocate of national supervision.

The resolution being referred to the committee on commerce, of which Mr. Smith was a member, the committee reported a bill embracing two separate enactments—the first of which, after considerable debate, was rejected, and read as follows:

1. "*Be it enacted, &c.*, The President of the United States be and is hereby authorized to direct, at what place or station in the vicinity of the respective ports of entry within the United States,

and for what duration and particular periods of time, vessels arriving from foreign ports and places may be directed to perform quarantine."

The second enactment was passed and approved May 27, 1796, and read as follows:

2. "*Be it enacted, &c.*, That the President of the United States be and is hereby authorized to direct the revenue officers and the officers commanding ports, and revenue cutters, *to aid* in the execution of quarantine, and also in the execution of the health laws of the states respectively in such manner as may to him appear necessary."

The adoption of this second enactment, and rejection of the the first, are significant facts, expressing the sentiment of Congress, that while the United States should render assistance, the states should enact and execute their own quarantine laws, and the rejection of this first enactment may have been to emphasize this right of the states which had been called into question during the debate.

In 1799 a quarantine bill was introduced in Congress by the Hon. Samuel Smith, of Maryland, chairman of the committe on commerce.

This bill became a law February 25th, 1799, and, in brief, directs collectors of customs and other officers of the general government to *aid* in the execution of the quarantine and health laws of the several states, and provides for the establishment of government warehouses for the deposit of goods and merchandise taken from vessels, subject to quarantine restraint. From this time until 1878, a period of seventy-nine years, no quarantine laws were enacted by Congress, and it should be mentioned that Jefferson, in 1804, in a communication to Congress on the state of the union, protested against the adoption of a code of laws to prevent the introduction of yellow fever.

In 1872, however, Congress passed a joint resolution providing for a more effective system of quarantine on the southern and gulf coasts, in accordance with which a medical officer of the army was detailed to make a report upon the subject. A national quarantine was proposed, and an act to prevent the introduction of contagious or infectious diseases into the United States passed the House of Representatives, but did not become a law.

In the winter of 1873 4 a strong effort was made in Congress to pass a quarantine act, and though unsuccessful, the discussions excited must have had some influence on later legislation.

It is pertinent to add that, in 1874, Congress ordered an investigation of the cholera epidemic of 1873.

But it was not until 1878 that special committees on epidemic diseases were appointed in the Senate and House of Representatives and a new quarantine law enacted.

Between these two periods of 1799 and 1878, however, the proper administration of quarantine, and other subjects bearing upon the public health, began to receive much discussion outside of Congress, and, notably in 1857, the first American convention called to consider sanitary reform was held in Philadelphia. This convention was composed of representative men from New York, Boston, Baltimore, New Orleans and other seaboard cities, and its avowed purpose was for conference in relation to the establishment of a uniform system of revised quarantine laws. Similar conventions were held in succeeding years, viz., at Baltimore in 1858, New York in 1859, and Boston in 1860, after which the breaking out of the civil war turned the attention of sanitarians and public health officers into other channels. As a result of these conventions greater uniformity in the quarantine regulations of the states was established, and the question of possession and control of a quarantine establishment by the general government received attention and discussion.

After the close of the war we find the same subject of national quarantine in its relation to state governments occupying public attention, and becoming a topic of discussion in the American Public Health Association, a body organized for " the advancement of sanitary science and the promotion of organizations and measures for the practical application of public hygiene." And, finally, February 14, 1878, at a convention of business men and physicians of the gulf coast and southern seaboard, held at Jacksonville, Florida, a resolution was adopted to the effect that a uniform system of quarantine was absolutely required, and that the system could only be enforced by the national government.

Based upon the action of this convention, a quarantine bill was passed by Congress and became a law April 29th, 1878, forbidding or restraining the entry of vessels from infected ports, and empowering the Surgeon-General of the Marine Hospital Service under direction of the Secretary of the Treasury to make necessary regulations. At that time the Russian plague was imminent and regulations were made which directed quarantine, isolation of infectious freight, disinfection and even burning if necessary.

In 1879 Congress repealed the act of 1878 so far as it gave power to the Surgeon-General of the Marine Hospital Service, and established a National Board of Health, and bestowed upon it a great deal of power in quarantine matters. But this act expired by limitation June 3rd of the present year. It may be well to state that there were two acts, the first March 3, 1879, establishing the board, and the other June 2nd investing it with its power. It is this last act which has expired by limitation, leaving the board its name only.

Now the expiration of this act leaves in force a portion of the law of 1878, but not that portion relating to its executive officer; so that the law of 1878 becomes practically a dead letter, there being no one charged with its execution.

Thus the laws of both 1878 and 1879 are practically of no avail.

However, the national quarantine operations are now very conveniently carried on, as shown in another portion of this paper, under the appropriation acts of 1882 and 1883, which authorize the president to use a sum not exceeding $100,000 each year in aid of local boards or otherwise, in his discretion, in preventing and suppressing epidemic disease. The president has in each of these two years entrusted this fund to the Secretary of the Treasury, to be used by the Marine Hospital Service.

In studying the question of state or national control of maratime quarantine, mention should not fail to be made of a rather recent decision made by the Superior Court of Louisiana (Judge Munro) bearing upon the subject. This decision is to the effect that municipal boards of health or state authorities have no constitutional right to levy a tax on vessels for quarantine purposes, and it may be that quarantine may therefore naturally and ultimately fall into the hands of the general government, unlesss states determine upon paying their quarantine expenses from their state treasuries.

But placing this view to one side, and looking at the present situation, it would seem that the precise relation which should exist between local and national quarantines will necessarily vary with each port, and remains to be determined by future legislation. In the meantime, and at present, the general government acts only as a powerful ally, and in the absence of local quarantine, assumes the jurisdiction and accepts the responsibility.

In conclusion, I desire to express my acknowledgments among other sources of information to the annual reports of the Surgeon General of the Marine Hospital Service, and to the able reports of Dr. Joseph H. Jones, president of the State Board of Health of Louisiana.

[NOTE—This paper was discussed by Drs. Bell of New York, and Steuart and Morris of Baltimore, and elicited much favorable comment. It is to be regretted that the reporter's notes, giving the full discussion, have been mislaid.—C. W. C.]

The next paper was by Dr. Richard Gundry on:

The Conflict of State Power and Individual Rights in Sanitary Matters.

The objects of this convention I take to be, to arrive at such agreement as may be possible as to the essential needs of the community in a sanitary point of view. Some, perhaps, would add that the main object is to formulate a *law* which, approved by us as a convention, should be presented to the legislature and passed by them to enforce certain practices and regulations for the improvement of public health. Now, the discussion of the sanitary wrongs suffered by the community, and suggestions for their remedy is an excellent thing if it shall open the eyes and understanding of the community in general to the importance of the subject—to the magnitude and constant increase of the sources of disease and degeneration—to the full recognition of the dangerous character of many of these things which people too often think to be of trivial weight and harmless, or at least only harmful to other people; if, I say, we can do anything to arouse public opinion to recognize and remedy these things, our convention will be a great success; but if we take for granted that as the self-elected instructors of the people it needs only our imprimatur to seal the success of a law—if the formulating of such a law be the do-all and be-all of this meeting we shall find that we only confirm the definition of the grammarian, who defined the word convention as a "noun of multitude, signifying many but not always signifying *much*." To have upon the statute book a good law for sanitary purposes is a good thing, provided you have a strong healthy popular opinion to sustain it—not otherwise. Better far, that the law be deficient in some detail, with an enlightened and aroused public opinion upon the subject, than the most perfectly devised law with an apathetic or hostile sentiment in the community where it is to be enforced. There is in reality no law so inefficient as that which is not fully supported by public opinion. If enforced it is regarded as tyrannical, and constant jarrings and frictions occur which increase the original dislike for it, and ultimately cause its disregard or repeal, or if they cannot be effected, revolt and anarchy. For it is a fallacy to suppose that because our laws are made by persons freely chosen by us (by the counting of noses) and therefore are the formulated expression of our will, and must be obeyed, and really are generally obeyed, laws are necessarily the expression of popular opinion. In reality they sometimes are; as often not. Public opinion is constantly changing from day to day, as the light of knowledge increases; its movements are oscillatory, but with a direction usually slowly determined. Not always is that direction ascertained. The eddies of the current often draw us out of the main stream, and that legislation as a rule is the most successful which keeps within sight, but just a little ahead of the wave--abreast or a little more—which discerning the shape popular opinion is assuming, has the apparel ready to clothe it with. Generally legislation follows in the wake of popular opinion, which has loudly demanded it, and when obtained, it is viewed with somewhat of distrust as extorted by force.

If the legislation should be too much ahead of the "popular wave," neglect and dislike follow. We are too apt to think that majorities, however obtained, are all that is needed to determine a question. Sir Robert Peel said, most philosophically, to Mr. Cobden, when he heard of the overthrow of Louis Phillippe by the French Revolution of 1848, "That comes of trying to carry on a government by means of a mere majority of a chamber, without regard to the opinion out of doors." From what I have heard, Maryland has had upon her statute books several good laws for sanitary purposes. Her law for boards of health and other sanitary purposes is good. How much of it is in operation, thoroughly and smoothly working with the support of the people? In how large a portion of the state are its operations felt or attempted?

So long as no epidemic is present, the law lies dormant, and the evils it was created to suppress are fostered by its neglect. The question itself is a subject of cheap wit and derision. When an epidemic breaks out in a community unprepared, then the strong arm of the law is evoked, its ministers censured, and with all the hurry and confusion of a panic, the provisions of the law hurriedly, and harshly, and expensively carried out. In proportion as the danger fades away, reaction sets in; the extent of the evil fought is contracted in the memory, the expense and harshness are only remembered and exaggerated, and thus sullen indifference succeeds to recrimination. But as a rule, all is not lost, some step has been gained and held, and thus gradually and slowly, step by step, is a system of law and regulation built up, and efficiency of its administration secured. Let us hope that the panic and terror of the late epidemic of small pox will lead to the more general practice of vaccination *when there is no epidemic,* instead of waiting till the enemy is at our doors. Let me illustrate the results of attempts to enforce sanitary laws in neighborhoods not enlightened upon the subject of their purport.

Two instances occur to me, drawn from very different states of society, but illustrating how the popular bias towards mistrusting sanitary doctrines and methods influences juries to give undue weight to adverse testimony. In the life of Lord Abinger, an instance is given of his astuteness in cross-examination, in the case of a nuisance fully proven—with expert testimony as to its deleterious effects upon the health of the community—and the case looked conclusive. The last witness put on the stand to prove the nuisance, or something connected with it, and who loudly complained of it, was a healthy looking matron, who gave her testimony clearly. Scarlett commenced his cross-examination as to her own history, who she was, how long she had been married, and how many children she had had, how she raised them, rousing her pride to describe them—as a mother would naturally—he was stopped by the opposing counsel, who objected to the scope of his examination as irrelevant; and the judge saying he really did not see how they bore upon the matter, he merely said he would like to continue and it would soon appear. Going on, he got from the witness that she had been healthy as the average; had raised a large family of healthy children, and then closed, saying: that is my case, a cause could not be unhealthy, which produces such results, and triumphantly defeated the opposite side, dispelling all the positive evidence of the ill effect of the complained nuisance by the negative testimony of one whom it had failed to affect. As well deny in a time of universal bankruptcy that there is a prostration of business because Astor and Vanderbilt had their millions in safety. Allowing for the tact and power of the lawyer, effective in making the worse the better cause appear, there is much due to the mistrust with which juries naturally approach such subjects on which their information is limited.

The other incident occurred about sixteen years ago, in a rich and intelligent county. A case was on trial where the nuisance complained of was a large distillery, with its enormous hog styes, contaminating the air and streams adjacent, making the lives of those in the adjacent village uncomfortable by reason of the bad smell, and some *few* cases of fever had been traced to its influence. The facts were made out to the jury. Expert testimony showed the probable effect from the continuance of such a state of things, and everything looked conclusive, when the defence put in the witness box a respectable looking farmer, who had succeeded in life and was well-to-do. He testified that the nuisance complained of was nothing at all to be feared; rather an advantage, giving the extraordinary reason that he owned a very bad smelling privy himself. He admitted it was terrible, and added he was subject to headaches, which he always cured by inhaling the odor from that privy (placing his face over the seat). The man was honest, and in ordinary things, intelligent; and his so-called practical knowledge outweighed the positive testimony of the other side, and all the theories of the experts, in the view of the jury. A year or two after, that neighborhood was scourged by an epidemic of fever, resulting from the state of things unredressed.

Juries only represent the average intelligence of the communities, they are drawn from, and go into the jury box, impartial enough, but impartial as the personal equation of each limits him, that is to say, biased more or less by his association, habits of thought and extent of cultivation. A community thoroughly aroused to the importance of sanitary questions, will furnish jurymen capable of investigating such questions in an enlarged and enlightened manner, and less liable to be swerved by secondary considerations or legal sophistries. It is to juries that the question will naturally come; or if to magistrates, will the result differ materially?

Gradually as occasion has been developed, there has sprung up a class of men who have given these subjects of sanitation their earnest study, and this class will gradually increase. Among them have been lawyers, engineers, clergymen, physicians, and scientists. Of course, the larger portion come from the medical profession, whose training should fit them for such investigations; but the study of state medicine, or the prevention of disease, is only in its infancy in our land. Wherever boards of health have been established, there should be, and generally is, a nucleus of organization for all workers in this direction. At first the power confided to them may be small, but gradually as the knowledge is disseminated, popular opinion, organized by intellect, influenced by morality, and devoted to high and noble aims, presses to their assistance either by encouraging voluntary efforts or by the authority of law, which then can be enforced. But these transitions in law to be safe, should be the gradual product of popular opinion, so as to secure the practical well-being of the community, and to allow its social and industrial forces to develope, unimpeded by unnecessary restrictions, thereby carefully avoiding the exciting of violent passions, provoking reaction, offending large classes and generating enduring discontent among the people of any class.

It is to the voluntary efforts of this class that all success hitherto achieved is due; that laws in certain directions have been enacted and carried out successfully as the expression of the will of the state. Agitate, constantly agitate, must be the sanitarian's cry. When we point reproachfully to what is done in other countries, and contrast the clean streets of European cities every day of the year, with the general condition of our cities in this respect—except, perhaps, for a few days before an election—we may perhaps sigh and wish for more direct power to enforce this law in these respects, but we must remember our limitation, and that the efficiency of such work here must be regulated by the standard our intelligence demands; but we also can reflect how rapidly that intelligence once aroused has redressed many errors, and hope for the future revives. Until it can be impressed upon our people generally, that these questions are really questions of life and death, of wealth and poverty, our laws simply encumber our books of statutes and ordinances.

The word state is not used in any special sense. I have nothing to do with state rights or wrongs, but I use the word to imply the personification of what Cicero described: "Multitudo juris consensu et utilitatis communione sociata," whether embodied in a general government, state government, municipality or township, making and enforcing laws, ordinances or regulations. In order to the promotion of general health or the health of each, what have all a right to demand from each? It will be found that practically the amount of the individual's surrender of his self-acting power is gauged by the proximity and number of the community he is a member of. A man dwelling apart with his family, forms a law unto himself practically—because his evil practices, if any, effect no one but himself and family—the rest of the community can only take cognizance of very grave practices whereby the health of members of his family may be vitiated. The other extreme is found in the crowded city, where practically every man's act affects every other man's health and comfort in a greater or less degree, and where, if he does not care for his neighbor's condition, that condition may re-act upon himself directly or indirectly with fearful effect. Between these two extremes of personal contact are intervals of every extent, modifying more or less inter-personal relations and reactions. It is from city life, therefore, that we must draw most of our illustrations of the conflict of state power and individual rights, as they are there brought close to the light and more generally recognized. In the country on a broader scale, may be the same evils, but these effects are not so immediate, and are therefore ignored with less resulting evil. But unfortunately the tendency of modern life is towards the cities, and this is rapidly increasing, especially among the poorer classes.

In the East, 35 per cent.; in the West, 15 per cent.; in the South, 7 per cent. are within the city limits. They are drawn by the gravitating force of city life. The hope of finding work, the fascination of city sights and sounds holds them. And when here, what then? There is a disturbance of the social equilibrium. They are, a part of the time, out of work. They live from hand to mouth. They can learn no provident habit, since they never have enough to save. They cannot afford to pay rent enough to live apart from other families. They crowd into small rooms, which have no adequate provision for sewerage, pure air or pure water. They come under the infection of imitation from other families. There are few open spaces for children to play in. Neatness and order disappear. The man frequents the corner or the saloon. The woman finds no companionship, save that of dirty, dishevelled women.

It was discovered by George Combe that when the rabbit warren was not properly cleaned, the female killed her young, and the male became quarrelsome. The organism of the animal was injured and rendered miserable by dirt, and nervous irritability akin to insanity was, the result, and he adds, "The deleterious physical condition in which many of the human poor habitually live, is the cause of some of their sufferings and crimes."

The steps of descent from self-help to crime and idleness, voluntary or involuntary, are discouragement; crowded condition; evil association impossible of avoidance; uncleanness; doles of food or money; increasing dependence; demand for public aid—crime. Thus many hard working men and honest women have broken under the social pressure, and become pauperized, or criminal, or both. Now as the state has at last to provide for this class of persons, and their provision entails trouble and expense, it is decidedly preferable to interfere before the last step is reached, and arrest this degeneration, and in one respect, at least, this interference regards points of sanitation. If lack of cleanliness leads to crime, clearly the state has a right to say the individual shall be required to be clean. To be clean again includes several factors, pure air, pure water, ventilated houses, means of disposing of filth excreted or made by necessary contamination. Without these, efforts at cleanliness are spasmodic and exceptional. Now if the state insists on this cleanliness, it must see that the necessary agencies for it are provided. First—water, as free as possible to the poor, not as a question of charity, but as a question of economy, for cleanliness is cheaper than pauperism or crime. Then not only the freedom of supply, but the purity of that supplied. That this is a matter of economy may also be urged as the result of experiments and investigations. The epidemic of cholera in London in 1848-9, and 1853-4, showed the effects of water distribution—by a comparison of areas supplied by two water companies. The Southwark and Vauxhall, and the Lambeth. Each of these companies during the epidemic of 1848-9 and one of them (Southwark and Vauxhall) during the epidemic of 1853-4, had supplied its customers with sewage-polluted water of the Thames—and the miscellaneous sewage with which the water was polluted, had of course included choleraic discharges. The statistics of the two outbreaks in relation to the two quantities of local population were as nearly as could be estimated these. The quantity of population supplied by the Southwark and Vauxhall company suffered in the epidemic of 1848-9 at the rate of 118 cholera deaths for every 10,000 of population, and in the epidemic of 1853-4, at the rate of 130 for each 10,000. The quantity of population supplied by the Lambeth company, suffered in the epidemic of 1848-9 at the rate of 125 for each 10,000 of population, but in the epidemic of 1853-4 only at the rate of 37. And what was the single discoverable difference of condition in favor of the one quantity of population which suffered comparatively so little when the second epidemic befell? The company which supplied it with water had in the interval since the first epidemic improved its supply to comparative excellence; whereas the other company were distributing water of even filthier quality than before. Dr. Simon adds: "It is in the highest degree probable, that of the 3,476 tenants of the Southwark and Vauxhall Company, who died of cholera in 1853-4, two thirds would have escaped if their water supply had been like that of their neighbors.

The necessity of baths brought within the reach of the poorest as an auxiliary in the work of cleanliness needs no lengthened argument. The spread of baths for the poor is due very much to the work of one poor woman, and illustrates the inception of popular opinion. In 1832, when the cholera first appeared in England, there was a poor woman named Catherine Wilkinson, who was so impressed with the necessity of cleanliness as a preventative of the disease, that she encouraged her neighbors to come to her comparatively better house, which comprised a kitchen, parlor, three small bed chambers and a yard, for the purpose of washing and drying their clothes. The good that was manifested, induced some benevolent persons to aid her in extending her operations. The large amount of washing done in one week in a cellar, under the superintendence of this excellent woman represented the amount of disease and discomfort kept down by her energetic desire to do good without pecuniary reward. Such was the origin of public baths and wash-houses in England, which Catherine

Wilkinson had the satisfaction of seeing matured in Liverpool in 1846 in a large establishment under the corporation, to the superintendence of which she and her husband were appointed. The system has spread so that for a few cents all over the larger cities, baths are within reach of the poor. Plenty of water for drinking, washing and bathing of a proper quality, means diminution of all epidemic diseases, and an increased self-respect, with decrease of pauperism and crime.

Then it is clearly impossible to have the full benefit of this increased supply without the power of carrying it off when used, without doing harm to the rest of the population. For this a proper system of sewerage must be devised—a system which will not contaminate either the air of dwelling houses or the stream from which potable water is supplied. Both the supply of water to dwellings and the discharge of excreta, require skilled operatives to arrange and put in the necessary pipes and apparatus. This, if deficient, is not only detrimental to the parties, but to other innocent parties, producing disease and death by introduction of sewage gas, and requires that it should be supervised by competent persons, for the work of the plumber is hidden to a great extent, and the damages are great but insidiously produced when the work is imperfect. Has not the state the right to determine upon what conditions the work shall be done? Moreover, the state claims the right also to supervise dwellings where large numbers congregate (tenement houses), first for the protection of the poor against wealth, but principally as a police right to keep down pauperism, disease and crime. When these tenement houses have been properly supervised, their ventilation looked after—cleanliness enforced and proper sanitary arrangements introduced (as far as possible), the death rate has been very materially lowered. In New York from 1868 to 1873, the percentage of the death rate among the tenement house population, fell from 75 to 64 per cent.—11 per cent.—in consequence of such supervision, while in private houses where no such supervision was exercised, the death rate increased in these years. "May I not do what I please with my own," is the historical exclamation of a ducal owner of rotten boroughs when reform was threatened. The limitation of this liberty is now believed in more largely when it conflicts with the interests of others; and this limitation seems to be in proportion as any harm results to a large or helpless portion of the community. In time I hope it will be thought a crime to take advantage of the necessities of the poor, to rent houses with wet cellars, damp walls, ill ventilation, dark rooms, imperfect supplies of water or means of sewage removal.

The adulteration of food has always claimed the attention of the state, and thus butchers, bakers and others are brought into the class which may require supervision. This supervision has existed from ancient times in nearly all states.

No great industry arises, conferring employment to vast multitudes of people and benefitting very materially the community in which it is situated, without in time also developing attendant evils peculiar to it. Sometimes, but rarely, these evils are detected and corrected as they are discovered, but too often it requires special press of public opinion or its embodiment, law, to enforce the proper remedy. The large canning establishments, slaughter houses, almost every industrial pursuit carried on by large numbers associated together, has at some time engaged special attention on account of some evil introduced or increased by them. The restriction of the hours of labor of children, the sanitary arrangements of the work places, the use of antidotes against poisonous substances employed in manufactures, the security of the neighborhood against contamination depends upon the right of the state to protect itself against wrong-doing.

The unversality of the elective franchise has brought with it the duty of placing the means of enlightenment within the reach of all; but if we expect our future citizens and voters to be intelligent and instructed, we must also see that the places provided for their instruction are suitable for such purposes in a sanitary point of view and not detrimental to their physical and mental health. School hygiene should be the study, not only of every teacher, but the anxious object of solicitude to every supervising officer connected with the schools.

To another point popular opinion should be earnestly aroused · the arrest of causes of preventable disease. If scarlet fever springs from animal contamination; if typhoid fever is disseminated from fecal sources; if typhus from excessive overcrowding, the immense loss occasioned to the state by sickness and death in the diminution of its resources, should lead it to seek out means of curtailment of these evils. Take one instance alone: the planting of the eucalyptus tree has comparatively banished ague from some of the places where it most prevailed, in Algiers and Italy. Where it is adapted to our climate, why should not its planting be urged and tried? If successful, laws encouraging and enforcing such culture would speedily follow until it would be considered wrong in certain places for malaria to exist. The owner of the soil would be forced to put a stop to the evil.

In all these, the conflict of the state on behalf of the many is constant against the claims of some individual, but as he is not exempt from the good or the evil flowing from all the conditions of society, he too, in another way receives his portion of the benefit.

As the time advances, greater enlightenment will reveal still more points of contact with each other; will teach us more and more duties in these respects towards each other, and illustrate more clearly the benefits flowing to all from their performance. Then we shall more readily assent to their embodiment in laws and insist upon their systematic enforcement against the refractory. Then, and not till then, shall we be able to realize the correctness of the description of the judicious Hooker when he exclaims: "Of Law, there can be no less acknowledged than that her seat is the bosom of God, her voice the harmony of the world. All things in heaven and on earth do her homage, *the very least as feeling her care and the greatest as not exempt from her power.*"

Maj. Chas. H. Latrobe read the following paper on:

Sewerage Systems.

GENTLEMEN: As I conceive it to be the duty of every professional man attending this convention, to add what he can to the information we desire to elicit on sanitary subjects, I have here noted down what I believe often of vital interest in connection with that most important branch of sanitation, viz: The particular system to be adopted for the sewerage of any city, town or public institution in regard to which this question may arise. I think we may safely start from one premise, viz; That each case necessitates a special study, and possibly a different mode of treatment.

No one system may be accepted as a panacea for all the problems which arise: This fact is, I think, recognized by most sanitarians, more emphatically every day, and, in fact, is analogous to the most advanced practice in all professions, including the medical; indeed, it may be said of the latter, that any remedy professing to be a panacea for all the ills which flesh is heir to, at once excites suspicion in proportion to the breadth of its claim. In regard to the choice of a system of sewerage, we may safely conclude that there are but two fundamental truths for our guidance, viz: which is the most efficient and economical as applied to each case which arises. In making this choice, the sanitary engineer and the sanitary physician, if I may be allowed the expression, should work in harmony; each can contribute knowledge gained in his particular branch; the engineer with his knowledge of physical forces, meteorological phenomena, adaptability of materials and economy of workmanship, must be aided by the physician's knowledge of the seeds of disease, their subtle dissemination and insidious modes of attack; together, they may hope to checkmate the enemy; singly, either may make grave errors.

The several systems for the collection and disposal of the sewerage of cities and towns, now before the public, are, the system of dry-removal as it is called; the water carriage system, and the pneumatic system; of each of these there are variations, but the statement is sufficiently clear as a generalization.

First. As to dry-removal: This system proposes simply to deal with human excreta, totally disregarding all other household waste as well as that from manufactories. At the very outset, such a system must of necessity be a failure for large cities, from its want of scope, after having equipped every house with dry earth-closets, you must of necessity, provide in addition a complete system of sewers to carry off the waste water of the household and the factory; that is, if this system is to be compared fairly with others which accomplish both.

But to return to the matter of human excreta alone, it may be said that the use of earth-closets, especially inside dwelling houses, and above the ground floor, can never be made acceptable to the great majority of people; the storing of the compost, even for twenty-four hours in the house, and the necessity for its daily removal would be, whether rightly or not, an insurmountable objection to its general use, and most people would probably prefer the old-fashioned cess-pool in the yard, to be emptied once in six months by the Odorless Excavating Company.

Again, the physical difficulties in the way of supplying the dry-earth, the constant hauling to and fro of the vast quantitity required, would demand a well drilled army of carts, horses and attendants. Mr. Bateman the celebrated English hydraulic engineer, intimated in 1860 that London would require two million cubic yards per annum of dry earth, and Liverpool four hundred thousand cubic yards, which means forty acres dug six feet deep. Baltimore would require about one hundred and fifty thousand cubic yards. Imagine the handling of this mass of material every year, and it must be dry to be absorbent, this implies drying apparatus. Again, suppose a strike among the employees, a siege or a pestilence. In short, unless this vast machinery moves with the regularity of a clock and the certainty of the force of gravity, it collapses. It is, I think therefore, plain that we cannot successfully apply the dry-system to a large community, and we must relegate it to its proper sphere, viz: To encampments, military, hospitals and some public institutions where strict discipline can be enforced, where the closets are in general external to the buildings, and when the amount of dry earth required is not excessive, and above all in situations where the water-supply is so limited and inaccessible that it is not available for sewerage purposes.

Second. Water carriage, that is all systems in which water is the sole vehicle, and gravity the principal motor; broadly, there are two systems of water carriage, the combined, and the separate.

The combined is that system in which a single set of drains or sewers is used to carry off household waste of every description (except ashes and solid garbage), which is pretty accurately gauged by the water supply to each house, the liquid refuse of factories, and the storm-water which falls upon the roofs, yards and streets.

This may be said to be the most time-honored of all sewerage systems exemplified in many ancient cities of the old world, and still extensively used everywhere. The history of this system would fill a volume; it is a legacy left us by our ancestors; it originated centuries before municipal or rather household water-supply had any existence in the modern sense of that term. Undoubtedly it originated in the necessity for covered water channels to carry off small streams in built-up districts, which had become foul with impurities, and to accommodate the accumulation of storm-water in low lying grounds. Gradually, and in quite modern times, coeval with the supply and use of water for household purposes, these storm-water channels were pressed into service as sewers in the true sense of the word, simply because they existed, were convenient, and economy forbid that they should be ignored. The defects of this system, I think, may be formulated in the statement that combined sewers are expected to perform two incompatible functions, viz.: to accommodate the moderate equable and constant flow of sewerage proper, and the violent, and at times enormous flow of storm-water.

It is true that egg-shaped combined sewers have been constructed and are now built, which eliminate as far as is possible the faults of the system; but there are inherents faults which no constructive skill or ingenuity can ever overcome. The debris of our streets must, to a great extent, enter them in spite of catch-basins, to clog the flow of the sewage proper, the large and uncovered extent of sewer wall must become coated to the flood-line with sewer-slime, whilst the large body of contained air must become contaminated by the contact, and be driven to and fro to seek an outlet in time of storm and flood. And yet, notwithstanding these defects, properly built and thoroughly cared for, combined sewers will probably be continued to be built in those places for which they are best fitted; and this brings us to the question, For what conditions are they best fitted? In my judgment, the reply is: In those places where the conditions require that the storm-water should be at once taken under ground and carried to a distant outlet, whilst economy and structural difficulties forbid the building of two distinct and equally extensive systems, one for sewerage proper, and one for storm-waters. This brings us to the second variety of the water-carriage systems, viz.: the separate. This system, which is based upon the complete separation of sewage proper from the storm-water, was proposed in 1847 by the chief surveyor of a large portion of the metropolitan (London) sewers, Mr. John Philips, and is said to have been advocated by Mr. Edwin Chadwick as early as 1842. It was resuscitated in England in 1865, since which time it has in more or less perfect form, been introduced into a number of towns in England, and some in this country; the city of Memphis furnishing the most notable example here. In this variety as in the combined, water is the vehicle, and gravity the motor, but here the similarity ends. The sewage is conveyed in small pipes of glazed earthern ware, ranging from six inches in diameter upward. accurately proportioned to do the work which is closely measured by the water supply; that which enters the house, clean and pure, by the water-pipes after passing through bath-tubs, kitchen sinks and water closets, leaves it as sewage.

Thus, when we know the average amount of water used per capita per diem in any town or city, we know exactly how large to make the pipes of the separate system so that they may run from two-thirds to three-fourths full. Cut off as these sewers are, absolutely from all storm-water flow, their dead-ends must be taken care of by artificial means; this need is well met by providing automatic flushing tanks, which empty at any interval desired into the dead-ends, and being filled with clean water only, send a purifying stream into every small artery of the system. The wonderful regularity of flow in the sewer-pipes of the separate system was exemplified at Memphis, where in the twenty-inch outfall main, the center depths of flow varied during a period of twenty hours from 6 A. M. till 1 A. M., from twelve and one-half inches to fourteen and one-half inches, whilst from 1 A. M. to 5 A. M., a period of four hours, it varied from eight and one-half inches to eleven and one-half inches, minimum area being one hundred and seven and six-tenths square inches, the maximum one hundred and eighty-six and nine-tenths square inches.

As to the character of the flow, I can speak from personal observation, it was in appearance simply muddy water, everything being dissolved, even a scrap of paper was hard to find. The entire absence of inlets for storm-water, of course effectually prevents the entrance of the silt-sand and debris, which by its specific gravity is precipitated on the bottom of the best built and guarded Combined Sewer as soon as the current slackens. Again the small air space in these pipes, and the rapidity of the current over their glazed surface, which hurries everything to its destination, and prevents deposit, makes it impossible that gases should be generated to any injurious extent: Again, in case the utilization of sewage is desired, we have a concentrated article unburdened with the floods of storm water, which enters the Combined system. That sewage will be utilized in many places and principally by irrigation, is to me clear. Gravity being the motor, it is true at the same time that there are places where this is impossible, but where the outfall main traverses an extensive farming country at a fair elevation, as it would do, should this system ever be adopted for Baltimore, it is certainly reasonable to suppose that irrigation with sewage would at least be given a fair trial, and so favorable would be the position of the main, that but little expense would be involved. It has been suggested that the flushing tanks necessary to this system, would be a heavy draft upon the water supply. This is a great error, there should be about one flushing tank for every two hundred of the population. Supposing in the case of Baltimore that this system reached three hundred thousand people, we would need one thousand five hundred flushing tanks, these tanks would use, say two hundred gallons each per diem (in Memphis one hundred and twelve gallons is the amount) which would be but one gallon per capita per diem, for flushing purposes.

Of course, in treating of this system, although we do not propose to take the storm-water into our pipes, it will not do to ignore them; the outlay at which this can be done varies with the topography of each place to be sewered; we may state, however, in general, that in cities with well-defined ridges and valleys, they can be kept on the surface to great advantage, until they accumulate at or near the low grounds whence they can be carried by short lines of sewer into the nearest water course.

Baltimore is especially well placed in this regard. As to the comparative cost of the combined and separate water carriage system, I will give a few data: The combined system of Brooklyn, N. Y., cost $25,600 per mile, that of Providence, R. I., cost $34,550 per mile. The separate system at Memphis cost but $685 per mile, owing, however, to the size of the place and consequently of the sewers, the comparison is hardly fair to Brooklyn and Providence.

For Baltimore where the comparison is entirely fair to Brooklyn and Providence, my estimated cost of the separate system, is: Exclusive of out-fall main, $4,730 per mile; including out-fall main, $9,790 per mile.

This out-fall main carries our sewage to the Chesapeake bay, and is a costly but necessary addition to our system. Brooklyn and Providence have no main out-fall, and discharge the sewage at many separate points. When they build mains intercepting sewers, the cost of this system will be enormously increased. The cost of the separate system may be stated approximately at from one-quarter to one-third of the combined.

In summing up the applicability of this system of water carriage, I would say that, whenever the topography of a city is sufficiently undulating to give good grades, and when the lines are short to the nearest water-course or harbor, so as to avoid the necessity of a complete second system for storm-water, and what is of vital importance, wherever the water-supply is constant, I believe the separate system to be pre-eminently the proper one.

We now come to the pneumatic systems. Of these there are three at this time before the public, the Shone, the Berlier, and the Liernur. The Shone is an English invention, first brought to notice, I believe, in a paper read before the Philosophical Society of Glasgow, in February, 1880. This system may be called a separate system from the fact that the sewage proper is separated from the storm-water, and is collected at convenient points into globular reservoirs by gravity; each reservoir contains a float which, being lifted by the inflowing sewerage, opens a valve which admits compressed air; this air pressing upon the surface of the sewage, closes the inlet and opens an outlet valve upon which the sewage is lifted to a higher level, and again travels by gravity to the next reservoir, where the same process is repeated, once and again if necessary, until the desired out-fall is reached; of course air-compressers and tanks with the necessary compressed air-ducts leading to each of the sewage collectors are necessary.

It will then be seen that this system is a succession of drops and lifts, compressed air being the motor. To quote the "Sanitary Engineer:" "It will readily be seen that the demand for this invention must be limited to those places where the topography does not allow a gravity system to convey the sewage to the desired point of outfall, or does not admit of giving sufficient slope to the collecting sewer and mains to insure their being self-cleansing; in other words it is an apparatus for lifting sewage, and if the ground is such that it will run away by gravity at a proper destination, we do not care to lift it." One thing can be said in its favor, viz.: that compressed air can be carried with less loss of power to distant points, than any other; and where a series of small elevations have to be overcome, it would be more economical to send compressed air from a central reservoir to numerous lifting points, than to use steam pumps.

THE BERLIER SYSTEM—This is also in the same sense a separate system, by which the sewage proper is collected into a cesspool temporarily under each house, from which at intervals it is drawn into distinct tanks from which the air has been exhausted.

The Liernur System—This has been more extensively applied than any of the pneumatic systems, and is undoubtedly the most ingenious and effective of its kind. It is the invention of Captain Liernur, a Dutch engineer, and has been used in Dortrecht, Leyden, and parts of Amsterdam. In applying this system the town is districted. At a suitable point in each district an iron tank of sufficient capacity is sunk, say in the intersection of two streets. From this tank street mains are extended in every direction to the limits of the district; to these street mains are attached the house pipes, there being a barometric trap in each house-pipe, all having the same rise. The process is as follows: The sewage from each house flows by gravity towards the district tank, running over the traps as it accumulates behind them, each trap of course always remaining full. At some stated period of the day the district tank is cut off from the street mains and exhausted of its air; this being done, the valve is again opened, and the entire contents of the street mains and house-pipes are driven by a violent shock into the district tank; the barometric resistance of the traps being the same in every house-pipe, as they all have the same rise or head. From the district tanks the sewage is conducted by the same means to the central station tank, where a vacuum is always kept up by the air-pumps, the flow of sewage being kept up by relays of vacuum applied from time to time as section after section of the sewage pipe is reached, there being two lines of pipe, one for air, and one for sewage. As there is a multiplicity of valves in this system, clock-work has been applied, by which they are operated at proper intervals.

From these brief descriptions, and taking the Liernur as the best and most ingenious, it will be seen that this system ignores, except to a very limited extent the force of gravity, substituting therefor an artificial motor in the shape of a vacuum.

This necessitates a very perfect system of piping, consequently nothing but iron can be used with leaded joints; the district tanks must be of iron well caulked. From every district tank, to the central station, there must be two lines of iron piping, one called the vacuum main and one the transport main; there must also be numerous valves with clock-work attachments. The central station must contain its iron reservoir, vacuum pumps, &c., &c. All these arrangements necessitates a very large outlay for construction, as well as close attention and expensive maintenance. Again this system, with its expensive appliances, only provides for the solid and fluid excreta of the household; there must be another system of pipes on the gravity plan provided for the household water, from bath-tubs, kitchen sinks, laundries; also the waste from factories, &c., or in short, what constitutes our gutter-flow in dry weather.

In case this system of pipes should be required to take care of the storm-water also, we have at once the pneumatic system for excreta alone, and a complete combined system of water-carriage sewers in addition. If the pneumatic system is proportioned to take care of the excreta, and the household water in addition, which the ordinary separate water-carriage system does do in one system of pipes, its cost would become prohibitory, besides which, its claim for the utilization of sewage proper by the manufacture of poudrette would be endangered, as the evaporation of so much water would be a serious hindrance.

Mr. Adam Scott's estimate of the cost of the Liernur pneumatic system alone, that is, the system which takes care simply of the excreta, is for England \$20 per capita of population; in this country it would probably reach \$25 per capita; to this must be added the cost of the subsidiary system for the household and manufactory water, which would probably raise it to \$35 per capita; whilst a liberal estimate for a separate water-carriage system including the out-fall main, would be \$10 per capita for a city situated as Baltimore is.

The cause for this is very apparent. The pneumatic system as applied to cities having an undulating surface, with good lines of drainage, substitutes the artificial motor of a vacuum for the all-powerful, ever-present and cheap force of gravity.

We hardly think the extra cost is compensated for by the possibility of manufacturing poudrette, and the intermittent exhaustion of the foul gases from the soil pipes, especially as the small amount of water used in the closets must leave them in a foul condition. Undoubtedly the pneumatic system has its sphere of usefulness. In the dead flats of Holland and elsewhere, and in certain districts of many of our own cities where gravity is unattainable and the sub-soil water near the surface, much good may be achieved by its introduction: Also, in connection with large public institutions and hospitals where an exceptional outlay is justified, and where water enough could be used and handled by the system to insure perfect flushing, and where the manufacture of poudrette is a secondary matter, it certainly would be far more efficacious in such institutions than any system of dry removal: It might also be used collaterally to suddenly exhaust the air from wards or rooms where violently contagious diseases were being treated, carrying off floating germs with a rush into a special receiver in connection with the air-pumps.

Having thus treated the various systems of sewerage with, I think, due regard to their merits, I will close with many thanks for your attention.

Referred for publication.

Col. Geo. E. Waring, jr., M. Inst. C. E., of Newport, R. I., occupied the next hour in reading a paper entitled:

The Liernur System of Sewerage for Baltimore.

Col. Waring said: Dr. Chancellor, Secretary of the State Board of Health of Maryland, recently read a paper on the "Sewerage of Cities, Liernur's Pneumatic System," before the State Medical Society.

He closes it with these words: "My only object in this paper has been to awaken interest in the matter, and thereby produce a general conviction of its importance in a sanitary point of view. If I have at all succeeded in this I shall be abundantly rewarded."

He has so far engaged my interest that I am disposed to second his effort to awaken public attention, by a brief discussion of the important points brought forward and the important statements made in his paper.

I learn with great regret that Dr. Chancellor is ill and unable to be present and take part in this discussion. This fact would deter me from presenting even the present moderate criticism of his paper, were it not that he threw down the gauntlet to the engineering profession in such an emphatic way that it would be unjust to my confreres of that profession to omit such an opportunity as this for parrying his thrust in the arena where it was delivered.

Dr. Chancellor says of water carriage sewerage, "It may be said to be a triumph of engineering short-sightedness, together with a non-observance of scientific facts." He also says that the most obvious scientific truths are totally ignored. He sums up the combined system and the separate system by regarding them both "in the light of hopeless makeshifts—an attempt to institute measures of cure upon wrong principles—and it is difficult to say who blunders most, the engineer who constructs such works, or the medical authority that recommends them." As one of many engineers who have advocated and executed works that are here condemned, it seems to me a duty to resist the charge of blundering and to throw the responsibility of error and false judgment on the medical authority that recommends a bad substitute for them.

He classifies the systems to be considered under three heads:

First, the Combined System.

Second, the Separate System.

Third, the Liernur System.

He makes many of his comments which should properly be confined to the combined system relate to the whole "water carriage" system, and therefore, by implication, applies them to the separate system. To a certain extent, what he says about the ebb and flood of the dry weather flow of sewage, the amount being less at midnight than at noon, is applicable to large sewers having a broad shallow stream at the bottom, with considerable difference of width between their ebb and flood levels. It is in no useful sense applicable to small pipe sewers where the difference of surface between the ebb and flood is much less and where that portion of the wall which would be left dry by the diminishing of the flow is too steep and too vitreous for the lodgment of fœcal matter. With such sewers, at least, the statement that fragments of fœcal matter are found "principally scouring closely along the sides of the sewer" is not correct. In such sewers, at least, they are found principally coursing down the middle of the current. Therefore, with such sewers, when properly flushed, the "coating" referred to does not occur to any such degree as is suggested. With an eye to the germs of deadly fevers which will be developed by the fungus growth rooted in this sliming, he apprehends that they will be taken up by "the moisture which arises from the putrid mass." This rising, I think, has been experimentally proven not to occur, the dislodgment of spores taking place only after dessication. In pipe sewers properly flushed there is no such dessication. The area that is reached by the sewage is covered and flushed too often to become dry enough to part with its spores. The fungus growth itself is probably very slight in pipe sewers. Even in the case of large sewers, observation does not sustain the doctor's apprehensions. Marie-Davy found that the atmosphere of the sewers of Paris contained fewer bacteria than the atmosphere of ordinary living rooms. Even supposing these organisms to exist in the atmosphere of an unventilated foul sewer, or even that they exist in a well flushed and thoroughly ventilated pipe sewer, their existence would, according to Dr. Chancellor's opinion, be of no consequence for the reason, which he seems to have misunderstood, that the ventilating pipes leading from the sewer to the roofs of the houses give an easy and direct channel for their transportation, scattered through a flood of pure air, directly to the open atmosphere, all communication between the *house* and the *soil pipe* being perfectly closed by the traps attached to each fixture. The mistake has been made in this case of assuming that in good modern work, which alone we need consider, the conditions as to the transmission of sewer air are the same as in old work, where a foul and unventilated and unflushed sewer is connected with unventilated soil pipes, and where, whenever any influence is brought to bear which may reduce the air capacity of the sewer, or may expand its air by heating, there is a forcing of house traps and an escape of sewer air into the dwelling In all properly arranged work the sewer has ample breathing facilities directly above the roofs of the houses, without bringing the least pressure to bear upon the traps. It is in a certain sense true that "mosquitos cannot be diluted with air or a whale diluted with water." The organisms in question, however, supposing them to become detached from the walls of the sewer and to float in its atmosphere, would be relatively so few, and are always so buoyant, that the feeblest movement of the column of air would transport them without the least difficulty, as mosquitos are carried by wind and as the whale would be carried by a torrent.

Dr. Chancellor makes this statement "The finest bays and harbors in the world have become stinking pools, and their surrounding shores, teeming with lovely villas and villages, once the homes of thousands of happy people, are now desolate and deserted, their owners and former occupants having fled in disgust from the sickening stench borne upon every recurring breeze. A notable instance of this kind is to be found in the once beautiful bay of Naples." So far as I am informed and believe, the bay of Naples is still beautiful and its shores are still teeming with a happy people, few of whom have fled in disgust. In Naples, furthermore, and I beg that you will remember this, the water closets and privies of the population are not connected with the sewers. That which produces the unmistakable stench immediately along the shore of the city is the result of the deposit there of street wash and household waters only; fœcal matter is not there a considerable factor.

The statement is made that an attempt has been made to remedy this evil in England by using sewage for the irrigation of land, or rather by using land as a means for the purification of sewage. This attempt has not only been made, it has been wonderfully successful wherever applied, and not only in England but on the Continent as well. I have visited the sewage irrigation works of Kendall, Leamington, Rugby, Croydon, Malvern and London in England and those of Paris, Berlin and Dantzic on the Continent. The only observation of Dr. Chancellor's concerning sewage irrigation with which I can agree, after a close study of the subject on the ground, is that ordinarily there is no resultant profit but generally a loss. The Berlin irrigation fields which he cites are, like all the others, not notable instances of the difficulties to which he refers, but notable instances of the easy control of the whole system and of complete success so far as purification is referred to, except where storm-water increases the volume to be treated beyond reasonable limits.

At Croydon the condition is not as Dr. Chancellor describes it, for this is, perhaps, the most eminent success of all that I saw, though nowhere was there anything approaching failure. The technical difficulties to which he refers are easily overcome where sufficient area can be obtained, by the application of sewage intermittently to one area and to another, or, where land is scarce, by the use of the intermittent *filtration* system.

Dr. Chancellor has little to say about the separate system, which to my mind is almost always the best system, and what he does say does not commend itself to my approval. For example, he says that its advantages are obtained at a "largely increased cost," the fact being exactly the opposite, that its cost is very much less than that of the combined system—often several times less. His statement that the city is under this system, "supplied with two generators of the germs of disease instead of one," seems to me not to be supported by any known facts and observations and to be distinctly controverted by all of the probabilities of the case. Here also I find myself obliged to differ with him absolutely, at least so far as well regulated separate sewers are concerned.

We now come to Dr. Chancellor's panacea—the pneumatic system of Captain Liernur, a man of great ingenuity in the devising of mechanical contrivances. We are told that this system "has been applied to some of the large continental cities with great success and seems destined to supersede all other systems now in use." It has been applied to a part of Amsterdam, a part of Leyden and a part of Dortrecht, and I think not elsewhere to any considerable extent.

I have myself given close attention to the development of this system almost from its inception. I was much struck with its ingenuity, and devoted some time to the investigation of its practical operation in Dortrecht and in Amsterdam, where, as well as in Leyden, it was in operation at the time of my visit, in 1875.

It is a system, so far as it has been practically applied, for the removal of the contents of water closets only. Captain Liernur has collateral devices for the removal of the coarser solid matters of kitchen waste and for the separate discharge of household waters of all kinds. These latter devices have not had the test of practical use. The system as it has been carried out relates to the removal of fœcal matter, together with a very small modicum of water, by means of iron pipes, about four inches in diameter, in which a partial vacuum is created by steam air pumps. There are at Dortrecht experimental appliances for dessicating the matters derived from water closets, so as to separate the solid matters in a dry condition for easy transportation and for use as manure. The mechanical arrangements for carrying out the whole of the work indicate a very high order of ingenuity. Soon after my examination I wrote as follows concerning this system:

"We have been so long relying on the system of water carriage, and we have so long ascribed to it every advantage, only to find it riddled and honey-combed with faults, as time has brought us better acquainted with it; and a large class has placed such implicit confidence in the dry-earth system, only to find it almost impossible of introduction in an average community, that no one who has long been interested in the general question can be expected to glow with enthusiasm over any new process that may be brought to notice. Liernur has struck out a new path, but it is a new path in an old field, in which we have learned to look out for pitfalls and ambushes at every step. We may well hope (and I unreservedly believe) that there is much in his invention that is of intrinsic value, and that it will perhaps accomplish all that we have so long sought. At the same time its success is certainly not to be achieved through a blind enthusiasm, ready to accept it as the final cure of the great and universal disease in our domestic economies against which it proposes to contend.

"While, therefore, it is to-day unquestionably the most interesting new fact in sanitary engineering, and is worthy of the most careful experiment and even the most expensive investigation at the hands of local governments, the investigation and the experiments should be made with a clear understanding that the time given to them and the money spent upon them may bring but little return. The difficulties we are contending with are so grave, and the dangers to life and health and usefulness are so threatening, that we may well afford to tax ourselves as largely as may be necessary in order to demonstrate whether this new process, for which so much is claimed and which has so many firm adherents among those who have been living under its daily operation for some years, is, or is not, to open the door for our escape. Much that has hitherto been written about it has been of that enthusiastic and confident character that made its success appear at first blush a foregone conclusion. It seems to be better that, however great our individual confidence may be—and I repeat that my own is very great—we should undertake this trial resolutely and determinedly, but should at the same time be quite prepared for entire or partial failure."

During the eight years that have passed since this visit, I have been familiar with the frequent writings of the friends and enemies of the Liernur system. I have had occasion more than once to converse with Dutch engineers on the subject. My general conclusion is that it has not commended itself in any special manner to the authorities of either of the three cities in which it has been tried. I believe that its use has not been extended in either Leyden or Dortrecht. I was told by the Town Engineer of Amsterdam that it was to be extended there because Captain Liernur had complained that its failure to give satisfaction had been due to opposition on the part of the city authorities. It was finally determined to give him his own way in making a further installation of the work. I have not heard from any engineering or official source that the new works have been more successful than the old. It certainly is not to be considered a failure. It does its work with much regularity and, though not economically, without inordinate cost. Mr. Hering, in his report on the drainage of Amsterdam, (1880) says that house owners pay an annual rent of $3 25 for connection; also 12 cents per hour for the labor necessary to remove obstructions in the house pipes. "The attendance upon the system consists of three machinists, two stokers and four laborers for the three engines, and one machinist, one stoker, one captain and two laborers for the steamboat. In addition, two persons attend to the reservoirs and valves and operate the collection of the sewage."

The cost of running the Liernur works in 1880 was $10,858 for a population of twenty-seven thousand nine hundred and forty-six, being equal to thirty-nine cents per head.

The works were recently visited by a committee of the Technical Commission of Paris, who reported, after an examination, that it was not suited to the needs of that city.

My own idea is that, while it permits the use of much less water than is necessary to keep closets in the cleanly condition to which we are accustomed, it is not objectionable in this respect for use among the poorer classes of people who are less nice in such matters. That closets such as I have seen in Holland would be satisfactory to the health authorities of Baltimore I do not believe.

The experiment in dessicating the product so as to make a dry manure has not been an economic success, nor is it likely that it ever could be, even with a population which is inadequately supplied with water. Under the liberal supply of water of American towns the difficulty would be greatly increased. It is an incident of the scant use of water in Liernur's closets, but a very important one, that the soil pipes descending from them are never adequately flushed. It is true that their escaping air is discharged into the air above the roofs of the houses; but if there is ever an objection to such discharge it must be, above all, in connection with this system which has no current of air through the soil pipes, and in which the amount of offensive decomposition and of bacterial growth must be very great.

The leading fallacy of many who have advocated Liernur's system and of many other writers on the subject of town sewerage lies in the common idea that the offensiveness and danger arising from matters discharged at the outlet of the sewer is due to human excreta. This is very far from being the case. It is true that fœcal matter is more offensive in its fresh condition than is the waste from the kitchen sink; but it is equally true that, given time and opportunity for decomposition, both become equally offensive and in most ways equally dangerous. Even the fouling of the beautiful bay of Naples, the devastated condition of which is held up as an example, is due not to fœcal matter, but, in small degree, to the surface-wash of the streets, and, chiefly, to the discharge of putrescible household wastes. These wastes, except so far as relates to their grosser particles, Captain Liernur delivers into the nearest water-course. Were his system applied in its entirety to Baltimore, the condition of the harbor would be hardly less offensive than it is now, its present offensiveness being due mainly to putrefying organic wastes other than water closet matter.

I think that Dr. Chancellor is wrong in the following points:

He is wrong in considering Liernur's system economical in construction or in annual expense.

He is wrong in supposing that its product can be used with much greater economy than can the discharge of a separate system of sewerage.

He is wrong in providing for the sewerage of a town without providing for the inexpensive removal of the wastes of manufacturing establishments. To require manufacturers to take care of their waste matters as he suggests, would impose a tax on industries which would to a great degree be fatal to the prosperity of a town—driving factories to rural districts.

He is wrong in supposing that the putrescible matters of household waters can be removed by straining and that diluted urine is unobjectionable. However well we may strain household wastes and however much we may dilute urine, they will both become active sources of offense when putrefying in the waters of a harbor.

He is wrong in supposing that the only way to prevent the pollution that comes from solid particles of food, etc., is to keep them out of the sewers altogether. The way to prevent their becoming offensive is to remove them entirely from the town in their fresh condition.

He is very wrong in supposing that a man can lift himself by his boot-legs, which is practically what Captain Liernur proposes when he suggests the moving of the contents of a horizontal sewer by discharging into it through standpipes, arranged as injectors, the liquid wastes of the houses along the line. We are told that "a series of water columns from two to three feet high, standing fifteen to thirty feet apart, press upon the sewer contents and give it, when the house drains discharge at the same time, the same velocity as if the sewer had a fall of two or three feet in fifteen to thirty feet. * * * * * * * * That the size of the sewer required for carrying the maximum quantity of water may be adjusted for a speed of current equal to that which would take place in a sewer with a fall of one in ten to one in fifteen as the case may be; and calculation shows that with this speed stoneware pipe of four inches diameter is quite sufficient for draining a length of street of some 1,600 yards of all the water used thereon, even in a densely built up area." This is a case where it would be well to check calculation by experiment. The fallacy involved here is one which it is curious to consider as having escaped the observation of its engineer inventor. Let me state the case absurdly: We have a dead level street one mile long; under it at a depth of three feet we lay a horizontal sewer four inches in diameter and having its mouth submerged so that it will always be full of water. At intervals of ten feet we erect standpipes bent at the lower end to discharge in the direction of the outlet at the axis of the sewer which, at the points of connection, is so enlarged as to leave an ample water-way around the injector bend. Captain Liernur's theory is that if water be delivered into the tops of these standpipes, the flow through the horizontal sewer will be the same that it would be if one of its ends were 1,584 feet higher than the other end. This would afford a ready means for overcoming the embarrassment of low grades. It is quite true that if we take the first ten feet of the sewer and consider only a single three-foot standpipe at its end, the fall would be equal to three in ten. The same is the case if we consider the second ten feet and its standpipe *by themselves*; but, unfortunately, when the head of the second standpipe has expended itself at the end of its own section, its own water is still to be taken care of by the first. As the force of the first section has been expended already we must look for other meaus to discharge the water of the second section through the horizontal ten feet of the first, and so on. The fact is that each of these standpipes is to be credited with a head in proportion, not to the next ten feet of the sewer, but to its distance from the outlet of the sewer, the most remote one having a fall of three feet in 5,280 feet and no more.

Dr. Chancellor tells us that no system of sewerage is acceptable to modern civilization which does not allow the use of water closets with all the water needed for purposes of cleanliness. That is very true, and it must be emphasized and carried to its logical conclusion. Not only must so much of the water closet as is visible be cleanly, but its trap and its connecting pipe and the soilpipe and drain into which it discharges must always be kept thoroughly clean. This can be done only with the use of an abundant sudden discharge of water; a single gallon will not do it, even if discharged suddenly, nor will ten gallons do it if dribbling in a little continuous stream. What we need is two or three gallons at least, discharged *en masse*, washing everything before it with certainty, and, what is equally important, wetting and lubricating the pipe in advance of the discharge of the foul burden. We are told that proper flushing may be given with less than seven-eighths of a gallon per day for each of the population. Allowing for toilet water, Captain Liernur provides for one and three-eighths gallons per head per day. This illustrates as well as anything that can be said, the fact that the Liernur system is not suited to the needs and habits of the American people. Some dependence is placed on the fact that the Dutch are a very cleanly people; that they use water more copiously than it is used elsewhere. This is true so far as the washing of their streets and house fronts and floors and utensils is concerned. It would doubtless be true with the introduction of our water closets with an abundant water supply. The requirements of the Liernur system step in here, however, to check their cleanly impulses, and to limit them to the use of a totally inadequate amount. It would be possible, of course, to increase the quantity of water indefinitely and to secure its complete removal by the more continuous action of the Liernur appliances; but this would defeat one of the main objects of the whole system, which is to reduce the amount of water to a point where dessication of the product will be possible from a commercial point of view, and it would add to the cost of working.

Even when limited to the quantity of water prescribed by the advocates of the Liernur system, I find that the cost of fuel for pumping and evaporation in a city of four hundred thousand inhabitants, with coal at $5 per ton, would be over $175,000 per annum, being the interest at four per cent. of a sum larger than the whole estimated cost of Mr. Latrobe's project for Baltimore. As an offset to this, we should have the agricultural value of the solid portions of the excreta of the population. There is no doubt that the wastes of each individual would be worth more than forty-four cents per annum if properly prepared for transportation and agricultural use; but it has never been demonstrated, and the attempt to demonstrate it at Dortrecht seems to be failure, that this result can be achieved for anything like forty-four cents per head.

To sum up, allow me to say, and I say it with much hesitation, for I know Dr. Chancellor's eminent attainments:

First. That he has allowed his agricultural enthusiasm and his devotion to scientific theory to carry him beyond the limits of wise discretion. He recommends for Baltimore a system which is of questionable success even in that single element of its development which has had a partial trial in three towns in Holland. He seems to have accepted the fact that Captain Liernur made a complete *project* for the fortifications and city of Luxemburg as equivalent to the *execution* and *trial* of the system there, I have never seen the statement, it certainly is not made by Captain Liernur's chief scientific advocate, Van Overbeek de Meijer, in a very recent pamphlet on the subject, that an attempt has ever been made to carry out the project in Luxemburg. This latter writer attaches great importance to the report of an official committee in Germany detailing its conclusions concerning the system, which report closes as follows: "The application of this system can be permitted so long as, and on the condition that, the results promised will be realized in practice."

Second. That he recommends a system which is still an interesting object of study, but which has not shown itself in a continuous trial for ten years or more to be nearly so good as he thinks it is.

Third. That however useful this system may be for the low-level cities of Holland, it would be absurd to resort to it in a city having such excellent slopes as has Baltimore.

Fourth. That his conviction as to the agricultural value of the product of this system is no stronger and no better found in scientific knowledge than was the conviction of the English school of sewage irrigators that great profit was to be derived from their system.

Fifth. That he has misjudged the results of irrigation in England, as he could not have done had he made it a subject of personal investigation, aided by the requisite agricultural knowledge.

I state one more conclusion, and this I state with especial hesitation, because of my personal interest in the subject, which is, that the plan proposed by Mr. Chas. H. Latrobe for the sewerage of Baltimore includes every advantage that present knowledge of sewerage works can compass, including the most economical and best facilities for the purification of the effluent before its discharge into the bay.

[NOTE—The paper of Col. Waring was referred to the State Board of Health for publication, it being a criticism of a paper heretofore published by Dr. C. W. Chancellor of Baltimore, on the "Liernur System of Sewerage," and Dr. Chancellor, being prevented by severe and protracted illness from being present to discuss the matter, has filed for publication his answer to Col. Waring's paper, which will be found below.

In regard to the statement of Major Charles H. Latrobe, touching the per capita cost of the Liernur system, Dr. Chancellor thinks they are so utopian that Maj. Latrobe, usually just and accurate in his opinions and statements, will, in justice to himself, make the proper correction when he reviews his figures and compares them with the *actual* cost of the system wherever it has been introduced]

Reply to the Paper of Col. George E. Waring, C.E., of Newport, R. I., on "The Liernur System of Sewerage for Baltimore"--An Important Question involving the Interests of Health, Commerce and Agriculture.

BY C. W. CHANCELLOR, M. D.,

Secretary of the State Board of Health of Maryland.

The title of Colonel Waring's paper seems to me to be a misnomer. It should have been "A Criticism of Dr. Chancellor's Paper on Liernur's Pneumatic System of Sewerage." Be this as it may, I cheerfully comply with Col. Waring's suggestion, and publish my reply, with his paper, in the report of the proceedings of the Maryland State Sanitary Convention.

Without having entered into a very critical examination of Col. Waring's paper, I shall attempt to give my views upon the merits of the question under discussion, notwithstanding the fact that I have already published a somewhat exhaustive paper on the subject, and also a reply to the sweeping assertions of Dr. John S. Billings of the U. S. Army, concerning the Liernur system.

Col. Waring starts out with the declaration that, in discussing the Liernur system in a paper read before the Medical and Chirurgical Faculty of Maryland last spring, I "threw down the gauntlet to the engineering profession in such an emphatic way that it would be unjust to his confreres of that profession to omit such an opportunity as this (the session of the State Sanitary Convention) for parrying the thrust in the arena where it was delivered." In a letter, he further characterizes my paper as "a very savage onslaught upon his profession." Before entering upon the merits of the question, I must be permitted to say that it was very far from my thoughts or intentions to reflect "savagely," or even unpleasantly, upon any profession, and I think if this fact *alone* induced Col. Waring's reply to my paper, he must be hypersensitive, or at least hyper-jealous of the reputation of his profession. At the same time, I would not have it understood that I object to the most liberal criticism. I am a cordial friend to the right of appeal from my opinions to the supreme tribunal of the public; and am equally disposed to pay all due attention to any motion for a re-hearing in my own court; or, of giving, as Col. Waring elegantly puts it, "an opportunity for parrying a thrust in the arena where it was delivered."

Col. Waring's sensitiveness still further manifests itself in the following paragraph: "As one of many engineers who have advocated and executed works that are here (in Dr. Chancellor's paper) condemned, it seems to me a duty to resist the charge of blundering and to throw the responsibility of error and false judgment on the medical authority that recommends a bad substitute for them." In this I quite agree with him, if he can substantiate the fact, which he has thus far failed to do, that the measure proposed is "a bad substitute." It will not do for the partisans of any particular scheme to expect that all opinions contrary to their own can be limited in such a manner as to leave them the power of suppressing all opposition to their particular "project." It is manifest, even at first sight, that no such limit will be set by public opinion. That truth, if it has fair play, will always triumph over error, and become the opinion of the world, is a proposition which rests upon the broadest principles of human nature, and therefore no one need fear the unveiling of *truth*.

In this connection, I am constrained to refer to the extreme unfairness of the criticism of my paper contained in the *Sanitary Engineer* of New York, November 29, 1883, with which, however, I am quite sure, Col. Waring had nothing to do. He is always frank, outspoken and courteous. In this instance the anonymous critic, who is supposed to be a "Sir Oracle" in sanitary matters, employed the press not to enlighten the public, but to accomplish his own ends, regardless alike of truth and justice. While ridicule and invective may stimulate partisans they are not likely to make one who seeks truth renounce an opinion, but usually have the contrary effect, and are therefore the least judicious weapons to be employed by sanitary journals having the interest of the health and life of the people at heart.

But to return to the paper of Col. Waring. He says that I have made many of my comments which should have been properly confined to the combined system relate to the "water-carriage" system; and therefore he thinks they are by implication applied to the separate system. While I cannot believe that the separate system is all that could be desired, I was certainly very emphatic in expressing the opinion that it was *a great improvement* over the combined system. The chief trouble of any water-carriage system of sewerage, as I stated, lies in the question of the ultimate disposal of the noxious sewage *after it is out of the city.*

Notwithstanding Col. Waring's special plea in behalf of the Bay of Naples,* there can be no doubt that the influx of sewage matter will pollute and render noxious any harbor or stream into which it flows. It is only a question of time and quantity, and no remedy will prevent it which does not exclude all sewage waste.

At Paris the river Seine, with its immense volume and frequent flushings by torrents of storm-water, gathered as far off as the western slope of the Jura mountains, has suffered greatly from the influx of sewage matter, which was discharged into the river by two "collectors" at St. Denis and d'Asnieres, respectively, in a quantity amounting to nearly three hundred thousand cubic yards every twenty-four hours, which formed banks in the bed of the stream below the "collectors." These deposits, representing a volume of at least one hundred and eighteen thousand cubic yards of material, which had to be removed at an annual expense of more than two hundred thousand francs; and it is said that even with this expenditure "the removal has been very incomplete, and the obstruction is increasing year by year, and extending further down the river, to the serious detriment of commerce." These banks occupy more than a quarter of the bed of the river from d'Asnieres to Chaton.

So much for the obstructions occasioned in the river Seine by the sewage of Paris. As to the *pollution* of the waters "the river from Clichy to Poissy," says the director of public works, "is converted into a vast bed of fermentation and infection, and offers nothing in this part of its course but a water too impure for domestic uses, mortal to the fish, and filling the air with fœtid exhalations, which are borne even to the gates of the capitol."†

*During my stay in Europe last winter I read in a French journal a letter stating that "the Bay of Naples had become a reeking cesspool from the sewage matter which flowed into it, and during the summer many of the owners or occupants of villas upon its banks had abandoned their homes in consequence of the sickening stench exhaled from the polluted waters of that once beautiful bay." Col. Waring denies the accuracy of the statement, and I shall accept his version of the matter, as I am not personally cognizant of the facts.

† Revue des Deux Mondes, 1880.

At London, where there is a tide of nearly twenty-four feet, the sewers at one time emptied into the Thames, some ten or twelve miles below the city, and that large river became a nuisance so intolerable that the government built sewers, at an expense of several millions of pounds, to carry the sewage more than twenty miles below the city. It was clearly shown by the reports of distinguished engineers, made to the Sewerage of Towns Commission, that "sewage discharged into the river two hours after high tide, reached the same point upon the next flood that the sewage did which was discharged into it two hours before the previous high tide."

At Montreal, where there is a current running at the rate of seven miles an hour, the sewage discharged into the St. Lawrence river so contaminated the locality as to be offensive to smell and injurious to health; and in one instance when a small sewer delivered its flow into a dock of La Chene Canal, which was constantly changing its contents by the passage of boats, the water became so defiled and offensive that the authorities found it necessary to construct a sewer far out into the river, and below the city.

The city of Boston had, a few years since, sewers emptying into the large rivers on its circumference, and into the harbor where the tide is twelve to fifteen feet, and although the sewage of the city was distributed over a line of many miles instead of into a contracted basin, it became so great a nuisance that a large tunnel has lately been built to remove the discharge to a point many miles down Massachusetts bay.

Many other examples of cities might be given where neither tide nor current afforded relief, but those cited are deemed quite sufficient.

The harbor of Baltimore has already been affected by the surface washing and other organic matter which passes into "The Basin," and it is a fair and irresistible deduction that should the sewage of the whole city, amounting in the aggregate to more than one million tons annually, be emptied anywhere into the Patapsco river or the upper bay, it will not only tend to obstruct the channel but will be brought back by refluent tides, converting not only the Patapsco river but all the tributaries of the upper bay "into beds of fermentation and infection," rendering their waters "too impure for domestic uses, mortal to fish, and filling the air with fœtid exhalations." Indeed with such an afflux of fœtid matter it is not unsafe to predict that, in the course of time, the waters of Chesapeake bay will become a distillation of all the filth of Baltimore city.

Few men, I think, not completely blinded by prejudice will reject the evidences which exist on this point, and if such evidence can be questioned, it is in vain to look for further testimony in sanitary affairs.

Col. Waring lays great stress upon the hypothesis that "in pipe sewers properly flushed" there is no dessication and, consequently, he argues, "there can be no dislodgment of spores" developed by the fungus growths which take place in sewer pipes generally, and which even intrude to the house side of the traps of water closets, &c., and are known to give off poisonous germs. These germs are borne here and there by sewer gas, when in a dry state, and by exhalations when moist. To deny that these germs or parasites can be transmitted from and by moisture, would be to deny the theory of *miasma*, which I scarcely think a gentleman of Col. Waring's intelligence and experience will undertake to do. The fundamental error in the argument seems to be this: He contends that in the small pipe sewers "the area that is reached by the sewage is covered and flushed *too often* to become dry enough to part with its spores." The volume of sewage matter flowing in the pipes is by no means a fixed quantity, consequently there can be no uniform "area" covered by the sewage, and it is quite impossible to determine whether the flushing is sufficiently "often" and voluminous to prevent the dislodgment of the spores or not.

Continuing his criticism of my views in regard to the escape of the germs of deadly disease from sewers, Col. Waring says: "Marie-Davy found that the atmosphere of the sewers of Paris contained fewer bacteria than the atmosphere of ordinary living rooms," and he goes on to say that "their existence would, according to Dr. Chancellor's opinion, be of no consequence," etc. I am certainly at a loss to understand the force of these remarks. It is, I believe, well established that organic liquids deprived of bacteria, may have infective properties in certain cases, and on the other hand, the presence of bacteria has not been demonstrated in all infectious diseases, hence we are not authorized to consider these organisms as the *sole* agents of infections. M. Bouchardat thinks that "if organic liquids in which no micro-organisms are found have contagious properties, either the organisms have escaped observation because of their tenuity, or the fluids contain organic poisons."

In confirmation of the theory that disease bearing germs cannot be rendered innocuous by dilution with air, Prof. Bouchardat remarks: "It is possible to modify micro-organisms by varying the external conditions around them; but if they become infectious after having passed through an infected medium they become practically disease germs, and *there is no reason why the process should not continue.*" Col. Waring's attempt to escape from this proposition by declaring that these disease germs, "supposing them to be detached from the walls of the sewer and to float in its atmosphere, would be relatively so few and are always so buoyant that the feeblest movement of the column of air would transport them without the least difficulty, as mosquitoes are carried by wind, and a whale would be carried by a torrent," appears to me to be, as a learned authority once observed, "one of those consecutors which are so intimately and evidently connected to or founded in the premises, that the conclusion is attained *quàsi per saltum*, and without anything of ratioscinative process, even as the eye sees an object immediately and without any previous process."

But grant that disease germs are diluted by atmospheric air and are carried, as Col. Waring says, like mosquitoes by wind, does it follow that they are entirely destroyed or become altogether innocuous? By no means! They may be reduced in number by "dilution," but not in virulence, and are therefore simply transferred from one locality to another to exert their baneful effect wherever they may lodge, as a mosquito will bite in any locality.

Col. Waring should have guarded this weak point in his argument. He is undoubtedly an excellent engineer, but he does not succeed as a medical logician.

His statement that using sewage for irrigation purposes has been "wonderfully successful *wherever applied*," is to me simply incomprehensible, especially with reference to the Berlin irrigation fields, which I am positive have proved a failure. I was not permitted to visit the "fields" myself, the interdiction, so far as strangers are concerned, being peremptory, on account, it is said, of their fearful insanitary condition. They are, as I was credibly informed, already over-saturated, and the authorities, both city and state, are bestirring themselves as to what shall be done under the circumstances. I was also informed by prominent citizens of Berlin last summer that a pestilence was feared unless speedy relief was afforded, either by increasing the area of irrigable surface or adopting another system of sewerage, and several commissions have been appointed to look into the matter.

But my surprise was still greater when I read the statement of Col. Waring that he had himself visited the sewage irrigation works at Paris, among others, and found them "wonderfully successful." This statement is, if possible, more astounding, *me judice*, than his representations in regard to the Berlin irrigation fields, inasmuch as the latter, like those of Croydon, were *for a time* looked upon with some favor, whereas the Paris "fields" have been a source of nuisance from the time the first "regulator" was laid, up to the present time, and have never been regarded as a success, except in so far as they served to divert the sewage flow from the Seine, which was simply transferring the evil from one locality to another; not curing it.

The observations of Col. Waring in reference to these works certainly do not coincide with the experience of the municipal authorities of Paris and the communities in the midst of which these irrigation fields are located. In 1866 the first experiment with irrigation fields at Paris was made, and the peninsula of Gennevilliers, and subsequently the barren wooded lands of St. Germain were selected for the purpose. It was estimated that some twenty thousand acres of irrigable surface would be required to absorb the total sewage of Paris, which amounted to about three hundred thousand cubic yards in twenty-four hours. "At first the 'Villegiature,' who owned or occupied and cultivated the lands proposed to be utilized in irrigation, regarded the scheme as an element of certain fortune, relying upon the statement of the minister of public works that the land would be enhanced in value from one hundred and fifty to four hundred and fifty francs per hectare; but in a short time after the inauguration of the system they were overdosed by sewage, and began to demand, at first, that the flow be stopped for one day, then for a week, and finally for a month, and even longer periods, in order that the land might absorb that which was already upon it. As this could not be done, the lower lands were transformed into seas of sewage, and many cellars were overflowed by the filthy liquid, which on some of the farms even rose above the fences. A great deal of sickness was produced, and the peninsula of Gennevilliers is still plagued with fevers, which had been hitherto unknown. Such were the evils experienced, that public inquiry into the facts resulted in bringing to light an almost unanimous opposition to the system." *

A commission appointed by the prefect of the Seine from among the general council of the department arrayed itself vigorously against the disastrous consequences of the irrigation works. They say that "the project has not succeeded in freeing the Seine from the evils of sewage pollution because the surface set apart for irrigation purposes is insufficient, but it has destroyed one of the richest districts in the department of the Seine, by introducing an intolerable nuisance and much sickness among the numerous and luxurious villas which adorn the locality. Of the thirty-two communities consulted, twenty-seven protested energetically against the continuance of the works, while the remaining five, viz., Argentenil, Ecquevilly, Meular, Verneuil and Versailles, were too remote to take an interest in the question, or were only interested in excluding the sewage from the Seine."

In the communities most interested, nearly 8,500 citizens signed a petition protesting against the continuance of the nuisance, and the residents of localities where the irrigation system had not yet been extended, looked with terror upon its encroachments. This terror was particularly participated in by the residents of "the park," where there is an immense collection of costly villas, on the borders of the beautiful forest of St. Germain. So great, indeed, is the opposition to the works that even the director of public works of Paris and the engineers of the city, who at first so earnestly favored the project, now advise an entire modification of it, which provides for a flow of the sewage upon the lands only at such times as it may be needed. At all other times the waters of the sewage to be drained off or purified and discharged by a canal into the river or the sea; the solid matter to be preserved or utilized for agricultural purposes. This, it will be observed, is not the "irrigation" under "easy control" which Col. Waring speaks of, but a purification of the sewage water which is diverted from the irrigation fields and the solid matter subsequently utilized as contemplated in the Liernur system. Such are the modifications deemed necessary by the director of public works and the engineers of

*See article on The Sewerage of Paris, by M. Villet, in *Revue des Deux Mondes.*

Paris, which is conclusion that they do not consider these works "*wonderfully successful.*"

In speaking of the sewerage of Paris, M. Aubry says: "Irrigation exacts an enormous surface on which it instills insalubrity, or at least certain causes for insalubrity which extend to the very gates of Paris, in the midst of a luxuriant and beautiful country where property is condemned to an inevitable depreciation in value; it mutilates a forest which offers to a numerous population resources and comforts, and that in a time when throughout all France there is complaint of the destruction of wood-land which the state has interposed to protect. Finally, it does an injustice to a large agricultural interest, at a time when agriculture has the most pressing need of encouragement and aid."

In the face of such testimony will Col. Waring longer maintain that the irrigation works at Paris are a "wonderful success?" The works at Berlin were, I think, only established in 1876, ten years after the Paris works, and I venture the prediction that they will be abandoned long before they reach the present age of the Paris works.

I would recommend to Col. Waring and those who wish information on the subject, the perusal of a report of Privy Councillor Schultz, chairman of the Berlin Sewerage Commission,* containing an exposé of the trouble and expense experienced with "water carriage and irrigation" at Berlin, and also official information about the Liernur system by the city authorities of Amsterdam.

We come now to consider what Col. Waring calls "Dr. Chancellor's panacea"—the pneumatic system of Liernur, which, in a former paper, I have described in detail, and which Col. Waring seems inclined to "damn with faint praise."

The chief objections urged by Col. Waring against this system are:

1. *That it has not been practically applied, except for the removal of the contents of water closets.*

This is in a measure true, but Col. Waring admits that there are mechanical arrangements for carrying out the whole of the work, which he says, "indicate a very high order of ingenuity." But while it is true that these "collateral devices," as he terms them,

---

* "*Anhalt-spunkte zur Beurtheilung der Canalisationsfrage,*" Berlin, Weigandt, Hampel and Parey, 1880.

have not been "practically applied," they have nevertheless been *experimentally tested*, and found to be thoroughly practicable and efficient in all their details, as will appear from the fact that the city of Amsterdam, after ten years of experiment and experience, has finally adopted the system in its totality, including all "collateral devices," and in addition to the twelve thousand or fifteen thousand houses which already connect with it, all new buildings within its limits are compelled, by order of the authorities, as is also the case in Dortrecht, to adopt it. In the former city, plans were being rapidly executed last summer for applying the system on a large scale, with a central station, where all the material will doubtless be eventually manufactured into "poudrette." This station consists of a substantial stone building, in the suburbs of the city, which contains the engines for working the pneumatic pumps, and all the machinery and appliances for operating the system. The experiments heretofore made at Dortrecht have demonstrated the fact that the great value of the system in a hygienic point of view consists in destroying completely all micro-organisms inimical to health, as well as the virus of contagious maladies contained in excretal matters, by the combined action of heat and acid. The fires of the boilers are so arranged as to burn all the air coming from the pneumatic pumps, as well as the bad emanations from other parts of the system.

The fact that Capt. Liernur's first experiments were not a *complete success*, and did not accomplish all that could be desired *instanter*, is no reason why he should be debarred from the field of progress and improvement. Not a year passes which does not afford fresh illustration of the value of science; which does not show by some new and unexpected application, the inexhaustibleness of its power to lessen the evils which are incident to man, and to add to the substantial happiness of his condition.

2. *That the closets are not satisfactory.*

When Col. Waring examined the system in 1875, it was at a time when the works were designed solely for testing the possibility of removing simultaneously out of a number of houses, by means of a single "main," fœcal matter in a far more concentrated state than common sewage. It is reasonable to suppose that within eight years great improvements may have been made, and as I know, from a personal inspection of the system in August, 1883, have been made. The system now allows the application of water closets with the use of all the water required for cleanliness and health. I found the closets exceptionally free from odor and extremely clean, especially in the better classes of houses; and even the *air closets* appear to give entire satisfaction to the people and the authorities. I could detect no more odor in them than is usually found in well kept water closets in America. In speaking of these pneumatic closets, one of the most eminent engineers of Holland, M. de Kops, says: "When they are properly constructed these closets are inodorous to such a degree that the people of Amsterdam do not hesitate to place them within their houses without the least communication with the outside air, except by a small ventilating tube. *They are perfectly inodorous.*"

I also saw them in operation in the grounds of the "International Exhibition" at Amsterdam, where they were in constant use by thousands of careless people, of all sorts and sizes and conditions and nationalities, from the fastidious Frenchman to the filthy Fejee Islander, and they were not offensive in a single case. But a still more striking illustration of the popularity of the system is the fact, as I was informed by the alderman of public works at Amsterdam, that landlords or agents having houses for rent would, as a great recommendation, advertise that they were "sewered by the Liernur system," which, in that city, is considered a great desideratum in point of health and comfort.

3. *That the experiments in dessicating the products so as to make a dry manure, have not been an economic success, and the plans have not been put into practical operation in Amsterdam.*

In all technical combinations and great inventions, the *principles involved* remain the same whether they are carried into execution or not. The following extract from an official report of the mayor and aldermen of Amsterdam, dated August, 1880, will explain why Capt. Liernur's plans for the utilization of fœcal matter had not, up to that time, been carried out in that city. The report says:

"In order to utilize the material at present obtained, it has been decided to concentrate it by partially evaporating the water, using the exhaust steam of the air pump engines to furnish the heat necessary for the purpose, and to reduce this concentrated mass to a compost through mixing it with street dirt and house rubbish, thus disposing at the same time of these latter substances. *The selection of this plan is based upon the agricultural peculiarities of the surrounding country, these offering a more ready market for such sort of compost manure than for poudrette.*"

As to the advisability of Capt. Liernur's particular method of utilizing the material in question, in comparison with all other modes, there can scarcely be a doubt. The method is based upon the theory that, as it is the duty of towns to get rid of their offal in such a manner that no nuisance can arise from it to others; it is also *their interest to give it such form and properties as to find ready buyers for it, without being compelled to submit to grievous sacrifices.*

When in Amsterdam I obtained a small jar of this "poudrette," which was manufactured at Dortrecht. The agricultural value by analysis, acccording to the component parts, is estimated in Europe at about $48 per ton, and I understand that Prof. Liebig, of this city, who has examined the specimen, places even a higher value upon it.

In discussing this question Dr. Alexander Müller, Professor of Agricultural Chemistry, Berlin, says: "The high agricultural value of this manure cannot be doubted. It contains all the ingredients required for the production of human food, for it is well known that all excremental matter is capable of growing the food required for the organism it was produced by, and the Liernur process consists solely in withdrawing from the fluid matter it collects its *superfluous water*, without losing anything of value. The poudrette contains therefore whatever the excreta themselves contained of manure substance, the percentage of the various ingredients depending upon the habits of the people which produced them, and the food they consumed."

Below will be found an analysis of the "Liernur poudrette," obtained from Mr. Adam Scott, who Major Latrobe, in his paper, quotes as authority against the Liernur system, and therefore, it cannot be considered as a prejudiced statement:

ANALYSIS supplied by ADAM SCOTT, Esq.:

Water		22.5
Nitrogen as ammonia	per cent., 4.26	per cent., 6.70
" in organic combination	" " 2.44	
Phosphoric acid		" " 1.6
Kali (potash)		" " 8.27

VALUE.

	s.	d.
Nitrogen........................	11	2
Kali	6	11
Phosphoric acid	1	0
	19	1 per 100 kilos. of manure,

equal to £9 10s. 10d. per ton.

As additional evidence that the Liernur "poudrette" is a valuable manure, and will prove a financial success, I give below the analysis and report of Mr. Alfred Sibson, Professor of Chemistry in the Royal Agricultural College, London:

LABORATORY. 11, EATON TERRACE, ST. JOHN'S WOOD, LONDON, N.W.

Moisture	15.34
Nitrogenized organic matter and Salts of Ammonia*................	64.13
Phosphates and Oxide of Iron, containing Phosphoric Acid equal to Phosphate of Lime 3.14..........................	5.40
Alkaline Salts, &c..........................	11.33
Insoluble matter..........................	3.80
	100.00

* Containing Nitrogen........................ 8.30
Equal to Ammonia........................ 10.08

"This is an excellent manure, containing, as will be seen from the above analysis, no less than ten per cent. of ammonia, with three of phosphates and other constituents of lesser value. It is superior to any sewage manures or similar products now in the market, since, from its being prepared from the actual excreta, it necessarily contains the whole of the fertilizing matter well known to be present in those substances, especially in the liquid portion. A little sulphuric acid only is added for the purpose of fixing the ammonia, and the pulverulent condition is attained by drying merely, without the aid of absorbent materials; hence the concentrated product represented by the above analysis is obtained.

"This sample is very suitable as a corn manure, and for all purposes for which guano and other ammoniacal manures are commonly employed in agriculture; and if prepared on the large scale of this, or even lower quality, cannot fail in my opinion to meet with a ready sale, as the demand for such manures, especially those of a nitrogenous character, is at present very large and steadily progressing.

"I consider this sample of special interest, inasmuch as I am informed it is obtained by a system now in successful use at several towns on the continent by which the solid and liquid excreta are removed and collected without the use of separate receptacles for every house, the numerous difficulties connected with the removal of which by hand having always proved a bar to this mode of dealing with sewage.

"If the present system therefore overcomes these difficulties of collection, and meets the sanitary requirements of the case, and at the same time allows of the production of a manure of this character, I think there can be no doubt of its commercial success if introduced into this country."

ALFRED SIBSON, F. C. S.

4. *That the putrescible matters of household or kitchen waters cannot be removed by straining.*

A series of experiments on London sewage has recently been carried on at the northern out-fall by the metropolitan board of works, under the immediate supervision of one of the board's officers, for the purpose of testing the possibility of purifying sewage, by precipitation and filtration, with the result of giving "an effluent perfectly clear and tasteless, in which fish can live." Analysis of the effluent showed that the "remaining solid was not higher than is sometimes found in potable waters, and more than satisfying the requirements of the rivers pollution prevention act." I therefore conclude that Col. Waring is "wrong" when he states that: "However well we may strain household wastes, and however much we may dilute urine, they will both become active sources of offense when putrefying in the waters of a harbor."

The arrangements made by Capt. Liernur for purifying the house waste is at once simple and effective. Prof. Müller, the distinguished German chemist, who examined the process and the effluent says: "The result is a liquid, which can hardly be called contaminated, and leaves no sedimentary deposit. Its level can rise and fall without polluting the town air, and the impure matter it contains is so little, and may be diluted so easily and homogeniously, that in most cases river pollution is quite out of the question. In fact this water is less impure or dangerous than the effluent, which is practically produced by surface irrigation."

"Should, however, a still greater degree of purity be demanded," continues Prof. Müller, "it can be easily attained. After removing the little quantity of suspended matter it still contains, by passing the water through any porous substance, the extraction of the organic matter in solution can be left to the *micro-organisms* in the water itself, through the agency of which the so-called 'self-purifying' of water always takes place; these organisms consuming the organic matter in question, as food."

Capt. Liernur makes use of "intermittent filtration" through beds of gas-coke, which he afterwards uses as fuel for his air-pump and poudrette apparatus; and it has been demonstrated by analysis that the effluent from the household or kitchen waste, after passing through his filters or strainers, do not contain more than .001 or at most .004 of nitrogenous matter. They are, therefore, much less obnoxious to the public health than the waters of many rivers, which in their course are exposed to various sources of pollution.

By the Liernur system the sewer serving for house and rain water is not only kept free from fœcal matter, but also from kitchen waste, manufacturing refuse and street dirt; and as the other pipe of the system, which carries off the excretal sewage, works by "suction," and is, therefore, not only *per se* sealed air-tight, but keeps itself so, it is evident that this system keeps air, soil and river practically free from pollution, by means which are simple to construct, convenient in use and highly effective.

This is a merit no other system at present known can lay claim to, not even the so-called *separate water-carriage system;* for by this arrangement the rain-water sewer is not kept free from street dirt, manufacturing waste, stable gullies, etc., which are a serious source of pollution, not only of harbors but of town air. Another serious evil of the "separate," or small pipe water-carriage system, is that the household sewage, including excretal matter, needs cleansing by irrigation or some other costly means, or it will pollute the water into which it is discharged. The loss to the agricultural interests of the country, as has already been shown, will also be very great.

But if the effluent from kitchen waste, after thorough precipitation and filtration by Liernur's method, will be still "an active source of offense in the waters of a harbor," what shall be said of Col. Waring's small pipe water-carriage system, which discharges not only the *unfiltered kitchen slops, but also the entire excretal sewage* into the nearest stream? If, as Col. Waring alleges, "the unmistakable stench in the bay of Naples is caused *only* by street wash and household waters," what is to become of our beautiful Chesapeake bay when all the sewage of Baltimore is emptied into it through Col. Waring's outlet sewers?

"Water," says Prof. Müller, "in contact with fœcal matter becomes itself contaminated, without making the latter less dangerous, and favors rather the process of putrid fermentation. The intended effect would only be produced, if the solid excrements were *highly comminuted and homogeneously mixed with large quantities of water, and this was again aerated.* Under these conditions a dilution of 1 in 10,000 would *perhaps* suffice. But in water-carriage sewers, the dilution is at the utmost only 1 in 200, and the 'solids,' far from being homogeneously mixed with the water, float in fragments more or less large on or near the surface. These fragments are mostly crowded, through the action of the current, towards the edges of the stream, leaving thus by virtue of its adhesive power, at a falling sewage level, a coating of excrementitious slime on the sides of the sewer. This coating putrefies very soon, or, which is the same, becomes a livid mass of *micro-fungus vegetation*, the minute spores of which are readily taken up by the sewer-air by virtue of their extreme movability, and this air is mechanically pressed out of the sewer by every rise of the sewage level. Thus, the atmosphere we live in and breathe, is daily polluted with germs, which are known to be inimical to health, and may be the carriers of positive contagion, constituting also, most probably, the poisonous agents which experience has taught us to fear in the so-called sewer gas.

"Sanitarily therefore, the water-carriage system is a *decided mistake*, this being due to the effect of water upon putrescible matter, and also of the effect of current water with fluctuating levels upon floating bodies."

5. *That the system of Liernur is expensive, both in construction and maintenance.*

The high working expenses which attended the first experiments of Liernur were not attributable to the system, but were due to the circumstances, that in Amsterdam it was applied to various small parts of the city, lying far apart from each other, in a temporary fashion, and without comprehensive plan, as will be presently shown. The consequence was that most of these small districts were supplied, each with its own pumping station, and that a steam tug, with pneumatic apparatus, had to be provided for others, thus making the cost of working very much higher than it will be when the works now in course of construction are completed, and the various districts are joined by a common pneumatic main, and the vacuum power concentrated in one engine-house. It should be remembered that Capt. Liernur's plans were not officially adopted by the municipal authorities of Amsterdam until December 31st, 1879, and the work of making the system permanent was only begun in 1881, after the crucial test of ten years experiment.

Referring to the reports of the high cost of the system, Von Eulenberg, Chief Privy Councillor of Sanitary Affairs to the Prussian Government, says: "I can state, upon the authority of one of the most eminent engineering firms in Germany, that the estimates hitherto made upon the working of the pneumatic pipe system of Liernur, are based upon premises which are wrong altogether, resulting in figures not less than *seven times too high.* The system embraces, unquestionably, all that technically and financially could be desired for a good arrangement for the removal of impure fluid, and it deserves every recommendation, since engineers of experience and respectability officially declare it to be *easy to construct, and cheaper in working and first cost* than the ordinary modes of water carriage sewers, which have been the source of so much perplexity and trouble, besides being sanitarily dangerous."

In referring to this question, Col. Waring says: "The cost of running the Liernur works (in Amsterdam) in 1880 was $10,858 for a population of twenty-seven thousand nine hundred and forty-six, *being equal to thirty-nine per cent. per head.*" In the official report of Dr. A. Schultz, chairman of the Berlin sewerage commission, December, 1880, he says: "In a quarter of Amsterdam of about ninety-four acres, the net work of fœcal sewers, with its engine-house or air-pump station and everything belonging to it complete, has cost per metre (1. 1-10 yards) of street not quite $5. The total cost of working this quarter of the city, for fuel, oil, wages and repairs amounts to $890, which, divided over a population of thirteen thousand eight hundred and sixty persons, makes *about six cents per head per annum.*" That such a discrepancy should exist, in estimates for the same year, between two gentlemen of scientific attainments is quite astonishing; but as the statements in Dr. Schultz's report are based upon replies which the mayor and council of Amsterdam returned to two series of questions which he addressed to them, as well as his own personal observations made upon the spot, it is fair to presume that Col. Waring's estimate was based upon incorrect information furnished him, or at least upon premises altogether wrong.

My own personal information, derived principally from the municipal authorities of Amsterdam with whom I conferred last summer in reference to the workings of the system in all its details, coincides so nearly with the statements of Dr. Schultz, that I must believe Col. Waring has unwittingly fallen into a great error, as he unquestionably did in reference to the irrigation systems of Paris and Berlin.

The chief engineer of the works stated that in the quarter of the city, between the Wetering and Utrechtsche, which he took me to see, and which forms as it were a district to itself, the expense of service, comprising also the interest on the capital of construction was about thirty-five Holland or fourteen American cents per head per annum, which is only about six and a-half to seven per cent. per head for working expenses.

The entire expense of collecting, transporting and converting the material into a dry "poudrette" for commercial purposes may be stated as follows:

COST PER PERSON PER YEAR.

For Evaporation....................$	45
Sulphuric Acid to fix Ammonia....................	12
Interest on cost of Evaporating Apparatus, 5 per cent. on $1 60.....	08
Repairs of Apparatus, 10 per cent. of $1 60....................	16
Miscellaneous expenses....................	05
Total....................$	86
To which add working expenses and interest on Capital of Construction	14
Gives a total per person per year of....................$1	00

Against this expense we have the revenue derived from the "poudrette," which contains eight per cent. nitrogen, two and a-half per cent. phosphoric acid and three and a-half per cent. potash, the market value of which is at least $2 per hundred, or

$2 per annum per person, as each person furnishes an average of 100 pounds per year of dry poudrette.

We may, therefore, state that the entire expense of construction and operation will not only be re-imbursed by the "poudrette," but a handsome profit will also be realized from this source alone.

The expense of the service in the three principal districts, of the city of Amsterdam with an aggregate population of twenty-three thousand two hundred and thirty-nine people is given in the report of the chief engineer for 1882 as follows:

Superintendence	$ 156.60
Labor	1,187.40
Fuel, grease for machinery, etc	628.80
Repairs of Machinery and Conduits	248.49
Gas	23.48
Water for boilers	81.84
	$2,326.61
Deduct amount paid by house-owners for cleaning house-pipes	95.90
	$2,230.71

This will make for the twenty-three thousand two-hundred and thirty-nine inhabitants of these three districts an average of nearly ten cents per inhabitant per year, which will be notably reduced when the various systems are joined to the central station now in course of construction. It is by no means a fair thing to include in the estimate the remote and outlying small districts, which are supplied each with its own pumping station, and steam tugs with pneumatic apparatus. It stands to reason that the present high working expenses of these will be greatly reduced after the completion of the works, when the various districts are joined by a common pneumatic main, and the vacuum power is concentrated in one engine-house, and without the necessity for steamtugs.

That the system has attracted and is attracting favorable attention in Europe will appear from the following reply of the Royal Ministers of State of the Kingdom of Prussia, recently made to a communication from His Honor L. Schwartzkopff, privy-councillor of commerce, Berlin. It will be observed that the sanction of the system by the Prussian government is based upon the judgment of the "Royal Scientific Commission for Sanitary affairs:"

BERLIN, April 20th, 1883.

"Your Honor having submitted several proposals relating to Liernur's system of sewering towns, dated 1st and 16th November, 1881, and the 16th March and 17th July, 1882, asking the government to declare its opinion of the compass and value of the said system, we take pleasure in replying that, in consideration of the great importance of this question for the sanitation of towns, a most exhaustive examination of the system has taken place and that the desirability of a speedy opportunity for its application in its entirety has been repeatedly manifested.

"Seeing that the plan, as designed by Captain Liernur and submitted to us, for the systematic sanitation of towns, comprises, besides sub-soil drainage, the removal of the human excrements (fæces and urine) and the meteor-water, household slops, and manufacturing waters in *separate* conduits, we have had, with reference to our regulations of sanitary police, every motive for having it examined by competent judges.

"This was done by the *Royal Scientific Commission for Sanitary Matters* and resulted as follows:

1. 'The removal of human excrements (fæces and urine) can by means of the proposed subterranean conduits, unquestionably take place *without* pollution of the air and the townsoil.

2. 'A waterusage in the closets sufficient for preventing pollution of air in dwellings is perfectly compatible with the demands of the system.

3. 'The mode of reduction of the human excrements (fæces and urine) to manurepowder for purposes of agricultural utilisation is *perfectly innocuous*.

4. 'Through the treatment of the household and rainwater, as proposed by the system, and the cleansing of industrial liquids by the respective manufacturers themselves, the removal of these fluids by subterraneous conduits can take place without polluting the town-soil or the air.

5. 'Captain Liernur's method for cleansing the fluids, mentioned Sec. 4, will possibly be sufficient to give them the required degree of purity for being discharged in public streams without sanitary objection. Should such not be the case, other methods may be employed at least for a discharge into the larger rivers.

6. 'Captain Liernur's system allows, when applied in the com-

plete state as designed by him, a sufficient control on the part of the government as to its working from a sanitary point of view.

7. 'So long as the results held in prospect are actually obtained the application of the system is permitted.'

"To this judgment of the *Royal Scientific Commission for Sanitary Matters* we give our adherence in every respect. We meet in doing so the proposals made to us, so far as allowed by considerations of state and sanitary police, and give full liberty to make of this declaration all public use you may deem requisite.

"Leaving the further development of the matter to your Honor we fail not, respectfully, to add that we will be happy to see your meritorious endeavors, in so important a question as the sanitation of towns, crowned with success."

(Signed.)

VON PUTTKAMER, *Minister of the Interior.*
MAYBACH, *Minister of Public Works.*
LUCIUS, *Minister of Agriculture.*
VON GOSSLER, *Minister of Educational and Sanitary Affairs.*

"To His Honor
L. SCHWARTZKOPFF,
Privy Councillor of Commerce, Berlin."

Finally, Col. Waring seems to think me as ignorant of physical laws as he would have the world believe I am of the principles of sewerage and agriculture. After enumerating many points on which he thinks I am wrong, he says: "He is wrong in supposing that a man can lift himself by his boot-legs." Whether Col. Waring or I represent that metaphorical personage, who spent his life in a vain endeavor to make dominoes out of bonny-clabber, the public must be the judge. Certain it is, I should not consider such an undertaking more Quixotic than the attempt to convince an enlightened community that "water carriage" is the only "panacea" for sewage evils. Of one thing, however, the public may be convinced, and that is, that Col. Waring is as much in love with his own ideas as Cobbett was with "Indian Corn," or Charles Lamb with "Roast Pig." This is not strange. It is a property of genius, not only to be in love with its chosen pursuit, but at the same time to make others in love with it. When Col. Waring loves he loves with all his heart and soul; the contemplation of the object of his affections warms his imagination into a glow, and he grasps it with the athletic power of a man to whom nature has been liberal in both physical and intellectual gifts. Like all true lovers, too, he finds no pleasure in aught else; he turns away with indifference, if not contempt from all but his favorite object and resents with energy the solicitations of any other claimant upon his attentions.

Conclusion of the Convention—Miscellaneous Business.

Dr. Morris offered the following resolution, which was adopted:

Resolved, That this convention strongly recommend the city authorities to establish a public morgue in the interest of decency and morality.

Dr. Steuart advocated the resolution, and Dr. McShane, assistant Health Commissioner, stated that a bill for a morgue had already been introduced in the Council. Dr. Benson, Health Commissioner, heartily concurred in the resolution.

Resolutions of thanks, on the part of the State Board of Health, were tendered to those who had attended and taken part in the convention, and especially those who had come from a distance to aid in the work; to the press of the city and the officers of the convention.

Dr. Steuart moved that "the convention do now adjourn *sine die*."

President McSherry said: "Before closing the exercises of this convention, by putting the motion to adjourn *sine die*, I desire to express the hope that this may be only the beginning of a series of such conventions. I have a very high appreciation of the work done here, and believe that when the proceedings go out to the public, through the reports of the State Board of Health, they will be productive of much good and awaken a new interest in sanitary matters."

The motion to adjourn was then formally put to the house and carried, and Dr. McSherry declared the convention adjourned *sine die.*

[NOTE—The next convention will probably be held at some point on the Eastern Shore of Maryland in October or November, 1884, and the physicians of that section of the state are earnestly requested to organize medico-sanitary associations in every county with the view of aiding the State Board of Health in this important work.—C. W. C.]

Officers of the Convention.

President—Prof. RICHARD MCSHERRY, M. D., Baltimore.
Vice President—HENRY C. HALLOWELL, Esq., Montgomery County.
Vice President—Col. EDWARD LLOYD, Talbot County.
Vice President—EDWARD STAKE, Esq., Washington County.
Vice President—Hon. S. H. COOMBS, St. Mary's County.
Vice President—Col. WM. KNIGHT, Cecil County.
Permanent Secretary—C. W. CHANCELLOR, M. D., Baltimore.
Acting Secretary—G. LANE TANEYHILL, M. D.

Executive Committes.

FROM THE STATE MEDICAL SOCIETY:

DR. RICHARD MCSHERRY. DR. G. LANE TANEYHILL.

FROM THE CITY BOARD OF HEALTH:

DR GEORGE W. BENSON. MR. A. R. CARTER.

FROM THE STATE BOARD OF HEALTH:

DR. J. ROBERT WARD. DR. JAMES A. STEUART.

DR. C. W. CHANCELLOR.

Committee of Citizens.

DR. JOHN MORRIS, Baltimore.
FRANCIS T. KING, Esq., Baltimore.
MAJ. CHAS. H. LATROBE, Balto.
HON. LLOYD LOWNDES, Allegany Co.
COL. HENRY PAGE, Somerset Co.
HON. HY. W. ARCHER, Harford Co.
JUDGE DAVID FOWLER, Balto. Co.
DR. GEO. W. BISHOP, Worcester Co.
HON. FREDERICK STONE, Charles Co.

Delegates in Attendance.

Jackson Piper, M. D., Baltimore County Board of Health.
A. Shelmon Warren, M. D., Baltimore County.
Chas. L. Leas, M. D., Glyndon, Md.
W. Stump Forwood, M. D., Medical and Chirurgical Faculty, Maryland.
Eugene F. Cordell, M. D., Medical and Chirurgical Faculty, Maryland.
Jas. Carey Thomas, M. D., Medical and Chirurgical Faculty, Maryland.
John C. Harris, M. D., Medical and Chirurgical Faculty, Maryland.
B. Bernard Brown, M. D., Medical and Chirurgical Faculty, Maryland.
Henry C. Hallowell, Esq., Montgomery County Board of Health.
G. H. Rohe, M. D., Medical Chronicle, Baltimore.
Richard Gundry, M. D., Maryland State Insane Asylum.
Walter Wyman, M. D, U. S. Marine Hospital Service.
Thomas A. Ashby, M. D., Maryland Medical Journal.
A. N. Bell, M. D., "The Sanitarian," New York.
E. E. Tucker, Civil Engineer, Stockton, California.
Dr. Miller, St. Michael's Maryland.
George W. Bishop, M. D., Snow Hill, Maryland.
J. D. Iglehart, M. D., Baltimore.
Thos. S. Latimer, M. D., Northern Central Railroad.
J. H. Grimes, M. D., Merchants and Manufacturers' Association, Baltimore.
Henry M. Wilson, M. D., Merchants and Manufacturers' Asso., Balto.
J. F. Supplee, Esq., Merchants and Manufacturers' Association, Balto.
C. H. Latrobe, Civil Engineer, City of Baltimore.
W. Chew Van Bibber, City of Baltimore.
Wm. Lee, M. D., City of Baltimore.
E. J Henkle, M. D., City Health Department.
Jas. F. McShane, M. D., City Health Department.
Prof. Samuel C. Chew, University of Maryland.
Wm. Dunnett, Plumbers' Association, Baltimore.
John F. McConnell, Plumbers' Association, Baltimore.
P. F. Leonard, Plumbers' Association, Baltimore.
J. W. Chambers, Plumbers' Association, Baltimore.
Chas. S. York, Plumbers' Association, Baltimore.

VITAL STATISTICS

OF

BALTIMORE CITY, 1881 & 1882,

REPORTED BY

G. W. CHANCELLOR, M. D.

SECRETARY STATE BOARD OF HEALTH AND REGISTRAR OF VITAL STATISTICS

FOR

THE STATE OF MARYLAND.

Office State Board of Health and Registrar of Vital Statistics.

BALTIMORE, January 1st, 1884.

To His Excellency, the Governor, and the
Honorable, the General Assembly of Maryland.

I have the honor to present herewith, in accordance with section 7, chapter 438, acts of 1880, a classified and tabulated statement of the vital statistics of the State, so far as it has been possible to collect the same under existing laws.

The amount appropriated for "collecting and recording marriages, births and deaths in the state," viz: $200 is wholly inadequate for the purpose, even if there were a law requiring a systematic report of the facts from each city, town, village and county. It has been estimated by other states having efficient registration laws, that the actual cost of collecting and recording the marriages, births and deaths, including the necessary books, blanks, postage, clerical work, &c., amounts to from ten to fifteen cents per name, according to the number of names and the completeness of the record.

Vital registration is the account kept by the state with its population, and is one of the most powerful aids in determining questions of health, the duration of life, the movement of population, &c.

By figures the health of a community is shown at a glance; by figures the efficiency of preventive measures, such as vaccination, is tested and the fatality of epidemics traced; by figures we ascertain the proportion of deaths to the whole population, and it is obvious that without the use of a system of vital statistics our knowledge of the number of deaths, births and marriages in a community must be vague, uncertain and often erroneous.

It is to be hoped that, in the interest of the health and safety of the people, this important subject will be placed on a better footing in our state, and that a compulsory system of vital registration may be enacted by the present legislature. Under existing laws it is quite impossible to collect statistics of value, and the attempt may be regarded as simply a waste of effort.

Respectfully your ob't serv't,

C. W. CHANCELLOR, M.D.,
Sec'y S. B. of H. and Registrar of V. S.

TABLE No. 1—*Annual Report of Deaths from all Causes in the City of Baltimore for the year* 1881.

CAUSES OF DEATH.	January.	February.	March.	April.	May.	June.	July.	August.	September.	October.	November.	December.	Totals.
Abscess	..	..	..	..	..	..	..	..	..	1	..	..	1
Abscess Brain	..	1	..	1	..	..	..	..	..	..	..	1	3
Abscess Ear	1	1	..	..	1	..	..	..	..	..	..	..	3
Abscess Ear and Throat	1	..	..	..	..	..	..	..	..	..	..	..	1
Abscess Mammary	1	..	..	..	..	..	..	..	..	..	..	..	1
Abscess Liver	1	..	..	..	1	..	1	..	..	4	..	..	7
Abscess Pelvis	..	1	..	..	..	1	..	..	..	..	..	..	2
Abscess Recto Pharyngeal	..	1	..	..	..	..	..	..	..	..	..	..	1
Abscess Intrauterine	..	..	1	..	..	..	..	..	..	..	..	..	1
Abscess Psoas	..	..	1	..	1	..	..	..	..	..	..	1	3
Abscess Peritoneal	..	..	..	1	1	..	..	..	..	..	..	..	2
Abscess Neck	..	..	..	..	..	1	..	..	..	..	..	..	1
Abscess Throat	..	..	..	..	..	..	1	..	..	..	..	..	1
Abscess Iliac	..	..	..	..	..	..	1	..	..	..	..	..	1
Abscess Thigh	..	..	..	..	..	..	1	..	..	..	..	..	1
Abscess Parietes of Abd'n	..	..	..	..	..	..	..	1	..	..	..	..	1
Abscess Scrotal	..	..	..	..	..	..	..	1	..	..	..	..	1
Abortion	3	..	..	..	..	..	..	..	..	..	..	..	3
Angina Pectoris	1	2	2	1	..	..	2	..	..	..	..	1	9
Apoplexy	13	14	18	9	14	7	19	11	6	11	8	11	141
Ascites	1	..	..	1	1	1	..	..	2	..	..	1	7
Asphyxia	2	1	..	..	2	..	..	2	2	..	..	5	14
Asthma	3	1	4	2	1	2	4	1	2	2	2	1	25
Asthenia	3	3	4	6	6	3	10	4	1	4	2	11	57
Atelectasis Pulmonum	2	3	..	1	..	1	1	..	..	1	1	..	10
Adenitis	2	..	..	..	..	..	..	..	..	..	..	..	2

Acute Miliary Tuberculosis	..	1	..	..	..	..	..	..	..	..	..	..	1
Amenorrhœa	..	1	..	..	..	..	..	..	..	..	..	..	1
Aortic Stenosis	..	1	..	..	..	..	..	..	..	..	..	..	1
Aneurism of Aorto	..	..	1	1	..	..	..	..	..	..	..	..	2
Aortic Regurgitation	..	..	..	1	..	..	..	..	..	..	..	..	1
Albuminuria	..	..	..	1	..	1	3	..	..	1	..	1	7
Anaemia	..	..	..	1	1	..	..	..	..	..	1	..	3
Adynamia	..	..	..	1	..	..	..	..	..	..	..	..	1
Aneurism of the Innominate Artery	..	..	..	1	..	..	..	..	..	..	..	..	1
Addison's Disease	..	..	..	1	..	..	..	..	..	..	..	..	1
Atrophy of Liver	..	..	..	..	2	..	1	..	..	..	..	..	3
Atrophy—Progressive Muscular	..	..	..	..	..	1	..	..	..	..	..	..	1
Atrophy	..	..	..	..	..	..	4	..	..	6	..	1	11
At Birth	..	..	..	..	..	..	..	..	1	..	..	..	1
Anthrax	1	..	..	..	..	..	..	..	..	1	..	..	2
Bright's Disease	8	9	12	14	8	10	6	7	10	9	4	13	110
Burns	4	3	5	4	1	..	..	4	..	1	2	4	28
Bronchorrhea	..	..	..	..	..	..	..	..	..	..	..	1	1
Cancer	1	..	..	..	..	..	..	..	..	..	..	..	1
Cancer Cerviv	1	..	..	..	..	..	..	..	..	..	..	..	1
Cancer Diffused	1	1	..	1	..	1	1	1	..	..	..	..	6
Cancer Breast	2	1	5	5	1	2	4	1	2	4	3	1	31
Cancer Liver	1	4	1	1	2	2	..	1	..	2	1	1	16
Cancer Uterus	1	3	1	7	3	1	4	4	3	3	2	1	33
Cancer Stomach	4	5	3	5	4	3	7	1	2	11	2	2	49
Cancer Pylorus	..		..	1	..	3	..	..	..	..	2	..	6
Cancer Face	..	1	..	..	..	..	..	..	..	..	..	1	2
Cancer Œsophagus	..	1	..	..	..	..	1	..	..	..	..	..	2
Cancer Bowels	..	..	1	..	..	..	..	3	..	1	1	1	7
Cancer Ovary	..	..	1	..	..	..	..	..	..	1	..	..	2
Cancer Ventricular	..	..	1	..	..	..	..	..	..	..	1	..	2
Cancer Mouth	..	..	..	1	..	1	..	..	..	..	..	..	2
Cancer Vagina	..	..	..	1	..	..	..	..	..	..	..	..	1
Cancer Rectum	..	..	..	1	..	..	..	1	..	..	..	1	3

TABLE No 1.—Continued.

CAUSES OF DEATH.	January.	February.	March.	April.	May.	June.	July.	August.	September.	October.	November.	December.	Totals.
Cancer, Cheek	..	..	..	..	..	1	..	..	..	..	..	..	1
Cancer, Lower Jaw	..	..	..	..	..	2	..	..	..	..	..	..	2
Cancer, Pectoralis	..	..	..	..	..	1	..	..	..	..	..	..	1
Cancer, Shoulder	..	..	..	..	..	1	..	..	..	..	..	..	1
Cancer, Caecal Valve	..	..	..	..	..	..	..	1	..	..	..	..	1
Cancer, Vulva	..	..	..	..	..	..	..	..	..	1	..	..	1
Cancer, Duodenum	..	..	..	..	..	..	..	..	..	1	..	..	1
Cancer, Axillary Gland	..	..	..	..	..	..	..	..	..	..	1	..	1
Cancer, Mesenteric Gland	..	..	..	..	..	..	..	..	..	..	1	..	1
Cancer, Bladder	..	..	..	..	..	..	..	..	..	..	..	1	1
Consumption of Lungs	126	81	102	122	83	76	104	83	104	94	74	157	1,206
Consumption of Bowels	1	..	..	..	..	..	..	..	..	1	1	..	3
Capillary Bronchitis	11	4	7	5	2	3	..	..	1	2	5	8	48
Calculus (Biliary)	1	..	..	..	..	..	..	..	..	..	..	..	1
Cirrhosis of Liver	2	1	2	..	3	..	3	2	3	..	2	1	19
Concussion of Brain	1	1	..	1	4	..	3	1	3	..	2	..	16
Congestion of Brain	8	3	8	8	3	3	9	6	5	7	4	6	70
Congestion of Lungs	5	2	4	4	2	3	3	5	6	7	3	5	49
Congestion General	1	..	..	..	..	..	..	..	..	..	..	..	1
Croup	20	17	13	17	8	4	11	9	17	35	42	49	242
Cyanosis	2	3	3	1	1	2	4	3	4	4	2	2	31
Chorea	1	..	..	..	..	..	..	..	..	..	..	1	2
Catarrh Bronchial	1	..	1	..	1	..	1	1	1	..	1	..	7
Catarrh of Stomach	1	..	1	..	..	..	..	..	..	..	..	..	2
Catarrh of Lungs	1	..	1	..	2	..	..	..	..	..	1	..	5
Catarrh Gastro Intestinal	..	..	..	..	1	..	4	6	..	3	..	..	14

Disease													
Catarrh Intestinal	..	..	..	..	..	1	..	1	..	..	2	1	5
Cholerine	..	..	..	1	..	..	1	..	..	..	..	..	2
Cirrhosis	..	..	1	..	..	..	..	..	..	..	..	..	1
Congestive Chill	2	..	..	..	2	..	..	1	1	1	..	..	7
Convulsions	36	37	36	26	32	39	45	37	29	37	27	38	419
Child Birth	..	2	1	1	..	..	..	2	2	1	..	1	10
Congestion of Liver	..	1	..	..	..	..	1	..	1	1	..	..	4
Caries of Femur and Ilium	..	1	..	..	..	..	..	..	..	..	..	..	1
Caries of Dorsal Vertebrae	..	1	..	..	..	..	..	..	..	..	..	..	1
Carbuncle	..	..	..	1	..	..	..	..	..	..	..	..	1
Compression of Brain	..	..	..	1	..	..	..	..	..	..	..	..	1
Colic	..	..	..	2	..	..	1	1	..	1	..	1	6
Cholera Infantum	..	..	..	..	3	37	279	119	70	40	6	4	558
Cholera Morbus	..	..	..	..	2	3	14	7	2	3	1	1	33
Congestion of Bowels	..	..	..	..	1	..	..	..	1	..	1	..	3
Congestion of Heart	..	..	..	..	1	..	..	..	..	..	..	..	1
Collapse of Lungs	..	..	..	..	1	..	..	..	..	..	..	..	1
Cramps	..	..	..	..	..	1	..	..	..	..	..	..	1
Colic (Biliary)	..	..	..	..	..	..	..	1	..	..	..	..	1
Colic (Renal)	..	..	..	..	..	..	..	1	..	..	..	..	1
Colitis	..	..	..	..	..	..	..	..	1	..	..	..	1
Chlorosis	..	..	..	..	..	..	..	..	1	..	..	..	1
Congestion of Stomach	..	..	..	..	..	..	..	..	..	..	1	..	1
Concussion of Spinal Cord	..	..	..	..	..	..	..	..	..	..	1	..	1
Catarrh, Nasal	..	..	..	..	..	..	..	..	..	..	..	1	1
Disease of Brain	1	4	..	..	..	..	2	1	2	1	1	..	12
Disease of Spine	3	..	1	1	..	..	..	..	..	1	..	1	7
Disease of Liver	..	1	..	2	1	1	1	..	..	..	1	..	7
Disease of Stomach	..	..	..	..	..	1	3	..	..	..	..	..	4
Disease of Hip	..	..	..	..	..	..	..	..	..	..	..	1	1
Dropsy, Peritoneal	..	..	..	..	..	..	1	..	..	..	..	..	1
Dropsy, Abdominal	..	..	..	..	..	..	1	..	..	..	..	..	1
Dropsy, Ovarian	..	..	..	..	..	1	..	..	..	..	..	..	1
Dropsy, General	6	5	4	3	7	4	8	7	4	4	4	6	57

TABLE No. 1—Continued.

CAUSES OF DEATH.	January.	February.	March.	April.	May.	June.	July.	August.	September.	October.	November.	December.	Totals.
Dropsy, Heart	..	1	..	..	1	..	..	..	1	2	..	2	7
Dropsy, Liver	..	..	..	..	2	..	..	..	..	..	..	..	2
Dropsy, Scarlatinal	..	..	..	1	..	1	..	1	..	..	..	..	3
Dropsy, Renal	..	..	..	..	..	1	..	..	..	..	..	..	1
Drowned	1	..	2	1	6	2	6	5	6	4	6	..	30
Dysentery	2	..	3	1	2	3	14	15	3	6	4	3	56
Diarrhœa	3	3	4	3	2	4	29	15	8	9	4	2	86
Dentition	6	5	5	7	8	10	27	19	14	8	3	3	115
Diphtheria	47	29	20	25	24	30	46	42	70	100	90	116	639
Debility	1	..	..	2	1	..	..	..	..	2	..	1	7
Dilatation of Heart	1	..	..	..	..	..	..	..	..	..	..	..	1
Delirium Tremens	..	3	1	1	3	..	1	1	..	1	..	3	14
Diabetes	..	1	2	..	..	..	..	..	..	..	1	1	5
Dyspepsia	..	..	..	1	..	..	..	..	..	1	1	..	3
Duodenitis	..	..	..	..	..	..	1	..	..	..	..	..	1
Dipsomania	..	..	..	..	..	..	..	..	..	1	..	..	1
Dropsy of the Pericardium	..	..	..	..	..	..	..	..	..	..	1	..	1
Disease of the Prostate	..	..	..	..	..	..	..	..	..	..	..	1	1
Emphysema	1	..	..	..	..	..	..	..	..	1	1	..	3
Entero Colitis	3	..	..	1	1	6	13	4	7	5	3	..	43
Endo Carditis	1	1	1	1	..	1	..	..	..	..	..	..	5
Endo Peri Metritis	1	..	..	..	..	..	..	..	..	..	..	..	1
Epilepsy	3	1	1	..	2	1	2	1	1	2	3	..	17
Erysipelas	4	4	3	10	1	3	4	1	4	..	4	1	39
Effusion of Brain	1	..	1	..	..	..	..	1	..	..	..	..	3
Exposure	2	..	..	..	..	..	..	..	..	..	..	..	2

Exhaustion	..	..	1	..	..	..	..	..	..	..	..	..	1
Eczema	..	..	..	1	1	..	..	..	..	..	..	..	2
Enlargement of Liver	..	..	..	1	..	..	..	..	..	..	..	..	1
Extra Uterine Pregnancy	..	..	..	2	..	..	..	..	..	..	..	..	2
Epistaxis	..	..	..	..	1	..	..	..	..	1	1	..	3
Excessive Heat	..	..	..	..	1	..	..	..	..	..	..	..	1
Embolism	..	..	..	..	1	..	..	..	1	..	..	..	2
Enteralgia	..	..	..	..	..	..	..	..	..	1	..	..	1
Excessive Vomiting	..	..	..	..	..	..	..	..	..	..	1	..	1
Fever, Scarlet	58	34	20	21	14	15	7	8	6	12	8	12	215
Fever, Typhoid	9	8	5	9	9	11	11	32	37	29	20	17	197
Fever, Congestive	3	..	..	..	..	..	..	..	..	2	..	1	6
Fever, Malarial	1	..	3	1	1	3	2	6	10	11	9	1	48
Fever, Typho Malarial	1	..	1	2	1	2	3	11	8	11	4	6	50
Fever, Gastro Enteric	1	..	..	..	1	..	..	..	..	..	..	..	2
Fever, Intermittent	2	1	1	1	2	1	..	..	1	..	..	1	10
Fever, Puerperal	1	1	2	..	..	..	3	1	1	1	..	2	12
Fever, Catarrhal	1	2	1	..	..	..	..	..	..	..	..	1	5
Fever, Remittent	..	..	2	2	..	..	..	1	6	4	2	..	17
Fever, Rheumatic	..	..	2	1	..	..	..	..	..	..	..	..	3
Fever, Typhus	..	..	..	1	1	..	..	..	1	..	..	..	3
Fever, Gastric	..	..	..	..	1	..	..	..	..	..	..	2	3
Fever, Brain	..	..	..	..	1	..	2	..	..	..	..	..	3
Fever, Bilious	..	..	..	..	..	..	1	2	3	..	..	..	6
Fever, Continued	..	..	..	..	..	..	..	..	1	..	..	..	1
Fracture of Ribs	1	..	..	..	..	..	..	..	..	..	..	..	1
Fracture of Skull	2	2	1	3	..	2	..	1	2	2	..	3	18
Fracture of Hip	..	1	..	..	..	..	..	..	..	..	..	..	1
Fracture of Humerus	..	1	..	..	..	..	..	..	..	..	..	..	1
Fracture of Neck	..	1	..	..	..	..	..	..	..	1	..	..	2
Fracture of Veterbrae	..	1	1	..	1	1	..	..	..	..	2	..	6
Fracture of Jaw	..	..	1	..	..	..	..	..	..	..	..	..	1
Fracture of Thigh	..	..	1	..	1	..	..	..	..	..	1	..	3
Fracture of Leg	..	..	..	1	1	..	..	..	..	..	..	..	2

Table No. 1—Continued.

Causes of Death.	January	February.	March.	April.	May.	June.	July.	August.	September.	October.	November.	December.	Totals.
Fracture of Tibia	..	..	..	..	..	..	1	..	..	..	..	..	1
Fracture of Ilium	..	..	..	..	..	..	..	..	1	..	..	..	1
Fracture of Frontal Bone	..	..	..	..	..	..	..	..	1	..	..	..	1
Fistula in Ano	..	..	..	..	1	..	..	..	..	..	..	..	1
Fissure Cervix Uteri	..	..	..	..	..	..	1	..	..	..	..	..	1
Forceps Delivery	..	..	..	..	..	..	1	..	..	..	..	..	1
Gangrene of Navel	1	..	..	..	..	..	..	..	..	..	..	..	1
Gangrene of Leg	..	..	1	..	2	..	1	1	1	..	..	..	7
Gangrene of Lungs	..	..	2	..	1	..	..	..	..	1	..	..	4
Gangrene of Face	..	..	..	..	..	..	1	..	1	..	..	..	2
Gangrene of Foot	..	..	..	..	..	..	1	..	..	..	..	..	1
Gangrene Senile	2	..	..	..	..	..	..	..	..	1	..	1	4
Gangrene Bowels	..	..	..	..	..	..	..	..	..	1	..	..	1
Gastro Enteritis	1	3	3	3	5	4	13	13	7	6	6	6	70
Gout	1	..	..	..	..	..	..	1	..	..	..	..	2
Hernia	..	1	..	..	..	1	..	..	..	..	..	..	2
Hernia Inguinal	1	..	..	..	..	..	..	..	..	1	..	..	2
Hernia Strangulated	..	2	1	1	2	1	1	..	3	1	2	..	14
Hemorrhage of Brain	3	2	1	..	1	..	3	..	1	..	..	2	13
Hemorrhage of Navel	2	..	2	..	..	1	2	1	..	1	1	3	13
Hemorrhage of Stomach	2	1	..	..	..	..	..	..	..	..	..	..	3
Hemorrhage of Lungs	1	..	1	2	..	..	..	2	3	2	..	2	13
Hemorrhage of Uterus	1	..	..	..	2	..	..	..	..	..	..	1	4
Hemorrhage of Bowels	..	..	1	2	..	..	1	1	..	1	..	..	6
Hemorrhage Post Partem	1	..	..	..	..	..	..	..	1	..	..	..	2
Hemorrhage Hæmorrhoidal	..	..	..	..	..	..	..	..	..	..	..	1	1

Hydrocephalus	8	..	6	3	6	4		7	2	6	1	3	48
Heart Disease	22	33	28	32	25	22	30	17	22	30	25	28	314
Hæmatemesis	..	1	..	..	1	..	..	1	1	..	..	..	4
Hydrothorax	..	..	1	..	..	..	..	1	..	1	2	2	7
Hydro Pericardium	..	..	..	..	..	1	..	..	..	1	1	..	3
Hypertrophy of Liver	..	..	..	..	..	..	1	..	..	..	..	..	1
Hæmoptysis	..	..	..	..	..	..	..	..	..	1	1	..	2
Heat Stroke	..	..	..	..	..	..	..	..	..	3	..	..	3
Hydrocele	..	..	..	..	..	..	..	..	..	..	..	1	1
Inflammation of Brain	..	1	3	3	1	2	2	..	1	..	..	..	13
Inflammation of Bladder	1	2	1	3	..	2	..	1	..	1	1	1	13
Inflammation of Bowels	2	3	4	2	4	4	12	9	8	5	6	2	61
Inflammation of Stomach	2	2	1	8	10	6	1	4	4	2	3	2	45
Inflammation of Bronchi	18	12	7	12	13	2	8	2	5	4	7	16	106
Inflammation of Kidneys	5	5	3	2	1	1	2	..	2	2	1	..	24
Inflammation of Larynx	1	1	1	1	1	..	1	1	..	1	..	..	8
Inflammation of Liver	3	2	1	4	..	..	1	2	..	1	..	3	17
Inflammation of Pericardium	1	..	1	1	4	1	1	2	1	1	1	..	14
Inflammation of Peritoneum	3	9	2	6	2	3	6	4	5	7	4	4	55
Inflammation of Pleura	1	1	2	1	2	1	..	..	1	1	3	4	17
Inflammation of Caecum Intestinum	..	..	..	..	..	..	..	1	..	..	..	..	1
Inflammation of Tonsils	..	..	..	..	..	..	..	..	..	..	1	..	1
Inanition	10	6	8	10	6	12	25	20	14	25	9	11	156
Intussusception	1	4	2	..	..	..	1	..	1	2	1	1	13
Intemperance	3	2	3	3	1	2	1	5	..	2	4	2	28
Insanity	..	3	..	..	..	..	1	..	..	..	2	2	8
Imperfect Development	..	..	..	1	..	..	..	..	..	..	..	..	1
Indigestion	..	..	..	..	1	..	..	..	2	2	2	..	7
Influenza	..	..	..	..	..	1	..	..	..	..	..	..	1
Insolation	..	..	..	..	..	..	2	..	..	..	..	..	2
Ileus	..	..	..	..	..	..	..	..	..	1	..	..	1
Jaundice	1	1	1	1	1	..	1	5	3	1	3	1	19
Leucocythæmia	1	1	..	..	..	..	..	..	..	..	1	..	3

TABLE No. 1—Continued.

CAUSES OF DEATH.	January.	February.	March.	April.	May.	June.	July.	August.	September.	October.	November.	December.	Totals.
Lithotomy	..	..	..	..	1	..	..	..	..	..	..	..	1
Malignant Sore Throat	..	..	..	..	..	..	..	..	..	..	..	1	1
Marasmus	11	6	10	19	12	10	27	33	29	38	16	23	234
Myelitis	2	..	..	..	..	1	1	..	..	..	..	..	4
Malformation	2	1	1	..	1	1	3	2	1	..	..	..	12
Measles	1	1	3	10	25	13	14	4	4	..	..	..	75
Meningitis	9	14	14	17	10	14	16	15	21	15	7	10	162
Meningitis Tubercular	9	8	8	6	6	5	5	3	3	5	5	9	72
Meningitis Cerebro Spinal	3	3	4	6	4	4	3	..	3	4	..	3	37
Meningitis Basilar	1	..	..	..	..	..	..	..	..	..	..	..	1
Malarial Chill	..	..	..	..	..	..	..	..	..	..	1	..	1
Murder	1	..	2	1	2	..	1	3	..	..	..	1	11
Mal-nutrition	2	..	..	1	2	2	9	1	2	2	1	3	25
Malaria	..	..	1	..	..	..	..	4	1	3	..	..	9
Mercurial Dyscrasia	..	..	1	..	..	..	..	..	..	..	..	..	1
Metro Peritonitis	..	..	..	1	..	..	..	..	.	..	..	..	1
Menorrhagia	..	..	..	1	..	..	..	..	..	..	..	..	1
Multiple Sarcoma	..	..	..	1	..	..	..	..	..	..	..	..	1
Metritis	..	..	..	..	..	..	1	..	1	..	..	..	2
Miscarriage	..	..	..	..	..	..	..	1	..	..	1	..	2
Metorrhagia	..	..	..	..	..	..	..	..	1	..	..	..	1
Malignant Disease of Mesenteric Gland	..	..	..	..	..	..	..	..	..	1	..	..	1
Morbus Cæruleus	..	..	..	..	..	..	..	..	..	..	..	1	1
Neuralgia	1	..	..	..	..	1	..	..	1	..	..	1	4
Nervous Prostration	..	2	2	..	..	..	..	..	..	..	..	2	6

Necrosis	..	..	..	..	1	..	1	1	..	2	1	1	7
Neurasthenia	..	..	..	..	..	1	..	..	..	..	..	..	1
Old Age	25	26	19	27	15	16	23	19	19	23	16	23	251
Œdema of the Lungs	1	..	1	..	..	..	..	..	..	1	1	1	5
Opium Habit	..	..	1	..	..	..	..	..	..	..	..	..	1
Osteosarcoma	..	..	..	1	..	..	..	..	..	..	..	..	1
Ossification of Heart	..	..	..	..	1	..	..	..	..	..	..	..	1
Overlaid	..	..	..	..	..	..	..	..	1	..	..	..	1
Orchitis	..	..	..	..	..	..	..	..	1	..	..	..	1
Occlusion of Intestines	..	..	..	..	..	..	..	..	..	1	..	..	1
Osteitis	..	..	..	..	..	..	..	..	..	..	..	1	1
Obesity	..	..	..	..	..	..	..	..	..	..	..	1	1
Œdema of the Glottis	..	..	..	..	..	..	..	..	..	..	..	1	1
Paralysis	13	12	10	22	7	3	14	12	9	10	11	13	136
Pneumonia	73	43	45	56	39	17	19	11	14	21	23	46	406
Pneumonia, Typhoid	5	3	3	2	1	2	1	2	..	2	4	1	26
Pneumonia, Broncho	5	..	2	3	..	..	1	..	1	1	..	..	13
Pneumonia, Pleuro	..	3	4	3	3	..	2	1	1	..	2	2	21
Pulmonary Effusion	..	..	..	..	..	..	..	..	..	..	..	1	1
Premature Birth	7	15	9	15	8	12	18	10	11	16	15	7	143
Parotitis	1	..	..	..	..	..	1	..	..	..	..	..	2
Phthisis Mucosa	1	.	..	..	..	..	..	..	..	..	..	..	1
Protracted Labor	1	2	3	..	..	2	1	..	1	..	..	..	10
Pyæmia	2	3	..	2		1	1	2	1	1	2	1	16
Puerperal Mania	..	1	..	..	1	..	..	..	..	..	..	..	2
Poison	..	2	1	2	1	..	2	4	1	..	1	..	14
Purpura	..	1	..	..	..	..	..	..	..	..	..	..	1
Pott's Disease	..	1	..	..	..	..	..	..	1	..	..	..	2
Puerperal Convulsions	..	..	2	..	..	..	1	2	1	..	..	..	6
Pulmonary Embolism	..	..	1	..	..	..	..	..	..	..	..	..	1
Puerperal Septicæmia	..	..		1	..	..	..	..	..	..	..	..	1
Phthisis Laryngeal	..	..	.	1	1	..	3	1	..	..	..	..	6
Progressive Locomotor Ataxia	..	..	..	1	..	..	..	..	..	..	..	..	1
Phrenitis	..	..	..	1	..	..	..	..	..	..	..	..	1

TABLE No. 1—Continued.

CAUSES OF DEATH.	January.	February.	March.	April.	May.	June.	July.	August.	September.	October.	November.	December.	Totals.
Puerperal Metritis	..	..	..	..	1	1	..	..	..	2	2	..	6
Pelvic Cellulitis	..	..	..	..	1	..	..	..	..	..	..	1	2
Puerperal Peritonitis	..	..	..	.	..	.	2	..	1	..	..	2	5
Parametritis.	..	..	..	..	..	..	1	..	.	..	..	..	1
Perityphlitis	..	..	..	..	..	..	..	..	1	..	..	..	1
Placenta Prævia	..	..	..	.	..	..	..	..	1	..	..	..	1
Preternatural Birth		..	..	..	..	..	..	..	..	1	..	..	1
Polypus of Uterus	..	..	..	..	..	..	..	..	..	1	..	..	1
Rheumatism	..	..	1	..	..	..	.	1	..	1	2	..	5
Rheumatism, Inflammatory	2	5	3	3	4	..	2	2	..	3	1	4	29
Rickets	..	..	1	..	..	..	..	..	..	..	..	..	1
Result of Parturition	..	..	2	..	..	..	..	..	..	..	..	..	2
Rheumatism of Heart	..	..	..	5	..	..	..	..	..	3	..	1	9
Rupture of Kidney	..	..	..	..	..	..	..	..	..	..	1	..	1
Rupture of Gall Duct	..	..	..	..	..	..	..	..	..	..	1	..	1
Rupture of Uterus	..	..	..	..	..	..	..	..	..	..	..	1	1
Shock from Fall	..	..	..	..	..	..	.	..	..	..	1	1	2
Scalds	2	1	..	1	..	1	..	.	2	..	3	1	11
Scrofula	6	..	7	5	8	2	6	1	2	3	2	2	44
Softening of Brain	1	5	1	3	1	1	1	6	2	3	7	..	31
Septicæmia	3	3	1	1	1	1	3	1	1	.	..	4	19
Suicide	2	2	1	3	2	4	3	3	..	2	..	1	23
Syphilis	2	2	7	3	1	2	2	1	4	3	1	2	30
Stricture of Œsophagus	1	..	..	..	..	..	..	..	..	..	..	..	1
Stricture of Intestines	..	1	1	..	1	..	..	..	1	..	..	..	4
Suffocation by Gas	..	..	..	..	..	..	..	..	..	..	1	..	1

Suffocation by Earth	..	..	..	..	..	..	..	..	..	..	1	..	1
Starvation	1	..	1	..	..	..	..	..	..	..	..	..	2
Spasms of Heart	1	..	..	..	..	..	..	..	..	..	..	..	1
Stomatitis Materna	..	..	1	..	..	..	..	..	..	..	..	..	1
Specific Consumption	..	..	..	1	..	..	..	..	..	..	..	..	1
Sun Stroke	..	..	..	..	2	..	1	1	4	2	..	..	10
Small Pox	..	..	..	..	..	1	..	..	..	..	5	5	11
Septic Peritonitis	..	..	..	..	..	1	..	..	..	..	..	..	1
Sciatica	..	..	..	..	..	..	1	..	..	..	..	..	1
Sarcoma	..	..	..	..	..	..	1	..	..	..	..	..	1
Sclerosis of Spine	..	..	..	..	..	..	..	..	..	1	..	..	1
Stomatitis Aphthosa	..	..	..	..	..	..	..	..	..	1	..	1	2
Spina Bifida	..	..	..	..	..	..	..	..	..	..	..	1	1
Tabes Mesenterica	2	..	1	..	1	1	..	1	2	7	3	3	21
Tetanus	3	1	1	2	4	4	23	5	1	3	3	3	53
Tumor, Mammary	1	..	..	..	..	..	..	..	..	..	..	..	1
Tumor, Ovarian	1	..	2	..	..	1	3	..	..	..	..	..	7
Tumor, Brain	..	1	..	..	..	..	..	..	..	..	1	..	2
Tumor, Chest	..	..	1	..	..	..	..	..	..	..	..	..	1
Tumor, Malignant	..	..	..	..	1	1	..	..	..	..	..	..	2
Tumor, Super Peritoneal	..	..	..	..	1	..	..	..	..	..	..	..	1
Tumor, Sub Peritoneal	..	..	..	..	..	1	..	..	..	..	..	..	1
Thrombosis Cerebral	1	..	..	..	..	..	..	..	..	..	..	2	3
Thrombrosis, Left Femoral Artery	..	..	..	..	..	1	..	..	..	..	..	..	1
Trismus Nascentium	..	1	..	..	1	2	4	4	1	4	6	4	27
Tuberculous Mesenterica	..	..	1	..	..	..	..	..	..	..	..	..	1
Toxæmia	..	..	1	..	..	..	..	..	..	..	..	..	1
Tuberculous Diathesis	..	..	..	..	..	..	..	..	1	..	..	..	1
Tumor of Abdomen	..	..	..	..	..	..	..	..	..	1	..	..	1
Thrush	..	..	..	..	..	..	..	..	..	1	..	..	1
Tumor of Stomach	..	..	..	..	..	..	..	..	..	..	1	..	1
Uræmia	2	2	3	..	3	..	..	3	1	6	3	5	28
Uræmic Apoplexy	..	..	..	..	..	..	..	..	1	..	..	..	1
Uræmic Convulsions	..	..	..	..	..	..	..	..	1	1	1	..	3

TABLE No. 1—Continued.

CAUSES OF DEATH.	January.	February.	March.	April.	May.	June.	July.	August.	September.	October.	November.	December.	Totals.
Unknown Adults	1	1	..	3	2	..	3	3	1	..	2	1	17
Unknown Infants	4	3	3	7	4	1	3	1	5	5	3	2	41
Ulcer of Leg	..	1	..	..	..	..	..	..	..	..	..	1	2
Ulcer of Stomach	..	..	..	..	1	..	..	..	..	..	..	..	1
Ulcer of Bowels	..	..	..	..	..	1	..	..	1	..	..	..	2
Ulcer of Throat	..	..	..	..	..	..	1	..	..	..	..	..	1
Ulcer of Chronic	..	..	..	1	..	..	..	..	..	..	..	..	1
Ulcer of Duodenum	..	..	..	..	..	..	..	..	..	1	..	..	1
Ulcer of Uterus	..	..	..	..	..	..	..	..	..	..	1	..	1
Varicella	1	..	..	..	..	1	..	..	..	..	..	..	2
Vesicular Emphysema	..	2	..	..	..	..	..	..	..	..	..	..	2
Whooping Cough	5	11	4	7	1	8	10	13	14	8	6	6	93
Wounds	5	5	5	2	4	4	12	8	9	6	1	4	65
Waxy Liver	..	..	..	..	1	..	..	..	..	..	..	..	1
Grand Total	762	615	6.4	714	581	537	1,116	792	757	855	639	834	8,816

TABLE No. 1—Continued.

AGES.	January.	February.	March.	April.	May.	June.	July.	August.	September.	October.	November.	December.	Totals.
Under 1 year	172	117	136	154	134	181	475	276	210	218	119	172	2364
Between 1 and 2 years	58	45	56	57	52	46	137	94	96	84	72	72	864
" 2 and 5 "	79	41	43	52	41	36	58	46	66	87	66	80	691
Total under 5 years	304	203	235	263	227	263	670	416	372	389	253	324	3919
Between 5 and 10 years	59	56	37	49	51	33	52	43	51	75	65	94	665
" 10 and 15 "	24	12	15	9	9	13	33	25	17	15	19	6	197
" 15 and 20 "	26	19	18	18	11	17	21	29	22	27	16	23	247
" 20 and 30 "	72	59	64	56	52	37	58	62	65	85	55	78	743
" 30 and 40 "	51	50	50	72	38	39	56	48	56	56	50	81	647
" 40 and 50 "	44	44	35	47	48	31	51	38	42	35	43	49	507
" 50 and 60 "	47	64	48	55	47	35	48	40	42	58	46	59	589
" 60 and 70 "	68	44	54	65	44	45	61	36	85	52	37	55	596
" 70 and 80 "	41	45	42	55	39	14	41	37	39	29	45	45	482
" 80 and 90 "	21	15	10	22	13	9	24	18	13	21	7	16	184
" 90 and 100 "	5	3	4	3	2	1	..	5	3	3	3	4	36
" 100 and 110 "		1	2	..	..	..	1	..	..	..	..	..	4
Totals	762	615	614	714	581	537	1116	792	757	855	639	834	8816
NATIVITY.													
United States—White	484	360	314	414	340	318	690	477	469	550	394	513	5353
" " Colored	168	159	181	178	128	134	286	214	182	163	127	177	2097
Foreign	110	96	89	122	113	85	140	101	106	142	118	144	1366
Totals	762	615	614	714	581	537	1116	792	757	855	639	834	8816

Still Births	68	49	60	69	36	47	67	40	46	59	45	65	651
White.													
Males	287	237	221	251	225	211	452	294	290	336	274	324	3402
Females	307	219	212	285	228	192	378	284	285	356	238	333	3317
Colored													
Males	66	80	88	85	65	74	137	102	80	77	57	97	1008
Females	102	79	93	93	63	60	149	112	102	86	70	80	1089
Totals	762	615	614	714	581	537	1116	792	757	855	639	834	8816
Marriages	261	286	209	292	260	284	211	260	271	306	370	352	3452
Births	824	660	587	650	583	565	834	710	715	938	637	804	8507

Estimated population, 393,796. White, 338,384; Colored, 55,412. Death rate per 1000, whole population, 22.37. White, 19.87; Colored, 38.12. Marriage rate per 1000 population, 8.76. Birth rate, 21.06.

TABLE No. 1—Concluded.—*Total Number of Deaths Monthly in each Ward.*

WARDS.	January.	February.	March.	April.	May.	June.	July.	August.	September.	October.	November.	December.	Totals.
First	58	40	41	60	49	31	82	66	63	78	42	58	668
Second	50	39	27	35	35	23	61	48	48	52	30	41	489
Third	26	16	14	21	42	22	47	32	27	42	25	22	336
Fourth	21	16	17	17	17	22	26	20	11	21	29	16	226
Fifth	32	31	26	46	20	22	42	35	21	26	21	32	354
Sixth	36	32	36	32	24	29	57	35	42	36	27	43	429
Seventh	53	46	53	56	36	38	93	83	80	83	56	71	748
Eighth	19	21	23	29	15	19	44	24	26	29	32	27	308
Ninth	25	17	28	29	24	28	48	22	24	31	23	33	332
Tenth	27	23	17	19	13	16	11	12	18	12	10	24	202
Eleventh	21	21	23	19	17	16	19	18	24	15	14	18	225
Twelfth	24	19	25	26	18	19	40	18	26	24	22	32	293
Thirteenth	23	19	23	17	19	15	33	26	29	25	17	27	273
Fourteenth	40	22	24	30	25	22	37	23	22	29	23	39	336
Fifteenth	36	45	35	40	25	18	73	47	32	38	21	41	451
Sixteenth	58	47	47	58	35	49	72	63	39	43	42	46	599
Seventeenth	36	15	20	40	39	37	66	49	63	82	79	72	598
Eighteenth	65	52	44	47	38	33	82	64	72	70	44	68	679
Nineteenth	64	45	46	46	54	41	111	75	49	74	60	70	735
Twentieth	48	49	45	47	36	37	62	32	41	45	29	54	535
Totals	762	615	614	714	581	537	1116	792	757	855	639	834	8,816

TABLE No. 2.

Deaths from Zymotic and Lung Diseases in each Ward in the City of Baltimore during the year **1881.**

ZYMOTIC DISEASES.	First.	Second	Third.	Fourth.	Fifth.	Sixth.	Seventh.	Eighth.	Ninth.	Tenth.	Eleventh.	Twelfth.	Thirteenth	Fourteenth.	Fifteenth.	Sixteenth.	Seventeenth.	Eighteenth.	Nineteenth.	Twentieth.
Small Pox	1	..	..	.	..	..	..	..	..	..		..	2	1		1		..	4	2
Measles	1	6	1	3	..	2	6	1	2	..	4	2	3	..	5	3	9	10	9	1
Scarlet Fever	10	2	2	8	14	28	30	17	7	5	1	7	4	9	6	17	5	18	22	7
Diphtheria	49	31	14	12	16	39	64	7	9	3	4	9	8	15	30	78	145	42	30	26
Croup	27	18	11	7	6	13	34	10	3	..	2	8	4	8	6	18	22	22	10	13
Whooping **Cough**	3	1	5	2	2	4	1	6	3	1	6	5	1	..	6	3	2	9	14	5
Typhus Fever	..	..	..	..	..	1	..	1	..	..	..	..	..	..	..	..	..	..	..	1
Typhoid Fever	14	21	11	2	6	8	21	1	6	5	4	8	8	7	11	11	13	23	9	11
Cholera Infantum	44	43	31	15	8	22	13	18	14	5	11	12	16	14	37	40	44	50	63	24
Cholera Morbus	2	6	1	..	3	1	1	1	3	1	..	1	..	..	1	8	2	..	1	1
Remittent Fever	3	..	..	..	..	1	3	..	1	..	1	1	1	..	1	1	1	..	2	..
Intermittent Fever	1	1	1	..	..	..	..	2	1	..	..	1	..	..	1	..	1	2	..	..
Malarial Fever	3	3	4	2	3	1	3	6	..	..	..		..	1	3	1	5	4	5	..
Typho-Malarial **Fever**	5	3	1	..	..	1	9	3	2	3	1	1	2	2	6	2	4	3	3	..
Puerperal Fever	1	1	..	..	1	.	2	2	1	..	..	1	..	1	1	1	3	..	..	..
Diarrhœa	7	11	1	3	..	1	10	..	12	2	1	2	1	2	4	3	7	7	10	8
Dysentery	6	1	3	1	2	1	7	5	3	1	..	1	1	3	3	3	8	3	3	..
Tonsilitis	..	..	..	..	1	..	..	..	..	..	..	..	..	..	..	..	..	..	..	..
Erysipelas	3	2	1	3	2	..	2	..	1	3	..	1	1	..	..	..	3	2	4	..
Pyemia	3	..	1	2	1	1	1	..	1	..	..	..	..	2	..	..	2	3	..	1
Septicæmia	1	1	.	..	..	..	4	2	2	.	..	1	5	2	1	..	..	1	1	1
Entero Colitis	2	2	3	..	1	..	4	1	6	1	2	2	..	3	..	2	1	4	3	4
Cerebro Spinal Meningitis	8	1	2	2	1	3	6	2	1	1	..	..	..	..	..		3	..	..	3
Totals	194	157	93	62	67	127	251	82	78	31	37	63	57	70	122	192	280	203	193	108

METEOROLOGICAL SUMMARY FOR THE YEAR 1881.

PRESSURE.

Mean Barometer..............30,066 inches, or nearly normal.
Highest " ....30,869 " on February 7.
Lowest " ... .29,036 " on March 30.
Range of " .... 1,833 "

TEMPERATURE.

Mean Thermometer...........57.1 degrees, or 1.3 degrees above normal.
Highest " ....101 " on September 7.
Lowest " .... 6 " below zero, on January 1.
Mean Winter (1880-'81) Temperature, 32.4 degrees—about 10 degrees below that of 1879-'80.
Mean Spring............ ....54.0 degrees.
Mean Summer.......................75.6 degrees.
Mean Autumn.......................63.0 degrees, about 7 degrees above normal.

RAINFALL.

Rain or snow fell on 159 days, measuring 49.12 inches—an increase of 7,22 inches over last year, and an excess of 7.12 inches above the normal. The wettest month was March, with 7.59 inches of rainfall; the driest, July, with 1.40 inches.

WINDS.

Prevailing direction of wind, west to northwest.
Highest velocity of wind, 28 miles per hour, February 23.
Mean velocity of wind, 5.6 miles per hour.
Total movement of wind, 48.844 miles.

HUMIDITY, ETC.

Mean Relative Humidity, 66.0 per cent.
First frost of season, October 6.
First ice, November 25.

Births Recorded for the Year Ending December 31, 1881.

January	824	
February	660	
March	587	
April	650	
May	583	
June	565	
July	834	
August	710	
September	715	
October	983	
November	687	
December	804	
		8,507

Deaths recorded for the year ending December 31, 1881............. 8,816
Still-births recorded for the year ending December 31, 1881.......... 651

Unknown Dead Recorded for the Year Ending December 31, 1881.

Unknown men	5
Unknown children	7

Transcripts from the Records of Births for the Year Ending December 31, 1881.

For litigation	1
For family record	1

Transcripts from the Records of Deaths for the Year Ending December 31, 1881.

For life policies of insurance	26
For army pension claims	25
To go to Germany to prove death	15
To go to Russia to prove death	1
To go to England to prove death	2
To go to Washington, D. C., U. S., to prove death	1
To go to City Court for litigation	1
For divorce case	1
For family record	7
For other purposes	3
	84

Tables for 1882.

TABLE No. 1

SMALL POX.

Whole number of Cases in each Ward reported each week, from the 1st of January, 1882, to the 1st of July, 1882; how many sent to Hospital, Died and Recovered.

CASES REPORTED	WARDS.																				Total.	Hospital.	Died.	Remained in City.
	First.	Second.	Third.	Fourth.	Fifth.	Sixth.	Seventh.	Eighth.	Ninth.	Tenth.	Eleventh.	Twelfth.	Thirteenth.	Fourteenth.	Fifteenth.	Sixteenth.	Seventeenth.	Eighteenth.	Nineteenth.	Twentieth.				
Week ending January 7	..			..		..	..	..	1		..	..	..	..	..	1	..	..	..	1	3	3	..	..
" " " 14	..			..		..	..	..	..		..	..	..	..	..	..	..	..	2	1	3	1	..	2
" " " 21	2			..		..	..	..	..	..	..	1	..	..	..	2	..	1	5	1	12	9	1	2
" " " 28	..			..	..	..	2	..	1	..	..	2	..	1	5	2	..	..	8	1	22	19	1	2
" " February 4	..			..	..	..	..	..	..	..	..	..	1	..	4	4	..	..	8	..	17	18	1	..
" " " 11	1		..	..	..	..	3	..	2	..	..	..	..	1	2	9	1	..	2	..	21	13	2	6
" " " 18	..		..	..	..	..	..	..	..	..	..	..	1	..	..	1	2	2	2	..	8	4	..	4
" " " 25	..		..	..	..	..	..	..	..	..	..	..	..	..	1	2	..	..	6	..	9	2	3	4
" " March 4	..		1	..	..	..	..	..	4	..	..	..	..	..	2	1	..	1	..	..	9	[illegible]	3	..
" " " 11	2		..	1	..	..	..	..	..	..	..	..	1	..	1	1	..	3	3	..	12	9	2	1
" " " 18	..		..	..	..	..	1	..	..	..	..	..	..	..	1	3	1	6	1	..	13	7	1	5
" " " 25	..		..	..	..	..	..	..	..	..	..	..	..	..	..	2	..	8	..	1	6	9	4	..
" " April 1	..		..	..	..	..	..	..	..	..	..	..	..	..	..	..	..	2	..	..	2	..	1	1
" " " 8	..		1	..	..	1	..	..	1	..	..	..	..	..	3	8	1	2	..	1	21	11	1	10
" " " 15	..		..	..	..	2	..	..	..	..	..	..	..	..	2	2	2	..	..	1	9	6	3	..

Week ending April 22..........	2	1	1	1	..	4	1	..	1	..	..	..	..	..	3	1	3	1	..	2	21	13	3	5
" " " 29..........	1	1	1	..	1	4	..	..	..	1	.	..	..	1	..	..	13	2	1	..	26	7	5	14
" " May 6..........	..	3	..	1	..	1	..	..	..	..	1	3	..	..	5	4	1	2	..	..	21	7	3	11
" " " 13..........	1	3	..	..	..	1	..	..	..	..	..	..	..	..	3	..	12	..	..	..	20	3	7	10
" " " 20..........	3	1	5	2	..	6	..	..	..	1	..	..	..	3	3	2	9	1	..	..	36	9	4	23
" " " 27..........	..	..	12	..	..	2	..	..	1	1	..	..	..	..	1	..	5	3	..	..	25	7	3	15
" " June 3..........	..	3	..	..	..	3	..	..	..	3	..	..	..	..	4	..	3	1	..	..	17	6	1	10
" " " 10..........	..	2	4	..	..	2	..	..	1	1	1	2	..	..	3	2	1	..	..	..	19	4	3	12
" " " 17..........	2	3	9	..	..	4	..	..	..	..	1	.	..	1	3	..	2	..	.	..	25	6	5	13
" " " 24..........	1	3	3	..	..	4	..	..	..	1	..	..	..	..	..	1	1	..	1	..	15	4	4	7
Totals for six months.........	15	20	37	5	1	34	7	..	15	8	3	8	3	7	46	48	57	30	39	9	391	184	61	157

TABLE No. 1.—Concluded.

SMALL POX.

Whole number of Cases in each Ward reported each week, from the 1st of July ***to the 31st*** *of December, 1882; how* ***many sent to Hospital, Died and Recovered.***

Cases Reported.	Wards.																				Total.	Hospital.	Died.	Remained in City.
	First.	Second.	Third.	Fourth.	Fifth.	Sixth.	Seventh.	Eighth.	Ninth.	Tenth.	Eleventh.	Twelfth.	Thirteenth.	Fourteenth.	Fifteenth.	Sixteenth.	Seventeenth.	Eighteenth.	Nineteenth.	Twentieth.				
Totals brought forward	15	20	37	5	1	34	7	..	15	8	3	8	3	7	46	48	57	30	39	9	391	184	61	157
Week ending July 1	9	1	9	..	..	3	..	..	3	4	..	..	..	..	7	4	3	..	1	..	44	5	4	35
" " " 8	3	..	1	..	3	..	..	..	..	..	..	..	..	..	3	2	3	..	..	1	16	18	6	..
" " " 15	5	2	4	..	..	3	..	..	1	..	..	..	..	..	1	..	1	..	..	..	18	4	2	12
" " " 22	23	4	1	..	1	2	..	..	1	1	..	..	..	..	2	..	..	..	..	..	35	5	3	27
" " " 29	10	1	5	..	2	1	..	..	..	..	..	..	..	..	11	..	..	..	1	..	31	5	8	18
" " Aug. 5	5	8	7	1	..	6	2	..	..	2	..	..	..	..	2	..	..	..	..	..	33	9	2	22
" " " 12	9	7	3	15	5	2	1	..	2	..	..	..	..	..	6	..	1	..	..	..	51	15	6	30
" " " 19	23	4	3	1	3	6	..	..	..	..	..	..	..	..	14	..	..	..	..	..	54	11	10	33
" " " 26	17	14	5	1	8	..	..	..	..	..	..	..	..	..	6	..	2	..	..	..	53	11	6	36
" " Sept. 2	22	15	8	1	2	5	..	..	2	..	..	..	..	..	6	1	..	..	..	..	62	10	15	37
" " " 9	13	21	9	1	2	7	..	..	..	..	..	..	..	1	8	..	1	1	..	..	64	9	17	38
" " " 16	27	18	7	..	..	4	..	..	..	..	..	..	..	..	7	..	..	1	..	..	64	19	14	31
" " " 23	17	14	5	..	2	4	..	..	1	..	..	..	..	..	11	..	..	..	..	..	54	16	15	23
" " " 30	14	15	14	1	1	..	..	1	1	..	..	..	..	..	13	..	..	..	..	1	63	10	10	43

Week ending Oct. 7	23	11	3	1	1	2	2	..	..	..	..	1	..	..	17	..	1	1	..	1	64	27	16	21
" " " 14	41	34	4	..	..	3	..	..	..	..	..	..	..	..	8	1	6	..	..	..	97	6	12	79
" " " 21	31	29	6	..	..	6	5	..	..	..	..	..	..	..	9	..	2	5	..	..	93	13	22	58
" " " 28	15	31	3	1	..	12	4	..	..	..	..	..	..	..	9	1	5	..	..	..	81	12	13	56
" " Nov. 4	10	35	1	..	..	6	2	..	2	..	..	..	..	..	9	..	6	2	..	..	73	9	21	43
" " " 11	31	29	11	..	1	7	5	..	..	..	..	..	..	..	8	4	12	4	..	..	112	12	20	80
" " " 18	25	33	4	..	1	12	2	1	1	..	..	..	1	..	14	2	9	6	..	..	111	26	32	53
" " " 25	32	30	14	1	1	5	6	..	2	..	..	1	1	..	7	7	32	2	..	..	141	27	21	93
" " Dec. 2	32	27	2	1	3	20	7	..	2	..	1	..	..	2	9	3	17	1	..	..	127	23	25	79
" " " 9	44	38	10	1	5	5	4	1	1	2	..	2	..	1	12	10	16	8	..	..	160	29	23	108
" " " 16	39	53	16	4	9	27	5	..	2	1	..	..	1	4	12	16	18	11	1	..	219	47	41	121
" " " 23	34	73	8	5	5	17	7	2	1	1	..	..	..	..	6	3	15	20	..	1	198	27	57	114
" " " 30	45	75	30	10	7	16	6	2	5	2	1	..	4	10	20	14	30	31	2	5	315	69	71	175
Total for 12 months	614	642	230	50	63	215	65	7	42	21	5	12	10	25	283	116	237	126	44	18	2825	658	551	1616

TABLE No. 2.

SMALL POX.

A Table showing the number of Cases and Infected Houses in each Ward, under care of this Department at the end of each week, from July 1st, to September 30th, 1882.

Week Ending.	Wards.																				Totals.
	First.	Second.	Third.	Fourth.	Fifth.	Sixth.	Seventh.	Eighth.	Ninth.	Tenth.	Eleventh.	Twelfth.	Thirteenth.	Fourteenth.	Fifteenth.	Sixteenth.	Seventeenth.	Eighteenth.	Nineteenth.	Twentieth.	
July 8—Cases	6	2	5	..	3	5	..	..	2	2			..	..	5	4	3	..	2	..	39
Houses	5	1	4	..	3	4	..	..	1	1			..	..	4	4	3	..	1	..	31
July 15—Cases ..	8	2	7	..	3	3	..	..	1	..			..	..	7	5	4	..	..	..	40
Houses	7	1	6	..	3	3	..	..	1	..		..	..	..	6	5	4	..	..	..	36
July 22—Cases	25	5	5	..	3	4	..	..	2	1		..	..	..	4	4	2	..	..	..	55
Houses	20	3	4	..	2	3	..	..	1	1		..	..	..	3	3	1	..	..	..	41
July 29—Cases	28	3	5	..	3	2	..	..	1	1		..	..	..	12	2	1	..	..	..	59
Houses....	20	2	4	..	3	2	..	..	1	1		..	..	..	8	1	1	..	..	..	46
Aug. 5—Cases	20	6	5	1	..	6	2	..	..	2		..	..	..	8	..	1	..	..	..	54
Houses....	18	5	5	1	..	5	1	..	..	1		..	..	..	7	..	1	..	..	..	44
Aug. 12—Cases	18	6	4	16	4	4	1	..	2	1		..	..	..	7	..	..	..	..	..	63
Houses ...	15	4	3	15	3	2	1	..	2	1		..	..	..	5	..	..	..	..	..	51
Aug. 19—Cases	32	6	6	5	5	3	..	..	..	2		..	..	..	5	..	1	..	..	..	65
Houses....	19	4	6	4	5	2	..	..	..	1		..	..	..	4	..	1	..	..	..	46
Aug. 26—Cases	28	10	8	3	10	6	..	..	2	..		..	..	..	..	..	4	1	..	..	72

Houses....	23	6	7	3	8	5	..	..	1	..	..		..	..	..	..	3	1	..	..	57
Sept. 2—Cases.....	35	13	9	2	6	7	..	..	2	..	..		..	..	6	..	2	..	..	..	82
Houses....	23	11	8	1	5	5	..	..	1	..	..		..	..	5	..	1	..	..	..	60
Sept. 9—Cases.....	33	19	4	2	3	12	..	..	1	..	..		..	1	10	1	2	..	..	..	88
Houses....	25	14	3	2	2	7	..	..	1	..	..		..	1	7	1	2	..	..	..	65
Sept. 16—Cases.....	21	20	5	..	..	10	..	..	..	..	..		..	..	10	..	..	1	..	..	67
Houses....	15	4	4	..	..	8	..	..	..	..	..		..	..	8	..	..	1	..	..	50
Sept. 23—Cases.....	20	20	8	..	2	6	..	..	1	..	..		..	..	16	..	..	..	..	..	73
Houses....	18	17	7	..	1	5	..	..	1	..	..		..	..	13	..		..	..	..	62
Sept. 30—Cases.....	18	17	16	1	1	2	..	1	1	..	..		..	..	18	..			..	1	76
Houses ..	17	15	14	1	1	1	..	1	1	..	..		..	..	16	..			..	1	68

TABLE No. 2—Concluded.

SMALL POX.

A Table showing the number of Cases and Infected Houses in each Ward, under care of this Department at the end of each week, from October 7th to December 31st, 1882.

WEEK ENDING.	WARDS.																				
	First.	Second.	Third.	Fourth.	Fifth.	Sixth.	Seventh.	Eighth.	Ninth.	Tenth.	Eleventh.	Twelfth.	Thirteenth.	Fourteenth.	Fifteenth.	Sixteenth.	Seventeenth.	Eighteenth.	Nineteenth.	Twentieth.	Totals.
Oct. 7—Cases	23	25	9	..	1	2	1	..	..	..	..	..	..	..	21	..	1	3	..	..	80
Houses....	16	17	8	.	1	2	1	..	..	..	..	..	..	..	14	..	1	2	..	..	56
Oct. 14—Cases	42	41	5	..	..	4	1	..	..	..	..	..	..	..	16	..	5	1	..	..	115
Houses....	29	28	5	..	..	3	1	..	..	..	..	..	..	..	11	..	2	1	..	..	80
Oct. 21—Cases	52	35	5	..	..	9	6	..	..	..	..	..	..	..	11	..	6	5	..	..	129
Houses....	40	22	4	..	..	8	4	..	..	..	..	..	..	..	10	..	3	3	..	..	94
Oct. 28—Cases	58	38	6	..	1	19	8	..	..	..	..	..	..	..	9	2	7	4	..	..	152
Houses....	42	28	5	..	1	15	5	..	..	..	..	..	..	..	5	2	4	2	..	..	109
Nov. 4—Cases	44	40	12	..	..	15	8	..	2	..	..	..	..	..	9	..	8	6	..	..	144
Houses....	35	35	10	..	..	10	6	..	1	..	..	..	..	..	7	..	8	6	..	..	118
Nov. 11—Cases	36	42	16	..	1	11	10	..	..	..	..	..	..	..	7	..	15	9	..	..	147
Houses....	24	31	12	..	1	8	10	..	..	..	..	..	..	..	6	..	15	7	..	..	114
Nov. 18—Cases	33	44	5	..	2	11	7	..	..	..	..	..	..	..	15	4	17	5	..	..	143
Houses....	27	35	5	..	2	10	7	..	..	..	..	..	..	..	14	3	17	3	..	..	123
Nov. 25—Cases	43	61	8	1	3	8	8	..	..	..	..	1	1	..	16	6	30	1	..	..	187

Houses....	28	44	6	1	2	8	6	..	..	..	..	1	1	..	15	6	20	1	..	..	139
Dec. 2—Cases	41	74	9	1	5	15	8	..	..	..	..	1	1	2	11	8	33	1	..	..	210
Houses ..	28	51	7	1	2	11	5	..	..	..	..	1	1	2	11	8	24	1	..	..	153
Dec. 9—Cases	60	78	13	3	5	20	8	1	1	2	1	2	..	2	12	12	35	15	..	..	270
Houses....	45	55	10	2	3	16	6	1	1	1	1	1	..	1	10	10	30	12	..	..	205
Dec. 16—Cases	60	78	16	2	6	37	9	..	..	1	..	2	1	4	14	15	39	18	..	..	302
Houses....	45	55	13	2	5	26	7	..	..	1	..	2	1	4	12	13	30	15	..	..	231
Dec. 23—Cases	70	115	15	7	3	30	9	2	1	2	..	3	..	1	10	10	14	17	..	..	309
Houses....	53	74	10	6	3	24	8	2	1	2	..	3	..	1	10	9	12	15	..	..	233
Dec. 31—Cases	75	118	25	8	9	35	11	1	2	2	..	2	..	3	18	13	35	32	..	4	394
Houses....	59	75	19	6	7	29	9	1	1	2	..	2	..	3	18	13	24	22	..	5	294

TABLE No. 3.

SMALL POX.

Whole number of Cases reported from January 1, 1882, *to July* 1, 1882, *per week and month; color, age, sex; vaccinated and not vaccinated.*

CASES REPORTED.	Per week.	Per month.	COLOR.		SEX.		AGE.		Vaccinated.	Not vaccinated.
			White.	Black.	Male.	Female.	Adult.	Minor.		
January 7	3	46	1	2	1	2	1	2	2	1
" 14	3		1	2	1	2	1	2	1	2
" 21	12		6	6	7	5	6	6	6	6
" 31	28		3	25	15	13	10	18	16	12
February 4	11	53	4	7	6	5	4	7	6	5
" 11	21		9	12	14	7	12	9	14	7
" 18	8		5	3	4	4	5	3	3	5
" 28	13		4	9	10	3	3	10	9	4
March 11	17	38	8	9	7	10	8	9	8	9
" 18	13		7	6	9	4	7	6	3	10
" 25	6		1	5	5	1	4	2	3	3
" 31	2		1	1	..	2	..	2	1	1
April 8	21	78	11	10	13	8	12	9	10	11
" 15	9		3	6	6	3	3	6	3	6
" 22	21		13	8	9	12	11	10	8	13
" 30	27		22	5	12	15	7	20	12	15

May	6	20	107	12	8	8	12	9	11	9	11
"	13	19		18	1	12	7	4	15	12	7
"	20	38		24	14	20	18	5	23	28	10
"	31	30		19	11	20	10	11	19	20	10
June	10	31	106	14	17	11	20	7	24	20	11
"	17	24		19	5	13	11	6	18	7	17
"	24	15		10	5	5	10	5	10	7	8
"	30	36		8	28	18	18	9	27	16	20
Totals for six months		428	423	223	205	226	202	150	278	224	204

TABLE No. 3—Concluded.

SMALL POX.

Whole number of Cases reported from July 1st to December 31, 1882, per week and month; the color, sex, age, vaccinated and not vaccinated.

CASES REPORTED.	Per week.	Per month.	COLOR.		SEX.		AGE.		Vaccinated.	Not vaccinated.
			White.	Black.	Male.	Female.	Adult.	Minor.		
Totals brought forward	428	428	223	205	226	202	150	278	224	204
July 8	24	114	14	10	13	11	6	18	9	15
" 15	18		13	5	10	8	3	15	7	11
" 22	35		30	5	24	11	7	28	12	23
" 31	37		22	15	21	16	14	23	20	17
August 5	27	237	17	10	16	11	5	22	14	13
" 12	51		30	21	19	32	9	42	27	23
" 19	54		41	13	28	26	10	44	9	35
" 31	105		84	21	56	49	18	87	47	58
September 9	74	255	63	11	39	35	14	60	34	40
" 16	64		50	14	31	33	16	48	36	28
" 23	54		40	14	27	27	10	44	32	22
" 30	63		49	14	31	32	13	50	44	19
October 7	65	362	52	13	31	34	35	30	40	25
" 14	96		86	10	50	46	9	87	57	39
" 21	93		76	17	44	49	25	68	57	36
" 31	108		89	19	59	49	25	83	50	58

Nov
"
"
"
Dec
"
"
"

TABLE No. 4.

SMALL-POX.

Total Number of Deaths Monthly in each Ward—Adult, Minor, Male and Female.

WHITE.

1868.	January.				February.				March.				April.				May.				June.				July.				August.				September.				October.				November.				December.				Totals.				
AGE.	Adult.		Minor.		Adult.		Minor.		Adult.		Minor.		Adult.		Minor.		Adult.		Minor.		Adult.		Minor.		Adult.		Minor.		Adult.		Minor.		Adult.		Minor.		Adult.		Minor.		Adult.		Minor.		Adult.		Minor.		Adult.		Minor.		
SEX.	Male.	Female.	Male.	Female.	Male.	Female.	Male.	Female.	Male.	Female.	Male.	Female.	Male.	Female.	Male.	Female.	Male.	Female.	Male.	Female.	Male.	Female.	Male.	Female.	Male.	Female.	Male.	Female.	Male.	Female.	Male.	Female.	Male.	Female.	Male.	Female.	Male.	Female.	Male.	Female.	Male.	Female.	Male.	Female.	Male.	Female.	Male.	Female.	Male.	Female.	Male.	Female.	Grand Total.
First Ward	[illegible]	[illegible]	[illegible]	[illegible]	[illegible]	[illegible]	[illegible]	[illegible]	[illegible]	[illegible]	[illegible]	[illegible]	[illegible]	[illegible]	[illegible]	[illegible]	[illegible]	[illegible]	[illegible]	[illegible]	[illegible]	[illegible]	[illegible]	[illegible]	[illegible]	[illegible]	[illegible]	[illegible]	[illegible]	[illegible]	[illegible]	[illegible]	[illegible]	[illegible]	[illegible]	[illegible]	[illegible]	[illegible]	[illegible]	[illegible]	[illegible]	[illegible]	[illegible]	[illegible]	[illegible]	[illegible]	[illegible]	[illegible]	[illegible]	[illegible]	[illegible]	[illegible]	[illegible]
Second Ward	[illegible]	[illegible]	[illegible]	[illegible]	[illegible]	[illegible]	[illegible]	[illegible]	[illegible]	[illegible]	[illegible]	[illegible]	[illegible]	[illegible]	[illegible]	[illegible]	[illegible]	[illegible]	[illegible]	[illegible]	[illegible]	[illegible]	[illegible]	[illegible]	[illegible]	[illegible]	[illegible]	[illegible]	[illegible]	[illegible]	[illegible]	[illegible]	[illegible]	[illegible]	[illegible]	[illegible]	[illegible]	[illegible]	[illegible]	[illegible]	[illegible]	[illegible]	[illegible]	[illegible]	[illegible]	[illegible]	[illegible]	[illegible]	[illegible]	[illegible]	[illegible]	[illegible]	[illegible]
Third Ward	[illegible]	[illegible]	[illegible]	[illegible]	[illegible]	[illegible]	[illegible]	[illegible]	[illegible]	[illegible]	[illegible]	[illegible]	[illegible]	[illegible]	[illegible]	[illegible]	[illegible]	[illegible]	[illegible]	[illegible]	[illegible]	[illegible]	[illegible]	[illegible]	[illegible]	[illegible]	[illegible]	[illegible]	[illegible]	[illegible]	[illegible]	[illegible]	[illegible]	[illegible]	[illegible]	[illegible]	[illegible]	[illegible]	[illegible]	[illegible]	[illegible]	[illegible]	[illegible]	[illegible]	[illegible]	[illegible]	[illegible]	[illegible]	[illegible]	[illegible]	[illegible]	[illegible]	[illegible]
Fourth Ward	[illegible]	[illegible]	[illegible]	[illegible]	[illegible]	[illegible]	[illegible]	[illegible]	[illegible]	[illegible]	[illegible]	[illegible]	[illegible]	[illegible]	[illegible]	[illegible]	[illegible]	[illegible]	[illegible]	[illegible]	[illegible]	[illegible]	[illegible]	[illegible]	[illegible]	[illegible]	[illegible]	[illegible]	[illegible]	[illegible]	[illegible]	[illegible]	[illegible]	[illegible]	[illegible]	[illegible]	[illegible]	[illegible]	[illegible]	[illegible]	[illegible]	[illegible]	[illegible]	[illegible]	[illegible]	[illegible]	[illegible]	[illegible]	[illegible]	[illegible]	[illegible]	[illegible]	[illegible]
Fifth Ward	[illegible]	[illegible]	[illegible]	[illegible]	[illegible]	[illegible]	[illegible]	[illegible]	[illegible]	[illegible]	[illegible]	[illegible]	[illegible]	[illegible]	[illegible]	[illegible]	[illegible]	[illegible]	[illegible]	[illegible]	[illegible]	[illegible]	[illegible]	[illegible]	[illegible]	[illegible]	[illegible]	[illegible]	[illegible]	[illegible]	[illegible]	[illegible]	[illegible]	[illegible]	[illegible]	[illegible]	[illegible]	[illegible]	[illegible]	[illegible]	[illegible]	[illegible]	[illegible]	[illegible]	[illegible]	[illegible]	[illegible]	[illegible]	[illegible]	[illegible]	[illegible]	[illegible]	[illegible]
Sixth Ward	[illegible]	[illegible]	[illegible]	[illegible]	[illegible]	[illegible]	[illegible]	[illegible]	[illegible]	[illegible]	[illegible]	[illegible]	[illegible]	[illegible]	[illegible]	[illegible]	[illegible]	[illegible]	[illegible]	[illegible]	[illegible]	[illegible]	[illegible]	[illegible]	[illegible]	[illegible]	[illegible]	[illegible]	[illegible]	[illegible]	[illegible]	[illegible]	[illegible]	[illegible]	[illegible]	[illegible]	[illegible]	[illegible]	[illegible]	[illegible]	[illegible]	[illegible]	[illegible]	[illegible]	[illegible]	[illegible]	[illegible]	[illegible]	[illegible]	[illegible]	[illegible]	[illegible]	[illegible]
Seventh Ward	[illegible]	[illegible]	[illegible]	[illegible]	[illegible]	[illegible]	[illegible]	[illegible]	[illegible]	[illegible]	[illegible]	[illegible]	[illegible]	[illegible]	[illegible]	[illegible]	[illegible]	[illegible]	[illegible]	[illegible]	[illegible]	[illegible]	[illegible]	[illegible]	[illegible]	[illegible]	[illegible]	[illegible]	[illegible]	[illegible]	[illegible]	[illegible]	[illegible]	[illegible]	[illegible]	[illegible]	[illegible]	[illegible]	[illegible]	[illegible]	[illegible]	[illegible]	[illegible]	[illegible]	[illegible]	[illegible]	[illegible]	[illegible]	[illegible]	[illegible]	[illegible]	[illegible]	[illegible]
Eighth Ward	[illegible]	[illegible]	[illegible]	[illegible]	[illegible]	[illegible]	[illegible]	[illegible]	[illegible]	[illegible]	[illegible]	[illegible]	[illegible]	[illegible]	[illegible]	[illegible]	[illegible]	[illegible]	[illegible]	[illegible]	[illegible]	[illegible]	[illegible]	[illegible]	[illegible]	[illegible]	[illegible]	[illegible]	[illegible]	[illegible]	[illegible]	[illegible]	[illegible]	[illegible]	[illegible]	[illegible]	[illegible]	[illegible]	[illegible]	[illegible]	[illegible]	[illegible]	[illegible]	[illegible]	[illegible]	[illegible]	[illegible]	[illegible]	[illegible]	[illegible]	[illegible]	[illegible]	[illegible]
Ninth Ward	[illegible]	[illegible]	[illegible]	[illegible]	[illegible]	[illegible]	[illegible]	[illegible]	[illegible]	[illegible]	[illegible]	[illegible]	[illegible]	[illegible]	[illegible]	[illegible]	[illegible]	[illegible]	[illegible]	[illegible]	[illegible]	[illegible]	[illegible]	[illegible]	[illegible]	[illegible]	[illegible]	[illegible]	[illegible]	[illegible]	[illegible]	[illegible]	[illegible]	[illegible]	[illegible]	[illegible]	[illegible]	[illegible]	[illegible]	[illegible]	[illegible]	[illegible]	[illegible]	[illegible]	[illegible]	[illegible]	[illegible]	[illegible]	[illegible]	[illegible]	[illegible]	[illegible]	[illegible]
Tenth Ward	[illegible]	[illegible]	[illegible]	[illegible]	[illegible]	[illegible]	[illegible]	[illegible]	[illegible]	[illegible]	[illegible]	[illegible]	[illegible]	[illegible]	[illegible]	[illegible]	[illegible]	[illegible]	[illegible]	[illegible]	[illegible]	[illegible]	[illegible]	[illegible]	[illegible]	[illegible]	[illegible]	[illegible]	[illegible]	[illegible]	[illegible]	[illegible]	[illegible]	[illegible]	[illegible]	[illegible]	[illegible]	[illegible]	[illegible]	[illegible]	[illegible]	[illegible]	[illegible]	[illegible]	[illegible]	[illegible]	[illegible]	[illegible]	[illegible]	[illegible]	[illegible]	[illegible]	[illegible]
Eleventh Ward	[illegible]	[illegible]	[illegible]	[illegible]	[illegible]	[illegible]	[illegible]	[illegible]	[illegible]	[illegible]	[illegible]	[illegible]	[illegible]	[illegible]	[illegible]	[illegible]	[illegible]	[illegible]	[illegible]	[illegible]	[illegible]	[illegible]	[illegible]	[illegible]	[illegible]	[illegible]	[illegible]	[illegible]	[illegible]	[illegible]	[illegible]	[illegible]	[illegible]	[illegible]	[illegible]	[illegible]	[illegible]	[illegible]	[illegible]	[illegible]	[illegible]	[illegible]	[illegible]	[illegible]	[illegible]	[illegible]	[illegible]	[illegible]	[illegible]	[illegible]	[illegible]	[illegible]	[illegible]
Twelfth Ward	[illegible]	[illegible]	[illegible]	[illegible]	[illegible]	[illegible]	[illegible]	[illegible]	[illegible]	[illegible]	[illegible]	[illegible]	[illegible]	[illegible]	[illegible]	[illegible]	[illegible]	[illegible]	[illegible]	[illegible]	[illegible]	[illegible]	[illegible]	[illegible]	[illegible]	[illegible]	[illegible]	[illegible]	[illegible]	[illegible]	[illegible]	[illegible]	[illegible]	[illegible]	[illegible]	[illegible]	[illegible]	[illegible]	[illegible]	[illegible]	[illegible]	[illegible]	[illegible]	[illegible]	[illegible]	[illegible]	[illegible]	[illegible]	[illegible]	[illegible]	[illegible]	[illegible]	[illegible]
Thirteenth Ward	[illegible]	[illegible]	[illegible]	[illegible]	[illegible]	[illegible]	[illegible]	[illegible]	[illegible]	[illegible]	[illegible]	[illegible]	[illegible]	[illegible]	[illegible]	[illegible]	[illegible]	[illegible]	[illegible]	[illegible]	[illegible]	[illegible]	[illegible]	[illegible]	[illegible]	[illegible]	[illegible]	[illegible]	[illegible]	[illegible]	[illegible]	[illegible]	[illegible]	[illegible]	[illegible]	[illegible]	[illegible]	[illegible]	[illegible]	[illegible]	[illegible]	[illegible]	[illegible]	[illegible]	[illegible]	[illegible]	[illegible]	[illegible]	[illegible]	[illegible]	[illegible]	[illegible]	[illegible]
Fourteenth Ward	[illegible]	[illegible]	[illegible]	[illegible]	[illegible]	[illegible]	[illegible]	[illegible]	[illegible]	[illegible]	[illegible]	[illegible]	[illegible]	[illegible]	[illegible]	[illegible]	[illegible]	[illegible]	[illegible]	[illegible]	[illegible]	[illegible]	[illegible]	[illegible]	[illegible]	[illegible]	[illegible]	[illegible]	[illegible]	[illegible]	[illegible]	[illegible]	[illegible]	[illegible]	[illegible]	[illegible]	[illegible]	[illegible]	[illegible]	[illegible]	[illegible]	[illegible]	[illegible]	[illegible]	[illegible]	[illegible]	[illegible]	[illegible]	[illegible]	[illegible]	[illegible]	[illegible]	[illegible]
Fifteenth Ward	[illegible]	[illegible]	[illegible]	[illegible]	[illegible]	[illegible]	[illegible]	[illegible]	[illegible]	[illegible]	[illegible]	[illegible]	[illegible]	[illegible]	[illegible]	[illegible]	[illegible]	[illegible]	[illegible]	[illegible]	[illegible]	[illegible]	[illegible]	[illegible]	[illegible]	[illegible]	[illegible]	[illegible]	[illegible]	[illegible]	[illegible]	[illegible]	[illegible]	[illegible]	[illegible]	[illegible]	[illegible]	[illegible]	[illegible]	[illegible]	[illegible]	[illegible]	[illegible]	[illegible]	[illegible]	[illegible]	[illegible]	[illegible]	[illegible]	[illegible]	[illegible]	[illegible]	[illegible]
Sixteenth Ward	[illegible]	[illegible]	[illegible]	[illegible]	[illegible]	[illegible]	[illegible]	[illegible]	[illegible]	[illegible]	[illegible]	[illegible]	[illegible]	[illegible]	[illegible]	[illegible]	[illegible]	[illegible]	[illegible]	[illegible]	[illegible]	[illegible]	[illegible]	[illegible]	[illegible]	[illegible]	[illegible]	[illegible]	[illegible]	[illegible]	[illegible]	[illegible]	[illegible]	[illegible]	[illegible]	[illegible]	[illegible]	[illegible]	[illegible]	[illegible]	[illegible]	[illegible]	[illegible]	[illegible]	[illegible]	[illegible]	[illegible]	[illegible]	[illegible]	[illegible]	[illegible]	[illegible]	[illegible]
Seventeenth Ward	[illegible]	[illegible]	[illegible]	[illegible]	[illegible]	[illegible]	[illegible]	[illegible]	[illegible]	[illegible]	[illegible]	[illegible]	[illegible]	[illegible]	[illegible]	[illegible]	[illegible]	[illegible]	[illegible]	[illegible]	[illegible]	[illegible]	[illegible]	[illegible]	[illegible]	[illegible]	[illegible]	[illegible]	[illegible]	[illegible]	[illegible]	[illegible]	[illegible]	[illegible]	[illegible]	[illegible]	[illegible]	[illegible]	[illegible]	[illegible]	[illegible]	[illegible]	[illegible]	[illegible]	[illegible]	[illegible]	[illegible]	[illegible]	[illegible]	[illegible]	[illegible]	[illegible]	[illegible]
Eighteenth Ward	[illegible]	[illegible]	[illegible]	[illegible]	[illegible]	[illegible]	[illegible]	[illegible]	[illegible]	[illegible]	[illegible]	[illegible]	[illegible]	[illegible]	[illegible]	[illegible]	[illegible]	[illegible]	[illegible]	[illegible]	[illegible]	[illegible]	[illegible]	[illegible]	[illegible]	[illegible]	[illegible]	[illegible]	[illegible]	[illegible]	[illegible]	[illegible]	[illegible]	[illegible]	[illegible]	[illegible]	[illegible]	[illegible]	[illegible]	[illegible]	[illegible]	[illegible]	[illegible]	[illegible]	[illegible]	[illegible]	[illegible]	[illegible]	[illegible]	[illegible]	[illegible]	[illegible]	[illegible]
Nineteenth Ward	[illegible]	[illegible]	[illegible]	[illegible]	[illegible]	[illegible]	[illegible]	[illegible]	[illegible]	[illegible]	[illegible]	[illegible]	[illegible]	[illegible]	[illegible]	[illegible]	[illegible]	[illegible]	[illegible]	[illegible]	[illegible]	[illegible]	[illegible]	[illegible]	[illegible]	[illegible]	[illegible]	[illegible]	[illegible]	[illegible]	[illegible]	[illegible]	[illegible]	[illegible]	[illegible]	[illegible]	[illegible]	[illegible]	[illegible]	[illegible]	[illegible]	[illegible]	[illegible]	[illegible]	[illegible]	[illegible]	[illegible]	[illegible]	[illegible]	[illegible]	[illegible]	[illegible]	[illegible]
Twentieth Ward	[illegible]	[illegible]	[illegible]	[illegible]	[illegible]	[illegible]	[illegible]	[illegible]	[illegible]	[illegible]	[illegible]	[illegible]	[illegible]	[illegible]	[illegible]	[illegible]	[illegible]	[illegible]	[illegible]	[illegible]	[illegible]	[illegible]	[illegible]	[illegible]	[illegible]	[illegible]	[illegible]	[illegible]	[illegible]	[illegible]	[illegible]	[illegible]	[illegible]	[illegible]	[illegible]	[illegible]	[illegible]	[illegible]	[illegible]	[illegible]	[illegible]	[illegible]	[illegible]	[illegible]	[illegible]	[illegible]	[illegible]	[illegible]	[illegible]	[illegible]	[illegible]	[illegible]	[illegible]
Totals	[illegible]	[illegible]	[illegible]	[illegible]	[illegible]	[illegible]	[illegible]	[illegible]	[illegible]	[illegible]	[illegible]	[illegible]	[illegible]	[illegible]	[illegible]	[illegible]	[illegible]	[illegible]	[illegible]	[illegible]	[illegible]	[illegible]	[illegible]	[illegible]	[illegible]	[illegible]	[illegible]	[illegible]	[illegible]	[illegible]	[illegible]	[illegible]	[illegible]	[illegible]	[illegible]	[illegible]	[illegible]	[illegible]	[illegible]	[illegible]	[illegible]	[illegible]	[illegible]	[illegible]	[illegible]	[illegible]	[illegible]	[illegible]	[illegible]	[illegible]	[illegible]	[illegible]	[illegible]

3
48
47
24
105
78
97
117
61

TABLE No. 4.

SMALL-POX.

Total Number of Deaths Monthly in each Ward—Adult, Minor, Male and Female.

COLORED.

November 4	46		43	4	29	17	16	30	7	[illegible]
" 11	112	483	91	21	61	51	28	84	64	48
" 18	111		86	25	52	59	21	90	64	47
" 30	214		16[illegible]	52	117	97	53	161	90	124
December 9	215		172	43	119	96	63	152	107	108
" 16	218	946	162	56	119	99	80	138	145	73
" 23	197		152	45	103	94	41	156	100	97
" 31	316		231	65	170	146	89	227	199	117
Totals for twelve months	2825	2825	2078	747	1495	1330	700	2065	1496	1319

Table No. 5—*Total number of deaths monthly in each Ward from Small-pox.*

Ward.	January.	February.	March.	April.	May.	June.	July.	August.	September.	October.	November.	December.	**Totals.**
First.......	..	..	1	..	..	2	6	11	15	11	26	47	**119**
Second.....	1	..	..	..	3	2	4	8	19	35	42	70	184
Third......	..	..	..	..	..	..	3	1	9	2	2	6	23
Fourth.....	..	..	..	..	..	..	..	2	..	..	..	4	6
Fifth.......	..	..	..	..	..	..	1	3	1	..	..	5	10
Sixth.......	..	..	..	5	2	1	1	1	5	2	8	13	**38**
Seventh....	..	..	..	..	..	..	..	..	1	..	1	4	**6**
Eighth	..	..	..	..	..	..	..	..	..	..	..	..	..
Ninth......	..	..	..	..	..	..	1	1	..	..	..	3	5
Tenth......	..	..	..	..	..	..	..	1	..	..	..	..	**1**
Eleventh ..	..	..	..	..	..	..	..	..	..	1	..	..	**1**
Twelfth....	..	..	..	..	..	1	..	..	..	..	..	..	**1**
Thirteenth..	..	..	..	..	..	..	..	..	1	..	..	2	**3**
Fourteenth .	..	..	..	1	..	..	..	..	..	..	..	1	**2**
Fifteenth...	..	1	..	1	..	2	1	3	11	10	2	14	**45**
Sixteenth...	1	4	2	2	2	..	..	..	1	2	4	8	**26**
Seventeenth.	..	..	..	1	11	6	2	..	1	3	15	11	**50**
Eighteenth .	..	1	4	..	..	1	..	..	..	2	3	14	**25**
Nineteenth .	1	1	2	..	..	1	..	..	..	..	..	..	**5**
Twentieth ..	..	..	..	..	..	..	..	..	..	..	..	..	**1**
Totals	3	7	9	11	18	16	19	31	64	68	103	202	551

TABLE No. 6—*Vital Statistics of the City of Baltimore for the year* 1882.

Population by U. S. Census, taken June, 1880—white, 278,487; colored, 53,703; total	332,190
Population estimated by police census, taken middle of May, 1882—white, 348,900; colored, 59,620; total	408,520
Marriages reported during the year 1882	3,634
Births " " " "	7,759
Still births " " " "	677
Total number of deaths—white, 6,878; colored, 2,045	8,923
Annual death-rate per 1,000 of the population	21.81
" " " " white	19.70
" " " " colored	34.00
" marriage-rate " " population	8.88
" birth-rate " " "	19 97
" still birth-rate " " "	1.65
Total deaths from small pox	551
" " " measles	71
" " " scarlatina	179
" " " diphtheria	707
" " " croup	222
" " " whooping-cough	43
" " " typhoid fever	165
" " " typhus fever	3
" " " typho-malarial fever	44
" " " cerebro spinal fever	38
" " " yellow fever	
" " " relapsing fever	
" " " cholera	
" " " phthisis pulmonalis	1,217
" " " pneumonia	517
" " " bronchitis	110
Total deaths of children under 5 years of age	3,755
Per centage of deaths of children under 5 years of age to the total mortality	42.07

TABLE No. 6—Concluded.

Diarrhœal Diseases.

Total death of children under 5 years of age	583
Total deaths of all ages	705
Total deaths from zymotic diseases	2,802
Per centage of deaths from zymotic diseases, to the total mortality.	31.40

Diseases of the Puerperal State.

Total deaths from puerperal fever	16
" " " " convulsions	11
" " " " metritis	5
" " " " peritonitis	6
" " " " mania	1
" " " " septicæmia	11
" " " child birth	13
" " " miscarriage	8
" " " post partem hemorrhage	2
" " " rupture of uterine artery	1

TABLE No. 7—*Meteorological Summary for the Year* 1882.

PRESSURE.

Mean Barometer	30,161 inches, .033 above normal.	
Highest "	30,918 "	on January 24th.
Lowest "	29,350 "	on February 21st.
Range of "	1,568 "	

TEMPERATURE.

Mean Thermometer	55.7 degrees, or only 0.2 below normal.	
Highest "	97 "	on June 25th.
Lowest "	7 "	on January 24th.

Mean Winter (1881 and 1882) Temperature, 39.9 degrees—7.5 degrees above that of 1880 and 1881, and 3.3 degrees above normal.

Mean Spring Temperature	52.1	" 1.6 degrees below normal.	
" Summer "	74.8	" 1.3 " " "	
" Autumn "	58.3	" 1.1 " above "	

RAINFALL.

Rain or snow fell on 174 days, measuring 42.11 inches, an excess of only .06 of an inch above normal. The wettest month was September, with 9.38 inches of rainfall; the driest, November, with 0.65 inches.

WINDS.

Prevailing direction of wind, northwest.
Highest velocity of wind, 28 miles per hour, January 22d.
Mean velocity of wind, 5.5 miles per hour.
Total movement of wind, 48,435 miles.

HUMIDITY.

Mean Relative Humidity, 67.9 per cent.
First frost of season, November 3d.
First ice, November 19th.

TABLE No. 8—*Annual Report of Deaths from all Causes in the City of Baltimore for the year* 1882.

CAUSES OF DEATH.	January.	February.	March.	April.	May.	June.	July.	August.	September.	October.	November.	December.	Totals.
Abscess Brain	1	..	..	..	..	..	..	..	..	..	..	2	3
Abscess Ear	..	1	..	..	..	..	..	..	..	..	..	..	1
Abscess Abdomen	..	..	1	..	..	..	..	..	..	..	..	..	1
Abscess Liver	..	..	1	..	..	..	..	..	..	..	..	..	1
Abscess Pericaecal	..	..	1	..	..	..	..	..	..	..	..	..	1
Abscess Pelvic	..	..	1	..	..	..	1	..	..	..	..	..	2
Abscess Lung	..	..	..	1	..	..	..	..	..	..	..	1	2
Abscess Parotid Gland	..	..	..	..	..	1	..	..	..	..	..	..	1
Abscess Toe	..	..	..	..	..	..	1	..	..	..	..	..	1
Abscess Perinephritic	..	..	..	..	..	..	..	..	..	..	1	..	1
Anaemia	2	..	..	..	2	..	..	4	..	..	..	..	8
Angina Pectoris	2	4	1	1	..	2	..	..	..	..	1	5	16
Apoplexy	11	11	15	11	8	8	11	9	19	8	5	8	124
Ascites	1	4	2	1	..	..	1	..	..	..	..	2	11
Asphyxia	1	3	2	..	..	2	1	1	2	..	2	1	15
Asthma	5	3	3	4	8	3	3	2	4	..	1	6	42
Asthenia	5	5	5	1	8	2	11	3	3	2	9	6	60
Atelectasis Pulmonum	2	..	..	1	..	..	..	..	..	..	..	..	3
Albuminuria	..	1	1	3	1	1	1	..	2	..	1	2	13
Aneurism of Aorta	..	1	..	..	..	..	..	..	..	2	..	3	6
Atrophy	..	..	1	4	1	..	2	1	1	1	..	..	11
Adynamia	..	..	1	..	..	1	..	..	1	..	..	..	3
Addison's Disease	..	..	1	..	..	..	..	..	..	..	..	..	1
Abdominal Distention	..	..	..	..	1	..	..	..	..	..	..	..	1
Amputation of Penis	..	..	..	..	1	..	..	..	..	..	..	..	1
Amputation of Arm	..	..	..	..	..	..	1	..	..	..	..	..	1

Aneurism of Umbilical Cord	..	..	..	..	..	..	..	1	..	..	..	..	1
Bright's Disease	8	10	6	13	8	15	14	8	13	6	19	5	124
Burns	3	3	3	2	2	1	2	1	1	2	6	10	36
Bronchorrhoea	..	1	..	..	..	..	..	..	..	..	..	..	1
Cancer, Kidneys	1	..	..	..	..	..	..	1	..	..	..	..	2
Cancer, Mouth	1	..	..	..	..	..	..	..	1	1	..	1	4
Cancer, Breast	2	1	..	4	1	1	3	3	..	3	1	4	23
Cancer, Liver	2	2	2	2	2	1	1	..	..	..	1	2	15
Cancer, Uterus	5	3	2	3	2	7	2	6	7	2	2	5	46
Cancer, Aesophagus	..	1	..	..	..	..	..	..	..	..		..	1
Cancer Axilla	..	..	1	..	..	..	..	..	..	..	..	..	1
Cancer, Groin	..	..	1	..	..	..	..	1	..	..	..	..	2
Cancer, Tibia	..	..	1	..	..	..	..	..	..	..	..	..	1
Cancer, Stomach	..	..	2	2	2	1	5	1	5	2	2	3	25
Cancer, Anterior Mediastinum	..	..	..	1	..	..	..	..	..	..	..	..	1
Cancer, Maxillary	..	..	..	1	..	..	..	..	..	..	..	..	1
Cancer, Penis	..	..	..	1	..	..	..	..	..	..	..	..	1
Cancer, Lip	..	..	..	1	..	..	..	..	..	..	..	..	1
Cancer, Heel	..	..	..	1	..	..	..	..	..	..	..	..	1
Cancer, Carcinoma over 10th Rib	..	..	..	1	..	..	..	..	..	..	..	..	1
Cancer, Nose	..	..	..	..	1	..	..	..	..	..	..	1	2
Cancer, Tongue	..	..	..	..	1	..	..	..	..	..	..	..	1
Cancer, Ventricular	..	..	..	..	1	..	..	..	..	..	..	..	1
Cancer, Omentum	..	..	..	..	..	1	..	..	..	..	..	..	1
Cancer, Face	..	..	..	..	..	1	2	1	..	1	..	1	6
Cancer, Diffused	..	..	..	..	..	2	..	1	..	1	..	..	4
Cancer, Larynx	..	..	..	..	..	1	..	..	..	..	..	..	1
Cancer, Pylorus	..	..	..	..	..	..	1	..	..	1	..	..	2
Cancer, Jaw	..	..	..	..	..	..	1	..	..	1	..	..	2
Cancer, Rectum	..	..	..	..	..	..	2	1	2	1	..	..	6
Cancer, Vagina	..	..	..	..	..	..	1	..	..	..	..	..	1
Cancer, Scrotum	..	..	..	..	..	..	1	..	..	..	..	..	1
Cancer, Abdomen	..	..	..	..	..	..	..	2	..	..	1	1	4
Cancer, Ovarian	..	..	..	..	..	..	..	..	1	..	..	..	1

TABLE No 8.—Continued.

Causes of Death	January.	February.	March.	April.	May.	June.	July.	August.	September.	October.	November.	December.	Totals.
Cancer of Neck	..	..	..	..	..	..	..	..	..	1	..	..	1
Cancer, Haemaitodes	..	..	..	..	..	..	..	..	..	1	..	..	1
Cancer, Bladder	..	..	..	..	..	..	..	..	..	..	..	1	1
Cancer, Leg	..	..	..	..	..	..	..	..	..	..	..	1	1
Capillary Bronchitis	13	5	6	3	1	1	3	1	5	4	2	9	53
Carbuncle	1	5	1	..	..	..	..	..	..	1	..	..	8
Child Birth	3	..	1	2	1	1	2	..	1	..	..	2	13
Cholera Morbus	1	1	..	..	..	4	6	7	2	..	..	..	21
Cholera Infantum	..	..	1	2	3	28	238	71	42	10	4	..	399
Cirrhosis of Liver	2	1	5	4	2	..	..	2	1	..	..	5	22
Concussion of Brain	1	1	1	1	1	2	1	..	2	..	..	1	11
Compression of Brain	..	..	..	..	..	1	2	..	..	..	..	..	3
Congestion of Brain	4	2	2	3	3	6	9	..	6	2	3	4	44
Congestion of Lungs	6	7	6	3	7	5	..	2	3	4	4	9	56
Congestion of Bowels	..	..	1	..	..	..	..	..	..	..	1	..	2
Congestion of Liver	..	..	..	1	..	..	..	1	..	..	..	..	2
Congestion of Stomach	..	..	..	..	..	..	..	..	..	2	..	..	2
Consumption of Lungs	110	111	86	120	97	87	117	78	104	85	89	133	1217
Consumption of Bowels	..	..	..	1	..	1	1	2	1	..	..	..	6
Consumption, Bronchial	..	..	..	..	..	1	..	..	..	..	..	..	1
Convulsions	25	24	24	27	30	28	48	25	36	26	29	40	362
Convulsions, Puerperal	1	2	..	..	2	..	2	1	1	1	..	1	11
Croup	28	16	12	25	10	4	8	5	21	24	28	41	222
Cyanosis	4	..	3	7	2	4	1	1	3	1	1	1	28
Congestive Chill	1	..	..	1	3	1	1	1	3	1	..	..	12
Catarrh	1	..	..	1	..	1	..	..	..	..	..	2	5

Catarrh Bronchial	2	..	..	..	..	1	..	..	..	..	..	..	3
Cramps	..	1	..	1	..	..	..	..	..	..	..	..	2
Catarrh Senile	..	..	1	..	..	..	..	..	..	..	..	..	1
Calculus	..	..	..	1	..	1	..	..	..	2	..	..	4
Collapse of Lungs	..	..	..	1	..	..	..	..	..	..	..	..	1
Coxalgia	..	..	..	..	..	1	..	..	..	..	..	..	1
Caries of Pelvis	..	..	..	..	..	1	..	..	..	..	..	..	1
Cholerine	..	..	..	..	..	..	1	1	..	..	..	..	2
Colic (Bilious)	..	..	..	..	..	..	1	1	..	..	..	..	2
Chorea	..	..	..	..	..	..	1	..	..	..	..	..	1
Caries of Vertebrae	..	..	..	..	..	..	..	1	..	..	..	..	1
Concussion of Spine	..	..	..	..	..	..	..	1	..	..	..	..	1
Colitis	..	..	..	..	..	..	..	..	1	..	..	..	1
Cellulitis of Penis	..	..	..	..	..	..	..	..	..	..	..	1	1
Disease of Hip	1	..	..	..	..	..	1	1	..	..	..	..	3
Disease of Heart	32	22	21	22	31	26	22	17	22	18	20	33	286
Disease of Spine	1	1	3	1	3	..	1	..	1	1	1	1	14
Disease of Brain	..	2	1	3	1	..	..	..	..	..	..	2	9
Disease of Liver	..	..	..	..	2	..	..	..	1	1	..	..	4
Disease of Prostate	..	..	..	..	..	..	..	1	..	..	..	..	1
Dyspepsia	1	..	..	..	..	..	1	1	..	..	..	1	4
Dropsy General	5	1	3	4	2	6	3	7	6	5	9	6	57
Dropsy of Heart	2	2	1	3	3	2	1	3	..	1	1	..	19
Dropsy Ovarian	1	..	..	..	..	..	..	..	..	..	..	..	1
Dropsy Renal	..	..	..	1	..	..	..	..	..	..	..	..	1
Dropsy Liver	..	..	..	..	..	..	..	1	..	..	..	..	1
Dropsy Abdominal	..	..	..	..	..	..	..	..	..	..	1	..	1
Drowned	2	1	1	4	1	2	10	6	7	5	1	2	42
Dysentery	2	2	1	3	2	4	19	10	5	6	7	1	62
Diarrhoea	3	3	2	5	2	5	22	4	11	3	5	2	67
Dentition	2	3	10	4	5	6	14	15	11	9	5	3	87
Diabetes	2	..	..	1	1	..	1	..	1	..	1	1	8
Diphtheria	78	52	30	35	35	31	23	43	80	107	93	100	707
Delirium Tremens	..	..	1	3	..	..	1	..	2	..	1	..	8

TABLE No. 8—Continued.

CAUSES OF DEATH.	January.	February.	March.	April.	May.	June.	July.	August.	September.	October.	November.	December.	Totals.
Debility	..		..		..	..	1	1	..	2	1	2	7
Empyema	2		..	..	..	..	..	..	..	..	..	..	2
Erysipelas	3	6	5	2	9	1	2	2	..	1	4	..	35
Epistaxis	1	1	..	..	..	2	..	..	..	..	..	1	5
Embolism	2	2	..	..	..	..	..	3	1	..	..	..	6
Epilepsy	..	2	1	1	..	2	..	3	1	..	1	..	11
Effusion of Brain	..	1	1	1	..	..	1	..	..	1	..	2	7
Entero Colitis	..	..	.	2	..	5	11	11	6	..	2	2	39
Endo Carditis	..	..	.	2	.	..	1	..	..	..	..	1	4
Eczema	..	..	..	1	.	..	..	..	..	..	..	..	1
Elephantiasis	..	..	.	1	..	..	..	..	..	..	..	..	1
Exposure	..	..	..	..	..	..	..	..	1	..	..	..	1
Fever, Scarlet	13	12	15	31	18	18	9	14	8	12	10	20	179
Fever, Typhoid	11	10	8	14	8	9	14	23	29	17	5	17	105
Fever, Asthenic	1	..	..			..	..	..	..	..	..		1
Fever, Bilious	1	..	..	.		1	1	..	..	..	1	.	4
Fever, Intermittent	1	..	3	1	..	3	1	..	2	1	2	..	14
Fever, Puerperal	1	..	4	3	1	2	..	..	..	1	2	2	16
Fever, Catarrhal	1	1	2	1	..	..	..	..	..	..	..	2	7
Fever, Pyogenic	1	..	.	..	..	..	..	..	..	..	..	..	1
Fever, Malarial	..	1	3	4	6	2	6	9	8	5	7	4	55
Fever, Brain	..	..	1	..	..	..	..	2	..	..	..	..	3
Fever, Remittent	..	..	1	..	1	1	..	1	1	1	2	.	8
Fever, Congestive	..	..	.	1	..	..	..	..	..	..	..	..	1
Fever, Typho-Malarial	..		.	6	..	1	4	4	18	6	3	2	44
Pernicious	..			1	..	..	1	..	..	1	..		3

Fever, Typhus	..	..	..	1	..	1	..	..	1	..	..	..	3
Fever, Continued	..	..	..	..	..	1	..	..	..	..	..	..	1
Fever, Gastric	..	..	..	..	..	..	1	..	..	..	..	..	1
Fever, Rheumatic	..	..	..	..	..	..	1	..	..	..	..	..	1
Fever, Eruptive	..	..	..	..	..	..	..	1	..	..	..	..	1
Fracture of Thigh	1	1	..	..	1	1	1	2	1	2	..	1	11
Fracture of Vertebrae	..	1	..	..	1	..	..	1	1	..	..	..	4
Fracture of Fibia and Tibula	..	..	1	1	..	..	..	..	..	..	..	..	2
Fracture of Skull	..	..	..	1	2	2	2	2	1	..	1	..	11
Fracture of Leg	..	..	..	..	2	..	..	..	..	1	..	..	3
Fracture of Legs and Arm	..	..	..	..	..	1	..	..	..	..	..	..	1
Fracture of Pelvis	..	..	..	..	..	1	..	..	..	..	..	..	1
Fracture of Neck	..	..	..	..	..	..	2	..	..	..	..	..	2
Fracture of Multiple	..	..	..	..	..	..	..	..	..	1	..	..	1
Fracture of Arm	..	..	..	..	..	..	..	..	..	..	..	1	1
Gangrene Senile	3	1	1	..	..	..	..	..	..	..	..	..	5
Gangrene of Navel	1	..	..	..	..	..	..	..	..	..	..	..	1
Gangrene of Lungs	..	..	..	..	1	..	..	..	..	..	1	1	3
Gangrene of Foot	..	..	..	..	..	1	1	..	..	..	..	..	2
Gastro Enteritis	..	4	2	2	1	7	17	5	8	4	3	2	55
Gastro Intestinal Catarrh	..	..	..	1	..	..	3	..	..	..	..	..	4
Gout	..	..	..	..	..	..	1	..	..	..	..	..	1
Gangrenous Cellulitis	..	..	..	..	..	..	1	..	..	..	..	..	1
Hemorrhage of Bowels	1	1	..	..	..	..	1	1	..	..	2	1	7
Hemorrhage of Uterus	1	..	1	..	1	..	1	..	..	1	..	..	5
Hemorrhage Post-Partem	1	..	..	..	..	..	1	..	..	..	..	..	2
Hemorrhage of Brain	..	3	..	1	1	..	..	1	3	1	..	2	12
Hemorrhage of Navel	..	2	2	1	..	..	..	1	1	..	..	..	7
Hemorrhage of Stomach	..	1	..	..	..	..	..	..	..	1	..	1	3
Hemorrhage of Lungs	..	1	1	1	..	1	..	2	2	1	2	2	13
Hemorrhage of Bladder	..	..	..	..	..	..	1	..	..	..	..	..	1
Hydrocephalus	1	1	5	4	2	4	5	2	..	3	1	1	29
Hernia	..	1	1	..	1	..	..	1	..	..	1	..	5
Hernia Strangulated	..	1	1	1	..	..	4	1	..	2	..	2	12

TABLE No. 8—Continued.

CAUSES OF DEATH.	January.	February.	March.	April.	May.	June.	July.	August.	September.	October.	November.	December.	Totals.
Hernia Femoral	..	..	1	..	..	..	..	..	..	..	..	..	1
Hernia Umbilical	..	..	..	..	..	..	..	..	..	1	1	..	2
Hydrothorax	..	..	3	..	..	1	..	..	..	1	2	..	7
Hypertophy of Prostrate Gland	..	..	..	1	..	..	..	..	..	..	..	..	1
Heart Clot	..	..	..	..	1	1	..	..	..	..	..	1	3
Helminthopyra	..	..	..	..	..	1	..	..	..	..	..	..	1
Haematoria	..	..	..	..	..	..	..	1	..	..	..	..	1
Hypertrophy of Liver	..	..	..	..	..	..	..	..	..	1	..	..	1
Haematemesis	..	..	..	..	..	..	..	..	..	..	..	1	1
Inflammation of Brain	2	2	..	..	..	3	4	1	..	..	3	1	16
Inflammation of Bladder	1	4	1	1	2	4	2	1	1	2	..	4	23
Inflammation of Bronchi	12	5	17	14	6	9	9	3	3	11	6	15	110
Inflammation of Kidneys	1	..	4	1	3	3	3	..	1	3	2	1	22
Inflammation of Liver	1	2	1	1	1	1	3	1	3	..	2	3	19
Inflammation of Peritoneum	7	2	6	2	3	4	6	1	6	1	4	3	45
Inflammation of Pleura	1	2	2	4	..	..	3	..	..	1	..	1	14
Inflammation of Tonsils	1	..	..	..	..	..	..	1	..	2	1	..	4
Inflammation of Bowels	..	3	1	..	5	2	14	12	9	6	5	5	62
Inflammation of Stomach	..	3	4	2	3	6	5	3	7	2	4	3	42
Inflammation of Larynx	..	1	..	1	1	..	..	..	..	1	..	3	7
Inflammation of Lungs	..	2	..	..	..	..	..	..	..	..	..	..	2
Inflammation of Pericardium	..	..	..	2	1	3	1	..	2	..	..	2	12
Inflammation of Throat	..	..	..	..	..	..	..	..	..	1	..	..	1
Inanition	9	12	6	9	7	10	32	15	21	10	7	10	148
Indigestion	1	..	1	..	1	..	..	..	..	1	..	..	4

Intussusception	..	1	2	..	..	2	1	1	1	..	1	..	9
Intemperance	..	5	1	1	3	5	2	4	2	2	3	5	33
Incontinence of Urine	..	..	..	1	..	..	..	..	..	..	..	..	1
Infanticide	..	..	..	1	..	..	..	..	1	..	1	..	3
Instrumental Labor	..	..	..	..	1	..	..	..	..	..	..	1	2
Ischuria Renalis	..	..	..	..	..	..	1	1	..	..	..	..	2
Insolation	..	..	..	..	..	..	2	..	..	..	..	..	2
Ileus	..	..	..	..	..	..	..	..	1	..	..	..	1
Insanity	..	..	..	..	..	..	..	..	..	..	1	1	2
Jaundice	2	2	1	2	1	1	..	1	1	..	..	1	12
Leucocythæmia	..	1	..	..	..	1	..	.	..	..	..	1	3
Malformation	1	1	..	1	1	..	1	1	..	1	3	3	13
Marasmus	7	10	8	7	7	13	42	27	25	27	16	15	204
Meningitis	11	11	14	17	5	10	27	16	14	11	5	10	151
Meningitis, Tubercular	2	10	5	8	6	7	4	7	7	5	5	4	70
Meningitis, Cerebro Spinal	1	..	3	1	5	5	12	2	2	2	2	3	38
Murder	1	..	..	..	..	1	1	..	2	1	..	1	7
Malnutrition	1	1	2	..	..	5	5	5	2	2	3	1	27
Myelitis	..	1	..	..	..	1	..	1	1	..	2	..	6
Measles	..	2	2	3	17	17	18	7	1	..	2	2	71
Malaria	..	1	..	2	..	..	2	..	2	..	1	3	11
Miscarriage	..	..	..	1	1	..	..	..	..	2	3	1	8
Morbus Cæruleus	..	..	..	..	..	..	..	..	..	1	..	..	1
Malignant Sore Throat	..	..	..	..	..	..	..	..	..	1	..	..	1
Metrorrhagia	..	..	..	..	..	..	..	..	..	..	..	1	1
Metritis	..	..	..	..	..	..	..	..	..	..	..	1	1
Necrossi	1	..	..	..	..	1	..	..	..	..	1	..	3
Nervous Exhaustion	.	1	..	1	..	..	1	..	..	..	..	..	3
Nausea Marina	..	..	..	..	..	1	..	..	..	..	..	..	1
Non Viable	..	..	..	..	..	..	..	1	1	..	..	..	2
Nasal Catarrh	..	..	..	..	..	..	..	..	..	..	1	..	1
Old Age	22	25	30	23	22	28	34	20	23	19	19	40	305
Œdema of Lungs	..	1	1	..	1	..	1	..	1	..	1	1	7
Œdema of Glottis	..	1	1	..	..	..	..	..	..	..	..	..	2

TABLE No. 8—Continued.

CAUSES OF DEATH.	January.	February.	March.	April.	May.	June.	July.	August.	September.	October.	November.	December.	Totals.
Œdema General	..	..	..	1	..	..	..		..	..	..	..	1
Œdema of Brain	..	..	..	..	..	..	1		..	..	..	..	1
Otitis	..	1	..	1	..	..	1		..	..	..	..	3
Ossification of Heart	..	..	..	..	..	2	..		..	..	..	..	2
Otorrhœa	..	..	..	..	..	..	..		..	1	..	..	1
Paralysis	10	12	12	16	13	9	19	14	11	11	10	23	160
Pneumonia	62	84	48	58	45	21	17	11	13	13	24	62	458
Pneumonia, Typhoid	3	3	3	4	7	..	4	..	1	1	2	2	30
Pneumonia, Pleuro	..	1		2	2	1	..	..	1	..	2	4	13
Pneumonia, **Traumatic**	..	1		1	..	..	..	..	..	..	..	..	2
Pneumonia, **Broncho**	..	..	..	1	6	1	..	3	2	..	..	..	13
Premature **Birth**	11	5	11	14	7	15	19	14	19	12	6	12	145
Pyæmia	2	1	1	1	4	2	2	1	1	2	1	3	21
Pelvic **Cellulitis**	1	..	..	..	..	..	..	..	..	..	..	..	1
Purpura Hæmorrhagica	..	2	..	..	1	..		..	..	1	..	..	4
Puerperal Metritis	..	..	2	2	1	..		..	..	..	..	..	5
Poison	..	..	1	2	..	1		..	2	2	2	..	10
Parotitis	..	..	1	1	..	..		..	..	..	..	..	2
Puerperal Peritonitis	..	..	..	1	2	..		..	1	..	..	2	6
Pneumonia Hypostatic	..	..	..	1	..	..		..	..	..	..	..	1
Progressive Locomotor **Ataxia**	..	..	..	1	1	..	1	..	..	..	..	1	4
Palcenta Prævia	..	..	..	..	1	..	..	1	..	..	..	..	2
Phthisis Laryngeal	..	..	..	..	2	..	1	1	..	..	..	..	4
Pneumothorax	..	..	..	..	1	..	..	..	..	..	..	..	1
Puerperal Mania	..	..	..	..	..	1	..	..	..	..	..	..	1
Pott's Disease	..	..		..	..	..	1	..	..	..	..	..	1

Prostatitis	..	..	..	..	..	..	..	1	..	..	..	..	1
Protracted Labor	..	..	..	..	..	..	..	1	1	1	..	..	3
Poison by eating Toad Stools	..	..	..	..	..	..	..	..	1	..	..	..	1
Preturnatural Birth	..	..	..	..	..	..	.	..	..	1	..	..	1
Putrid Sore Throat	..	..	..	..	..	..	..	..	..	1	..	..	1
Prolapsus Funis	..	..	..	..	..	..	..	..	..	..	..	1	1
Rheumatism	..	..	1	..	1	..	1	..	..	..	..	..	3
Rheumatism, Inflammatory	2	3	1	4	..	1	1	..	2	..	..	5	19
Rheumatism, Heart	2	2	..	2	..	..	..	1	1	..	..	..	8
Rheumatism, Syphilitic	..	..	..	..	..	..	..	..	..	..	1	..	1
Rupture of Uterine Artery	..	1	..	..	..	..	..	..	..	..	..	..	1
Rachitis	..	..	..	..	1	1	..	..	..	..	..	..	2
Ricketts	..	..	..	..	1	..	..	..	..	1	1	..	3
Scalds	1	1	..	..	1	..	.	..	1	..	2	2	8
Suffocation by Gas	1	..	1	..	..	..	..	..	..	..	..	..	2
Scrofula	4	3	3	7	2	6	6	4	2	1	..	3	41
Small-Pox	2	6	10	12	17	13	22	24	71	63	94	217	551
Softening of Brain	4	3	4	2	1	4	4	2	3	..	2	1	30
Septicæmia	2	1	..	2	1	2	1	1	..	1	..	3	14
Septicæmia, Puerperal	..	..	2	..	..	5	2	..	..	1	..	1	11
Stricture of Intestines	1	..	..	1	1	..	..	1	1	..	1	1	7
Stricture of Œsophagus	1	..	..	..	..	..	..	..	..	..	..	..	1
Suicide	1	..	4	3	1	4	4	..	4	..	2	7	30
Shock	1	..	..	..	..	..	..	..	..	..	..	..	1
Syphilis	..	3	2	..	2	2	3	3	3	2	.	3	23
Suppression of Urine	..	1	..	..	..	..	..	..	..	..	..	..	1
Stomatitis	..	1	..	1	..	..	3	3	..	1	1	1	11
Spinal Apoplexy	..	1	..	..	..	..	..	..	..	..	..	..	1
Splenic Leucæmia	..	..	..	1	..	..	..	..	..	..	..	..	1
Scorbutus	..	..	..	..	..	1	..	..	..	..	..	..	1
Sun Stroke	..	..	..	..	..	..	..	3	..	..	..	..	3
Starvation	..	..	..	..	..	..	..	..	..	1	..	2	3
Spina Bifida	..	..	..	..	..	..	..	..	..	..	1	1	2
Suffocation	..	..	..	..	..	..	..	..	..	..	..	1	1

Table No. 8 Continued.

Causes of Death.	January.	February.	March.	April.	May.	June.	July.	August.	September.	October.	November.	December.	Totals.
Sarcoma	..	..	..	..	..	..	..	..	..	..	..	1	1
Tetanus	2	2	1	1	1	1	3	4	3	4	1	..	23
Trismus Nascentium	1	4	3	2	1	2	4	5	4	2	4	3	35
Tumor of Eye	1	..	..	..	..	..	..	..	..	..	..	..	1
Tumor of Uterus	..	1	..	..	..	..	1	..	..	..	..	..	2
Tumor of Throat	..	..	1	..	..	..	..	..	..	..	..	..	1
Tumor of Abdomen	..	..	..	1	..	..	1	..	..	..	..	..	2
Tumor of Brain	..	..	..	2	..	..	1	..	..	..	..	1	4
Tumor of Liver	..	..	..	..	..	..	..	..	..	..	1	..	1
Tumor, Ovarian	..	..	..	..	2	1	..	..	..	..	..	2	5
Traumatic Pleuritis	1	..	..	..	..	..	..	..	..	..	..	..	1
Tabes Mesenterica	..	1	..	3	1	..	1	..	1	..	1	..	8
Thrombosis	..	..	1	..	..	..	..	..	..	..	..	..	1
Typhomania	..	..	..	..	..	..	..	..	..	..	1	1	2
Unknown Adults	1	..	2	1	1	..	1	..	1	..	..	..	7
Unknown Infants	6	2	4	1	3	1	4	9	6	3	6	8	53
Uræmia	..	1	2	4	1	..	1	1	1	1	2	1	15
Uræmic Convulsions	..	..	..	..	..	1	..	..	..	..	..	..	1
Ulcer of Bowels	..	..	1	2	2	..	..	1	..	..	1	..	7
Ulcer of Stomach	..	..	..	1	1	1	..	3	..	..	2	..	8
Ulcer of Uterus	..	..	..	..	1	..	..	..	..	..	..	..	1
Ulcer of Heel	..	..	..	..	..	..	1	..	..	..	..	..	1
Ulcer of Leg	..	..	..	..	..	..	2	..	..	..	..	1	3
Vesicular Emphysema	..	1	..	1	..	..	..	..	..	..	..	..	2
Vasico Vaginal Fistula	..	..	..	..	..	..	..	..	1	..	1	..	2
Whooping Cough	4	4	3	3	3	5	7	3	5	2	1	3	43

TABLE No. 8—Continued.

AGES	January.	February.	March.	April.	May.	June.	July.	August.	September.	October.	November.	December.	Totals.
Under 1 year	145	141	134	126	124	176	471	204	205	144	134	194	2198
Between 1 and 2 years	52	66	35	52	44	45	98	87	88	95	76	106	844
Between 2 and 5 years	52	49	36	67	42	43	62	44	66	61	79	112	713
Total under 5 years	249	256	205	245	210	264	631	335	359	300	289	412	3755
Between 5 and 10 years	65	42	45	51	56	44	48	48	84	85	87	145	800
Between 10 and 15 years	6	9	12	12	10	11	18	8	17	15	23	20	161
Between 15 and 20 years	15	18	15	23	19	21	28	17	29	·15	16	41	257
Between 20 and 30 years	58	57	63	62	60	60	72	57	80	52	54	92	767
Between 30 and 40 years	63	62	36	65	42	44	60	51	63	45	56	80	465
Between 40 and 50 years	·39	50	45	48	46	45	48	38	47	45	47	63	561
Between 50 and 60 years	41	39	49	68	54	31	54	44	53	32	35	61	561
Between 60 and 70 years	56	46	47	66	44	48	63	48	52	36	45	64	615
Between 70 and 80 years	40	51	42	56	46	41	54	32	44	38	28	55	527
Between 80 and 90 years	18	14	21	20	12	21	19	20	17	9	16	27	214
Between 90 and 100 years	1	3	2	3	4	2	5	2	3	....	1	8	34
Between 100 and 110 years	....	....	1	1	....	....	....	1	....	1	1	1	6
Totals	651	647	583	720	603	632	1100	701	848	673	696	1069	8928

NATIVITY.													
United States—White	398	371	333	409	349	366	684	427	524	438	450	686	5435
United States—Colored	143	167	146	185	138	166	262	167	174	143	138	216	2045
Foreign	110	109	104	126	116	100	154	107	150	92	108	167	1443
Totals	651	647	583	720	603	632	1100	701	848	673	696	1069	8923
Still Births	53	44	49	62	51	47	71	48	72	47	51	81	677
WHITE.													
Males	260	256	315	288	249	251	443	275	355	304	269	441	3606
Females	248	224	222	247	216	215	395	259	319	226	289	412	3227
COLORED.													
Males	61	87	66	95	73	80	134	88	84	77	59	103	1007
Females	82	80	80	90	65	86	128	79	90	66	79	113	1038
Totals	651	647	583	720	603	632	1100	701	848	673	696	1069	8923
Marriages	306	305	216	298	283	277	257	302	351	300	391	348	3634
Births (reported)	624	667	613	674	608	467	604	606	799	615	703	779	7759

Total Mortality during the year, 8,923. United States, White, 5,434; Foreign, 1,443; Colored, 2,046; Total, 8,923.

Annual Death-rate per 1,000, whole population, 21.81; White, 19 70; Colored, 24 10.

Total Births, (reported) 7,759; Birth-rate per 1,000 population, 18.97.

Total Marriages, 3,634; Marriage rate per 1,000 population, 8.88. Total Still Births, 677.

TABLE No. 8.—Concluded.

Total Number of Deaths Monthly in each Ward.

WARDS.	January.	February.	March.	April.	May.	June.	July.	August.	September.	October.	November.	December.	Totals.
First	43	50	36	31	33	32	75	71	83	64	64	107	689
Second	22	19	17	32	29	37	64	50	72	75	86	133	636
Third	17	24	19	24	34	36	66	32	50	33	29	57	421
Fourth	24	14	11	16	32	21	42	25	36	24	26	39	310
Fifth	30	23	32	24	33	27	53	41	35	25	30	51	404
Sixth	36	20	21	40	31	34	55	42	36	35	40	57	447
Seventh	59	64	61	64	37	35	69	35	40	26	25	47	562
Eighth	26	18	33	32	23	24	43	24	30	26	21	33	333
Ninth	22	23	23	38	37	43	56	31	44	31	31	51	430
Tenth	15	22	21	21	26	23	44	35	48	16	32	40	343
Eleventh	20	23	19	32	27	25	67	25	28	30	19	30	345
Twelfth	27	33	17	32	34	37	71	42	32	29	34	54	442
Thirteenth	29	18	14	30	33	34	65	38	34	29	41	60	425
Fourteenth	18	17	25	46	11	21	46	29	29	23	28	33	326
Fifteenth	39	36	35	29	32	45	48	44	66	54	34	53	515
Sixteenth	38	32	39	37	24	29	46	28	33	42	25	43	416
Seventeenth	39	46	31	41	44	30	66	32	63	36	51	58	537
Eighteenth	54	48	35	51	37	43	54	36	37	35	40	57	527
Nineteenth	57	65	51	53	33	28	46	27	33	23	24	40	480
Twentieth	36	52	43	47	13	28	24	14	19	17	16	26	335
Totals	651	647	583	720	603	632	1,100	701	848	673	696	1,069	8,923

C. W. CHANCELLOR, M. D., *Secretary State Board of Health and Registrar of Vital Statistics.*

Important Rules.

APPENDIX.

Important Rules.

The following rules will afford valuable information to the public, and should be thoroughly studied and conspicuously posted in every house:

SANITARY RULES FOR THE PREVENTION OF SCARLET FEVER.

Scarlet fever is an infectious and dangerous disease. The mildest case may spread its fatal infection, and cause the most malignant cases.

The danger of communicating this disease continues during convalescence as well as in the height of the fever. Whatever is discharged or comes from the patient is liable to infect persons who have not had scarlet fever. The clothing, furniture, and the air of the sick room, may impart the infection. Clothing, bedding, closets and closed rooms may retain the infectious poison for a long time. Strict sanitary rules are urgently required on this account.

Parents, teachers, school officers and all persons who have the care of children, can do much to guard against the occurrence of infection, and they frequently are responsible for the spread of scarlet fever. The State Board of Health appeals to all who are thus responsible to do whatever they can to prevent this disease. This is to be attempted by the isolation or quarantine of the sick, and by disinfection, cleansing and ventilation.

Isolation and Quarantine of the Sick.—The sick with scarlet fever should be placed in an upper room with the best ventilation, and kept secluded from all except those who have charge of the case.

Children in the family, not affected, must be prevented from mingling with other children, and especially must be kept from schools and meetings. Children of other families in the same house should submit to this rule, yet it is earnestly recommended that uninfected children be sent away from the house in which there is scarlet fever to families in which there are no persons liable to the disease.

Infected Materials.—Carpets, curtains, trunks, clothing and all stuffed furniture and bedding should be removed from the room, and the part of the house in which the sick, or dead, with scarlet fever are to be placed.

The contagious matters thrown off from the surface of the patient's body is to be controlled as much as possible by such anointing of the body with oil, vaseline or lard, as the physician may direct, and especially, by disinfecting all discharges as they issue from the patient, and placing all clothing, towels, etc., removed from the sick, immediately in the disinfecting fluid of zinc-salt.

Disinfection.—Apply the methods and means described in the circular on disinfection. Follow the same rules as for diphtheria. The disinfectant made by dissolving one-fourth pound of sulphate of zinc and two ounces of salt in a gallon of water is best and cheapest.

Thorough cleansing and ventilation must be enforced. All drains, sewers and privies about the house should be kept thoroughly disinfected.

Restrictions upon Convalescents.—As the liability to infect others continues as long as there is any desquamation, or peeling of the skin, and possibly even longer, the recently sick should not attend any school, church or company, or ride in a public conveyance while the skin is peeling, the throat and eyes sore, or any symptoms of dropsy are present. A competent physician should decide what special cleansing, by warm baths with vaseline soap or chlorinated washes, should be used. In all cases let the physician decide, and certify in writing, that the patient is safe to others, before any child recently suffering from scarlet fever is permitted to attend school.

Whoever attends upon scarlet fever patients, and whoever enters the room where they are, should not mingle with persons liable to take this fever, without changing all clothing, after thorough ablution of hands and head.

Burial of the dead from scarlet fever should be strictly private, with the corpse wrapped in a sheet saturated with the zinc disinfectant, or inclosed in an air-tight coffin. When a death from this disease is announced in print, the notice should state the cause as "from scarlet fever," to prevent attendance at the funeral or visits to the house.—[*Circular Massachusetts Board.*]

PROPHYLACTIC IN SCARLET FEVER.

To prevent scarlet fever, give belladonna in small doses—say three grains of the extract of belladonna to two tablespoonsful of water, and give of this, daily, twice as many drops as there are years in the patient's age. In treating the disease, keep the sick chamber at an even temperature, not exceeding sixty degrees. Do not allow the patient to be covered with heavy bedclothes; freshen the air in the room frequently, and have the patient carefully sponged or bathed once or twice daily in tepid water. The best drink is pure cold water or lemonade. As nourishment, first, give chicken broth, bread and stewed fruit; later, give mutton or beef broth, milk, &c. If there be constipation give an enema of tepid water, avoiding active purges.

Dr. Elisha Harris, Secretary of the State Board of Health of New York, in commenting upon the dangers from this disease, says: "A destroyer of precious lives and a most harmful and permanent cause of injury to the bodies of children who survive its attack, scarlet fever must be treated as an enemy of childhood and of the family. We must endeavor to 'stamp out' and exterminate the known contagion by which it spreads. Separation, purification, ventilation and disinfection of the sick and all that pertains to them, as well as the rooms and bedding they have occupied, and the special sanitary care of all persons who have been exposed or near to them, are necessary for arresting the spread of this disease. Promptly report all cases of scarlet fever to the nearest health officer, and at once order the isolation and sanitary care of the sick as advised by these rules and the physician."

Prevention of Diphtheria.

Diphtheria is an infectious and dangerous disease, readily communicated by the sick and by clothing from the sick-room. The room itself is apt to retain and communicate the infection. Its spread is prevented by great care to have the sick, their clothing, and the persons who nurse them, kept entirely away from others, especially from children; and to such care should be added cleansing.

The sick must be nursed in a clean and airy room, on a floor where there are no other children.

Every cloth and cup, and all clothing and bedding used in the sick-room, must be cleansed and disinfected before being handled or used by other persons. The house itself must be disinfected as soon as the sick recover or die. Cleanliness and ventilation should be enforced night and day.

The Cleansing and Disinfection.—Open windows, and open fire-places—with fire in them day and night—protect the sick and all who attend them. The cloths and dishes used by the sick should be put into boiling-hot water, as soon as removed, without being taken to another room. The soiled clothing from the sick and the bed, that can be boiled, should be thrown into a disinfecting fluid, made by dissolving four tablespoonsful of sulphate of zinc ("white vitriol"), and two tablespoonsful of common salt in a gallon of boiling water (one-fourth pound of sulphate of zinc to two ounces of table-salt, to the gallon). When the time for washing comes, thoroughly boil the clothing, etc., before washing.

The woodwork, chairs and stools of the sick-room should be washed with the disinfecting fluid. The chamber vessels and spit-cups used by the sick should be drenched with this fluid before they are removed from the room.

The grounds surrounding the house, the ditches and drains and the privy and chip-yard, must be drenched with the cheap solution of green copperas (sulphate of iron), made by dissolving five pounds of the dry copperas in a large pailful of water

As soon as the sick-room is vacated let it be fumigated with sulphur, and let all rugs, beds, blankets and other furniture remain in the room and near where the kettles or pans of sulphur are placed. From two to five pounds of sulphur, or broken brimstone, laid upon ashes and coals in iron vessels (set into large tubs that contain a few inches depth of water), will be necessary for fumigating an ordinary chamber. The physician will direct how to do this; but it will be well done if the rooms to be fumigated are so closed that the suffocating fumes do not escape from flues and crevices, and the burning of the sulphur at last ceases for want of fresh air before all the sulphur is consumed. Let the fumes be kept shut in all day. Finally, let all plastered portions of the room be well white-washed with fresh-slaked lime. Let the bottom and sides of cellars be sprinkled thickly, and repeatedly, with quick-lime. All house-drains, ditches, filthy grounds, garbage-tubs, and decaying materials should be cleared out and disinfected, and waste-pipes, drains and sewer-connections so improved, that no gases from them shall enter the house.

The sick should be nursed by adults who have no children about them. Avoid the patient's breath and matters ejected in coughing.

Children and visitors should keep away from the house where there is diphtheria. The burial of those that die should be strictly private. The corpse should be wrapped in a sheet saturated with the zinc disinfectant.

Children who recover from diphtheria should not visit or be visited, attend school or meetings, nor mingle with others of the family from which separated, until the physician permits.

The mother, father, or other member of a family who needs to become the attendant upon the sick, when quarantined for diphtheria, should practice all possible precautions to prevent spreading the infection in the family. Nurses of such patients should keep away from other families and from other children of the same family.

It must be remembered that not only the mild cases, but the convalescent, may and frequently do infect others fatally, and that by this means diphtheria is thoughtlessly spread from place to place.

It is a public as well as domestic duty to apply these sanitary rules wherever a case of diphtheria occurs. This disease should be treated as an enemy, to be conquered in every house it enters.

Note—Perfect drainage and cleanliness, thorough ventilation and dryness, and repeated disinfection of all the house-drains and foul places, are necessary to the safety of the family and the neighborhood.

Ask your physician to notify the local health officer of the occurrence of diphtheria, also to inform the State Board of Health concerning the cases and discovered causes.

Sanitary Precautions to Prevent the Spreading of Infectious Diseases.

Cleanliness and ventilation are, in all cases and everywhere, of the first importance. The diseases which are spread chiefly from place to place and from person to person by means of their own infection or contagion, are to be regarded and treated as enemies, to be resisted and stamped out. The propagation of some of them, with the help of local causes, seen or unseen, and the fatality, as well as spread, of each one of them, is increased by personal uncleanliness and local unhealthfulness. Diphtheria, measles, scarlet fever, typhoid fever, puerperal fever and small pox are the most pestilent of these infectious diseases in this state. But typhoid fever and malignant cholera are infectious by means of excremental matters rather than from bodily emanations. Typhus spreads by its personal contagion, and originates among crowded and uncleanly people. These diseases, and all infections and contagions, require disinfection, and all sanitary precautions that prevent infection.

Small Pox, Scarlet Fever, Diphtheria or Measles.—The patient should be kept in a separate room (preferably on an upper floor), from which, if possible, carpets, curtains, stuffed furniture, clothing and other articles not required for immediate use should be removed beforehand; and no person, except the physician, nurse or parent, should be allowed to enter the sick room, or to touch any of the articles used therein, until after thorough disinfection.

To Disinfect Clothing, etc., in the Sick Room.—Keep in the room a tub containing a quarter of a pound of sulphate of zinc and two ounces of common salt to each gallon of water. All bed linen, towels, clothing, handkerchiefs, etc., used about the patient, should be allowed to soak in this solution for at least an hour before removal from the room, and afterwards be thoroughly boiled, separate from the rest of the family washing. Never send such articles to a public laundry.

To Disinfect Discharges from the Patient.—Use the same disinfecting fluid as in disinfecting clothing, but three times stronger, or use copperas water, made by dissolving a pound and a half of copperas in a gallon of water. The latter answers for all excremental discharges, while the former is best for all articles of clothing and furniture. All vessels used in the sick room should be disinfected with one or other of these disinfecting fluids, unless immediately immersed in boiling water. Disinfect the discharges and clothing immediately.

Typhoid Fever.—The poison lies in the discharges from the bowels, which should be at once disinfected with the solution of the zinc-salt or of copperas. Particular care should be exercised to prevent any possible contamination of sources of drinking water with these discharges. Bed-clothing or other articles soiled by the evacuations should be treated with the zinc solution, and be boiled.

Dysentery and Cholera.—Adopt the same regulations as in typhoid fever.

Typhus Fever.—Enforce free ventilation, and disinfection of clothing, as above described. Attend to the fumigation of the sick room and its bedding.

To Prevent the Body of the Patient from Spreading Contagion.—In the eruptive diseases, especially in scarlet fever, the patient's body should be anointed at least twice a day with oil, lard or vaseline, containing about ten grains of carbolic acid, or of thymol, to the ounce. This process should be maintained until all bran-like scaling of the skin is at an end. The zinc-salt solution should be used as directed. Before again associating with unprotected persons, the patient should have several complete ablutions, including thorough washing of the hair with soap or borax; and none of the clothing worn for several days, before the disease declared itself, should be again used until disinfected and ventilated in the open air several days.

Avoid visiting houses where there are any of these diseases. Occupants of such houses should not visit.

Disinfection of Houses and Apartments.—Fumigation with sulphur is the only practical method for disinfecting the house, as well as furniture, bedding, etc., that cannot be steamed or boiled. For this purpose the rooms to be disinfected must be vacated. Close the rooms as tightly as possible, place the sulphur in iron pans, supported upon bricks, in wash-tubs containing a little water; set it on fire by hot coals, or with the aid of a spoonful of alcohol, and keep the room tightly closed twenty-four hours. For a room of dimensions equal to ten feet square, or one hundred square feet of floor space, at least two pounds of sulphur should be used; for larger rooms, proportionally increased quantities. After fumigation, the freest possible ventilation should be practiced. All woolen clothing, silks, furs, stuffed bed-covers, beds and other articles which cannot be treated with zinc solution, should be hung in the room during fumigation, their surfaces thoroughly exposed, and their pockets turned inside out. Afterward they should be hung in the open air, beaten and shaken. Pillows, beds, stuffed mattresses, upholstered furniture, etc., should be ripped open, the contents spread out and thoroughly fumigated. Carpets are best fumigated on the floor, but should afterward be removed to the open air and thoroughly beaten. Many of such articles may be disinfected in an oven or steam-heated tank, at a temperature of from two hundred and twelve to two hundred and fifty degrees Fahrenheit, maintained for five or six hours.

Disinfection of Premises, etc.—Cellars, yards, stables, gutters, privies, cesspools, water-closets, drains, sewers, etc., should be repeatedly and profusely drenched with copperas solution, which is easily kept ready for use, at full strength, by hanging a basket containing about sixty pounds of copperas in a barrel of water, and renewing the supply from time to time.

Corpses should be thoroughly washed with a zinc solution of triple strength; should then be wrapped in a sheet wet with this strongest disinfecting solution, and buried as soon as practicable.

NOTE.—There are no substitutes for cleanliness and fresh air. The deodorizers, which are much used as disinfectants, are deceptive.

Warning Against Small Pox.—The small pox contagion which is being spread by tramps and vagrants, threatens much harm. Each of the cities and counties of the state should require their health officers to be watchful and ready to adopt all necessary sanitary precautions for isolating and controlling this disease at its first appearance. Tramps should not be permitted to enter dwellings and lodging houses as they wander from the cities. They should be cleansed and directed by the superintendent of the poor. Every small pox patient should be so quarantined and provided for as to prevent the spread of infection. All lodging houses and dwellings should be thoroughly cleansed beforehand; and wherever a case of small pox occurs the disinfection of the clothing, bedding and sick-rooms should be as prompt and thorough as possible.

Special Instructions for Disinfection.

Disinfection is the destruction of the poisons of infectious and contagious diseases.

Deodorizers, or substances which destroy smells, are not necessarily disinfectants, and disinfectants do not necessarily have an odor.

Disinfection cannot compensate for want of cleanliness nor of ventilation.

I. DISINFECTANTS TO BE EMPLOYED.

1. Roll sulphur (brimstone) for fumigation.
2. Sulphate of iron (copperas) dissolved in water in the proportion of one and a half pounds to the gallon, for soil, sewers, etc.

3. Sulphate of zinc and common salt, dissolved together in water in the proportions of four ounces sulphate and two ounces salt to the gallon, for clothing, bed-linen, etc.

II. HOW TO USE DISINFECTANTS

1. *In the Sick Room.*—The most available agents are fresh air and cleanliness. The clothing, towels, bed-linen, etc., should, on removal from the patient, and before they are taken from the room, be placed in a pail or tub of the zinc solution, boiling hot, if possible.

All discharges should either be received in vessels containing copperas solution, or, when this is impracticable, should be immediately covered with copperas solution. All vessels used about the patient should be cleansed with the same solution.

Unnecessary furniture, especially that which is stuffed, carpets and hangings, should, when possible, be removed from the room at the outset; otherwise they should remain for subsequent fumigation and treatment.

2. *Fumigation* with sulphur is the only practicable method for disinfecting the house. For this purpose, the rooms to be disinfected must be vacated. Heavy clothing, blankets, bedding and other articles which cannot be treated with zinc solution, should be opened and exposed during fumigation, as directed below. Close the room as tightly as possible, place the sulphur in iron pans, supported upon bricks placed in wash-tubs containing a little water set it on fire by hot coals or with the aid of a spoonful of alcohol, and allow the room to remain closed for twenty-four hours. For a room about ten feet square, at least two pounds of sulphur should be used; for larger rooms, proportionally increased quantities.

3. *Premises.*—Cellars, yards, stables, gutters, privies, cesspools, water-closets, drains, sewers, etc., should be frequently and liberally treated with copperas solution. The copperas solution is easily prepared by hanging a basket containing about sixty pounds of copperas in a barrel of water.

4. *Body and Bed Clothing, etc.*—It is best to burn all articles which have been in contact with persons sick with con-

tagious or infectious diseases. Articles too valuable to be destroyed should be treated as follows:

(*a.*) Cotton, linen, flannels, blankets, etc., should be treated with the boiling-hot zinc solution; introduce piece by piece, secure thorough wetting, and boil for at least half an hour.

(*b.*) Heavy woolen clothing, silks, furs, stuffed bed-covers, beds and other articles which cannot be treated with the zinc solution, should be hung in the room during fumigation, their surfaces thoroughly exposed, and pockets turned inside out. Afterwards they should be hung in the open air, beaten and shaken. Pillows, beds, stuffed mattresses, upholstered furniture, etc., should be cut open, the contents spread out and well fumigated. Carpets are best fumigated on the floor, but should afterwards be removed to the open air and thoroughly beaten.

5. *Corpses*, especially of persons that have died of any infectious or malignant disease, should be thoroughly washed with a zinc solution of double strength; should then be wrapped in a sheet, wet with the zinc solution, and buried at once.

Metallic, metal-lined or air-tight coffins should be used when possible; certainly when the body is to be transported for any considerable distance.

Rules for the Management of Infants.

CLEANLINESS.

An infant should be bathed every morning in warm water. If it is feeble, or if the weather is unusually hot, it should also be bathed again before being put to bed at night. After washing, the body should be wiped thoroughly dry. As the child grows older the temperature of the water should be gradually lowered, so that by the time the baby is four months of age, water shall be used to which only warm water enough has been added to take the chill off.

Let the diapers be frequently changed, and have them always washed before used a second time. If possible, never have the diapers dried in the room occupied by the baby.

FRESH AIR.

Give the child all the fresh air possible. Keep the windows of the room open day and night in hot weather, unless the heat of the outside atmosphere is greater than that within the room. Avoid as much as possible any overcrowding of the room occupied by the baby, especially at night. Have the baby taken out every day when the weather is fine. Do not keep the child in the same room in which cooking or washing is going on.

CLOTHING.

The clothing of a baby should be light, loose and warm. Except during the summer months the arms and legs should be covered. Have the night-dress thoroughly aired during the day, and the day-clothes aired during the night. Use only safety-pins. Do not keep the child's head heated by any covering except when exposed to unusual heat or cold. Never allow the child to be exposed to the direct rays of the sun.

SLEEP.

Every baby requires considerable sleep. Never wake a sleeping child. It should never be allowed to sleep with any other person. Regularity in reference to its hours of sleep is as necessary as for its times of feeding. At those hours it should be put to bed, where it should be left to go to sleep, unaided by any rocking or nursing in the arms as a preliminary to being placed in its bed. A child very quickly acquires the habit of going to sleep on being put to bed.

DIET.

As a rule, until a child has its eight centre teeth, it should receive no food but milk.

Breast-milk is better than cow's milk, and the mother's milk the best of all. Observe regular hours for feeding. Never nurse a child when overheated or fatigued.

Until the child is six weeks old, feed it every two hours during the day, and three hours during the night. After this gradually lengthen the intervals between the meals, so that, by the time the baby is four months old, it is fed every four hours during the day, and, if necessary, once during the night.

Do not consider that every time a child cries it is necessarily hungry. In hot weather, or if the child is feverish, allow it to drink freely of cold water.

If the mother has not breast-milk sufficient for the child, let the child be fed twice a day with the bottle. A flat bottle, its open mouth covered with a rubber nipple, is all that is required. Complicated nursing bottles should never be used, owing to the difficulty which will be found in keeping them properly cleaned.

At first equal parts of milk and warm water should be used, with the addition of half a teaspoonful of sugar. The quantity of the mixture necessary for a meal should not at first exceed a sixth of a pint. As the child grows older the amount of water added should be lessened, and the sugar be altogether omitted. By the time the child is two months old it should have pure milk, which in very hot weather need not be warmed. Immediately after using the bottle always wash it thoroughly. The rubber nipple should be kept always in cold water when not in use. In very hot weather a little soda should be added to the water with which the bottle is washed, and also to that in which the nipple is kept.

In very hot weather the milk should be boiled as soon as received from the milkman. It is also well to add, during the extreme heat of the summer, especially if the child is at all troubled with diarrhœa or vomiting, a teaspoonful of lime-water to each bottleful of milk.

If the child is to be brought up by hand, it should be fed with the bottle, as described above, and at the same times as, in the other case, it would have been nursed.

The best milk is obtained by allowing the can to stand about an hour after receiving it, and then pouring off for use the upper two-thirds.

If pure milk cannot be obtained, condensed milk may be tried. It should always be kept in a cool place, and is best prepared by adding one teaspoonful to six tablespoonfuls of boiling water. As the child grows, the strength of the mixture should be increased.

All prepared varieties of so-called infants' food are to be avoided. There is no proper substitute for milk.

WEANING.

As soon as the centre teeth begin to come, the child should have, in addition to its milk, one or two meals a day. These should consist only of bread, either fresh or stale, or crackers with the milk. Gradually the mother's milk should be withdrawn from the child, so that it should be completely weaned by the ninth month, unless that period should happen to fall in the midsummer. Milk should still be its main diet. After the child is ten months old, it may have one meal a day of simple broth (mutton or chicken), or beef tea with bread. When the child is a year old, it may have daily a little meat, cooked rare, and cut up fine. The yolk of a fresh, rare-boiled egg may also be given daily. Even at that age, however, milk should be freely given, and should form the main part of its diet.

GENERAL ADVICE.

Have the child properly vaccinated when young.

Never, under any circumstances, except by medical advice, give a child soothing syrups, sleeping drops, cordials, spirits or any of the numerous so-called carminatives.

If a child is suddenly taken sick with vomiting and diarrhœa, send immediately for the doctor. Until he arrives give no medicine, but, if the child seems in pain, wring out flannels in hot water and place them over the belly. Keep the child's body, arms and legs, warm. Keep cool, and do not give the child the various things which will be suggested by the neighbors.

To make lime-water put half a pound of quick-lime into an earthen vessel, pour over it slowly a gallon of cold water, stir it well and allow it to stand twenty-four hours; then skim it and pour off the clear liquid into clean bottles, which should subsequently be well corked.

Rules for the Management of Children over Two Years of Age.

Regularity as to the hours of eating and sleeping should be insisted upon in children after, as well as before, they are weaned.

Children should be bathed freely, and should be allowed plenty of fresh air and exercise. The sleeping apartment should always be well ventilated. Each child should have its own bed, if possible.

Plenty of good, substantial food should be given, and children should not be allowed to eat confectionery, cake, pies or similar articles. Unripe or over-ripe fruit should be forbidden. Tea and coffee should not be given to them.

Exposure to sudden changes of heat and cold, to wet and dampness, or to the direct rays of the summer's sun, should be avoided at all times.

In the colder months of the year flannel should always be worn next to the skin, at least over the child's chest.

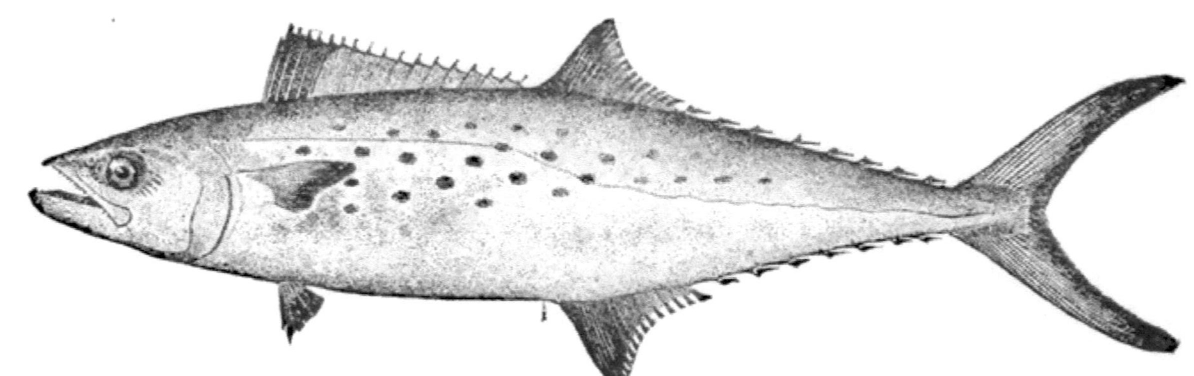

SPANISH OR BAY MACKEREL (1/3 natural size). *Cybium maculatum.*

www.ingramcontent.com/pod-product-compliance
Lightning Source LLC
Chambersburg PA
CBHW032116230426
43672CB00009B/1750

* 9 7 8 3 3 3 7 2 6 9 2 0 3 *